D0593057

FOR REVIEW

With the compliments of

GOWER PUBLISHING CO.

OLD POST RD., BROOKFIELD, VT. 05036

802-276-3162

Please send two (2) copies
of any review or mention
THANK YOU

Price: $41.50

European Philosophy and the Human and Social Sciences

Edited by
SIMON GLYNN

Gower

Published by
Gower Publishing Company Limited,
Gower House, Croft Road, Aldershot, Hampshire, England.

Gower Publishing Company Limited
Old Post Road, Brookfield, Vermont 05036, U.S.A.

British Library Cataloguing in Publication Data

European philisophy and the human sciences.
   1. Social sciences —— Philosophy
   I. Glynn, Simon
   300'.1   H61

ISBN 0 566 05023 4

Printed in Great Britain by Blackmore Press, Longmead, Shaftesbury, Dorset

Contents

CONTRIBUTORS

Rudolf Makkreel, Professor of Philosophy at Emory University, Atlanta, Georgia, is editor of the Journal of the History of Philosophy, author of Dilthey, Philosopher of the Human Studies, co-editor of the six volume edition of Dilthey's Selected Works, and author of several articles on Kant's aesthetics. He is presently working on a book on Kant's theory of imagination entitled Kant and the Life of the Imagination.

Klaus-Peter Koepping, Baldwin Spencer Professor of Anthropology and Asian Studies at Melbourne University was formerly Reader in the Department of Anthropology and Sociology at the University of Queensland, and has been an Associate Professor of Anthropology in the California State University system, and Guest Professor at the Universities of Bielefeld and Mainz. Professor Koepping has undertaken extensive ethnographic field-work in Japan, Afghanistan and among Australian Aborigines, and is interested in the epistemological foundations of such field-work and particularly in Hermeneutics, Phenomenology and Semiotics. Extensively published on both substantive and methodological aspects of anthropology, and author of a study of Adolf Bastian and the Psychic Unity of Mankind, Professor Koepping is currently studying German migrant communities in Australia.

Wolfe Mays, formerly Reader in Philosophy at Manchester University is currently director of the Intellectual Skills Project at Manchester Polytechnic. He has been visiting Professor of Philosophy at Northwestern University and the University of Wisconsin, Visiting Professor of Science, Technology and Human Values at Purdue University, Research Associate at Clark University and Worcester State Hospital, Mass., as well as assistant to Professor Jean Piaget at the University of Geneva, where he was a founder member of the International Centre for Genetic Epistemology. Author of three books, co-editor of two and co-author, with Jean Piaget, of a further two, Dr. Mays has also translated four books by Piaget, and has published some hundred articles and notes on a wide range of philosophical topics. A student of Wittgenstein's at Cambridge, Dr. Mays is editor of the Journal of the British Society for Phenomenology as well as currently chairman of the Society.

Dieter Misgeld is a faculty member of the Ontario Institute for Studies in Education, a research institute affiliated to the University of Toronto, where he has taught Philosophy and Social Theory. Co-editor of German Sociology (forthcoming)

Dr. Misgeld has published extensively on Hermeneutics with particular reference to the Critical Theory of Jurgen Habermas, ,and is presently working on a reinterpretation of Hermeneutics and Critical Theory in relation to the applied Social Sciences.

Simon Glynn, who teaches philosophy at Liverpool University was formerly a lecturer in Philosophy at Manchester University. He has also been a Research Fellow in the Epistemology of Creativity and Imagination at the Open University where he has, in addition, researched and taught aspects of Technology. His major research interest is in the implications of Hermeneutics, Phenomenology and Existentialism for the Philosophy of the Physical, Human and Social Sciences, although he has also published on the Social Philosophy and Ethics of Technology, and the Epistemology of Creativity and Imagination. He is currently editing a volume on Sartre.

James J. Valone is Professor of Philosophy at Ballermine College, Louisville, Kentucky, and has taught at Boston College and at Loyola University in Chicago. His areas of interest are Phenomenology, Existentialism and the Philosophy of the Social Sciences. Professor Valone has published a book, The Ethics and Existentialism of Kirkegaard: Outlines for a Philosophy of Life, and numerous articles on Phenomenology.

Roger McLure, who teaches French at Keele University, has just completed a book on Nathalie Sarraute, and has pulished extensively on French literature and philosophy, and is particularly interested in the relationship between French and German phenomenology. Dr. McLure is currently engaged in applying phenomenological epistemology to the French syntax of motion.

Helmut Loiskandl is chairperson of the department of Sociology at the University of Queensland, and combines research in the Sociology of Religion with a keen interest in the philosophical foundations of Sociological Theory. His latest works in this area are a translation of and introduction to Georg Simmel's 'Schopenhauer and Nietzsche' (with D. Weinstein and M. Weinstein), and Religionssoziologie which is to be published shortly.

Preface

Hermeneutics, phenomenology and existentialism constitute the mainstream of modern European philosophy. Not only is the work of those such as Dilthey, Husserl, Heidegger, Sartre, Merleau-Ponty and others in this tradition of major philosophical interest and significance in its own right, but, providing as it does the epistemological foundations for verstehen, critical theory, struturalism, post-structural deconstruction and other methodologies, it has of late been attracting increasing attention from practitioners of the human and social sciences, particularly those who oppose the ethnocentric, behaviourist, functionalist and other reductivist tendencies of positivistic and neo-positivistic approaches.

Following the success of Galileo, Newton, Bacon and others from the sixteenth to the eighteenth centuries, many suggested that it was only by adopting the 'objective' epistemologies, quantitative methods and explanatory goals of the physical sciences, that the human and social sciences could hope to achieve similar success. Against this view it may however be argued that the methods of the physical sciences, developed as they were for the study of objects, make them singularly inappropriate to the study of human subjects and social relations, and that the wholesale importation of 'objective' epistemology and quantitative methods into the human and social sciences would render them necessarily incapable of finding any evidence of those 'subjective' experiences of qualitative significance and meaning, or of values, feelings, purposes etc., which each and every one of us experiences as an integral part of our everyday existence and social interaction. It may further be argued that while physical events may be subject to causal determination and explanation, human and social experiences and actions are the product of free choices - albeit choices circumscribed by concrete situations and made for more or less 'compelling' reasons - and that therefore they only become comprehensible and predictable in so far as we understand the feelings, values, attitudes, purposes, goals etc. of the individuals and groups involved.

In light of such objections to the reductionist's programme, it has, following Dilthey, been argued that instead of attempting causally to explain human and social experience and behaviour as one would physical events, the human and social sciences should adopt as a model philological hermeneutics, and seek to understand human and social experience and behaviour by interpreting it in terms of its context, a context which, some have argued, ought to include those apparently 'subjective' elements referred to above.

The dependence of the meaning of a 'text' upon it's 'context' is also recognised by the structural linguists who, following Saussure, insist that a particular linguistic act (Parole), is dependent for its meaning on the totality of linguistic structures, (Langue), and concomitantly that the meaning of a 'signifier' is dependent upon its synchronic difference from other signifiers, to which in turn the same applies. This, as Derrida and the post-structuralists have pointed out, implies that relations or differences are in some epistemological sense prior to the 'entities' or identities which they subsequently constitute; a view which, while it may appear somewhat paradoxical has much in common with the field theoretical holism characteristic of much quantum and particle physics.

Nor is the priority of relations over the 'things' related confined merely to what we may, with some metaphorical license, call the 'lateral' or observed field, but applies equally to what we may call the 'perpendicularly' field between the observer and the 'lateral' field. Thus phenomenology recognising the priority of the intentional relation - of experiencer (or subject) to experienced (or object) in experience - argues that we can not know the subject and object 'poles' of experience independently of the empirical _relation_ in which they are exclusively given. Consequently the transcendental perspective of the objective _spectator_ inevitably gives way to the historic-socio-culturally situated _participator_ in the 'life-world' which we find in the works of the hermeneutic philosophers and of the later Husserl.

The point was taken by Heidegger who showed that the ontological context or relation of human being-in-the-world (_Dasein_), with others (_Mitsein_), is prior to the attempt to distinguish them in epistemological reflection, a view which, as Sartre recognised, clearly implies nothing short of a 'deconstruction' of the individual ego which, no longer a 'thing,' is _Nothing_ other than a totality of cognitive, evaluative and active capacities (e.g. to perceive, value, choose, judge, posit goals, initiate physical acts etc.) or ways of being related to the world and others, to whom, in turn, the same applies.

The significance of such philosophical insights for the human and social sciences is clear. In place of the reified subject of the positivists and neo-positivists, an originally isolated entity who only _subsequently_ enters into relations with the physical and historico-socio-cultural world, we now confront a subject who, although _epistemologically_ _distinguishable_ in reflection, is in reality _ontologically_ _inseparable_ from a physical and historico-socio-cultural context of some sort or other; a context from within which, to come full circle, the very identity of the subject is _originally_ constituted. No longer conceived of as a rootless individual standing over against, and consequently alienated from, an objective world, of things and persons, devoid of all 'subjective' (which is to say human) value, meaning and significance, the subject is now seen instead as participating in a world of historico-socio-cultural meaning, values and significance, a world of which he or she is an intrinsic part. Clearly such an insight has both profound _substantive_ implications for the human and social scientist's understanding of those individuals and societies which they study, and profound _methodological_ implications for _our_ understanding of the _human and social_ scientist's relations to, and consequent _understanding of_, such individuals and societies.

Those in the human and social sciences who's approach has been influenced by such considerations include Levi-Strauss, Schutz, Luckmann, Garfinkel, Eliade, Foucault, Piaget, Binswanger, Boss, Lacan, Laing, Cooper, Althusser, Marcuse, Adorno, Habermas and many others. Furthermore, somewhat ironically, one can detect in the work of a number of sociologists and philosophers of the physical sciences such as Kuhn, Hesse, Radnitzky, Capra, Margeneau etc., and not a few physical scientists themselves such as Heisenberg, Bohm, Bohr, Stapp and arguably even Einstein, increasing evidence that positivist or neo-positivist epistemologies are being deserted, and not always unconsciously either, in favour of more or less hermeneutic and phenomenological approaches.

In light of all this there has been a recent surge of interest, among philosophers as well as practitioners of the human and social sciences, in anti-reductionist methodologies, and in the philosophical foundations upon which such approaches are grounded, and it is to such interest that this volume caters. It would of course be absurd to hope that one book alone could provide systematic and sustained coverage of such a wide-ranging topic, and even to attempt this task in a single book would result, at best, in a survey of the most superficial kind. This volume therefore has no such pretensions, but rather, drawing contributions from both philosophers and human and social scientists, it attempts to provide selective insights into modern European philosophy and into its application to a few of the methodological problems and substantive issues of the human and social sciences. This, I hope, will provide individual chapters of considerable interest to the specialist reader while also more generally demonstrating something of the nature and potential of such philosophy.

The University of Liverpool, 1986   Simon Glynn

1 Dilthey and universal hermeneutics: the status of the human sciences*

RUDOLF A. MAKKREEL

The term 'human sciences' has become generally accepted today as describing a set of disciplines that includes history, literary criticism, philosophy, psychology and sociology, but the status of these sciences is as much in dispute as ever. When they are contrasted to the natural sciences this is often done to claim that only human sciences are interpretive. However, recent reflection on the history of natural science has made it clear that facts are theory laden and observations paradigm dependent. It seems then that all theoretical science is interpretive. This thesis of universal hermeneutics or theoretical holism has led Mary Hesse, Richard Rorty and others to greatly devalue the distinction, initially made by Wilhelm Dilthey, between the natural and human sciences.

According to this recent view, we cannot simply distinguish between the human sciences interpreting the meaning things have for us and the natural sciences providing causal explanations for them. Dilthey's <u>Verstehen-Erklären</u>

*This article was first published in <u>The Journal</u> of the <u>British Society for Phenomenology</u>, vol.16, No.3, (Oct. 1985), and appears here with the permission of the editor.

1

distinction led him to contrast the human sciences to the natural sciences of the late nineteenth century which operated with a linear, deterministic conception of causality. This contrast admittedly uses an outdated conception of natural science, and must now collapse according to the holists for lack of a supporting opposition.

Charles Taylor does not agree with this prognosis of collapse, for clearly other ways of articulating the distinction are possible. Yet he provides a graphic picture of the supposed situation:

> Old-guard Diltheyans, their shoulders hunched from years long resistance against the encroaching pressure of positive natural science, suddenly pitch forward on their faces as all opposition ceases to the reign of universal hermeneutics.1

What Taylor is imagining ironically could only happen if everything a Diltheyan claimed about the human sciences were based on negative contrasts with the natural sciences. This is, however, not the case. Several points need to be made here:

1. Dilthey did not establish as rigid a distinction between the human and the natural sciences as is often thought.

2. Dilthey himself anticipated theoretical holism without abandoning his claims about the special nature of the human sciences. He distinguished between a classificatory circle common to all sciences, and an interpretive circle peculiar to the human sciences.

3. Much of what Dilthey claims about the human sciences is not negative but is based on positive insights into the relation between understanding, and interpretation, lived experience and the development of world-views.

In this paper I will attempt to elaborate these points and consider how far the efforts to unify the natural and human sciences should be carried.

I. DILTHEY'S EXPLANATION/UNDERSTANDING DISTINCTION

In the Introduction to the Human Sciences (1883) and the Poetics (1887) Dilthey still thought that the human sciences could be explanative in the sense of developing laws of general scope. However, in the Ideas for a Descriptive and

Analytical Psychology (1894) Dilthey comes to the realisation
that laws can only be general and powerful in explaining if
they relate a limited number of well-determined elements.2
He considers this to be possible in the natural sciences, but
not in the human sciences. In the natural sciences our
Erlebnis or lived experience is reduced to external
experience - we isolate what can be observed and measured.
In human sciences like psychology we must preserve the
fullness of lived experience and not sever the relation
between inner feelings and outer events. Whereas it is
relatively easy to analyse external experience into a small
number of constant and measurable elements, analysis of the
more complex givens in the human sciences leaves us with an
indefinite number of possible components most of which cannot
be fully isolated from their context.

Hypotheses proposing general relations among the
deterministic elements of external experience can be easily
tested and gradually enable us to formulate causal laws about
nature. Hypotheses proposing general relations among the
indeterminate components of inner and lived experience are
very much more difficult to corroborate. But according to
Dilthey these components are indeterminate precisely because
they are already interrelated. We do not need hypotheses to
explain how our lived experience is connected. This
experience already comes with an understanding of its
connectedness. Thus Dilthey makes the oft-quoted claim: 'We
explain nature, but we understand psychic life.'3

The distinction between understanding (Verstehen) and
explanation admits of no simple formulation; it is certainly
not reducible to the simple form of immediate versus mediate
knowledge so often suggested. When Dilthey writes in the
Ideas for a Descriptive Psychology that 'we explain through
purely intellectual processes, but we understand through the
co-operation of all our psychic powers...,' it is apparent
that intellectual operations are not excluded from the
process of understanding. Although our lived experience
comes with a direct sense of the psychic nexus of which it is
part, the meaning it has for us results from the
accumulations of past experience. The connectedness of lived
experience is a function of its 'fundedness,' to use a
Deweyan term. Our understanding of the connectedness of
lived experience is thus not simply intuitive, but involves
what Dilthey calls 'elementary logical operations' which
allow us to discern relations among parts and wholes.

In understanding we proceed from the context of the
whole as given in its vitality, in order to make the
parts comprehensible on the basis of it.... All

psychological thought contains the basic feature that
the apprehension of the whole makes possible and
determines the interpretation of the individual.4

Broadly, it could be said that explanation involves
subsuming the particular data or elements that can be
abstracted from our experience under general laws, whereas
understanding is more concerned with focusing on the concrete
contents of individual processes of experience to consider
how they function as part of a larger continum.

Although Dilthey's proposed psychology is based on
understanding, explanative hypotheses are not banished from
it. Dilthey is willing to grant certain hypotheses from
traditional explanative psychology a subordinate role in his
descriptive psychology. It can, he acknowledges, incorporate
those hypotheses which explanative psychology arrived at with
respect to single groups of phenomena.5 If hypotheses are
restricted to questions of details, they are able to fill in
the overall structures provided by descriptive psychology.
Thus explanations can be integrated into the framework
provided by understanding. Later, Dilthey would draw from
this the conclusion that if hypotheses are able to predict
recurring processes in the domain of human action and
production, their scope will have to be severely limited to
specific cultural or social systems.

A proponent of holism might respond by claiming that the
situation is similar in the natural sciences, i.e., that the
laws of physics involve abstract systems. It is true that
the success of natural science depends on being able to
isolate a few key variables and finding correlations between
them. Yet having done that, physicists can arrive at
generalisations which are supposedly valid for all times and
places. This is exactly what is not possible for cultural
and social systems. Empirically warranted generalisations in
the human sciences are restricted to specific systems limited
in time and space. There are no laws of history in general,
as there are laws of nature. At best one will be able to
formulate certain generalisations about the development of a
specfic cultural system like capitalist economies in the
Western world. Thus there is a mere surface analogy between
the natural and human sciences on this point. In Diltheyan
terms, the natural sciences are hypothetical and explanative
from the ground up, whereas human sciences like psychology
are based on the understanding of connections which only
require hypotheses to explain or fill in certain details.

It is precisely when psychological understanding breaks
down that physiological explanations become necessary. It

would be foolish to deny the relevance of all kinds of scientific theories to our understanding of human life. The workings of the body as discovered by the biologist cannot be disassociated from human behaviour. Yet which biological results are brought to bear in our explanations must be determined by a meaning framework established by a human science like psychology or sociology.

Dilthey's distinction of the natural and human sciences is not based on a metaphysical dualism between nature and spirit. Dilthey's claim, that the natural sciences can delimit a number of clearly definable elements and that the human sciences cannot, may sound metaphysical. But in fact, he is only distinguishing two types of experience and what can be anlaysed in them. The content of lived experience cannot be analysed into constant elements, because in lived experience, fact and meaning are inseparable. Thus even when we wish to explain certain historical facts causally, we must at the same time consider their meaning. Dilthey writes:

> When we seek the complex of causes to account for German literature moving away from its Enlightenment phase, then we distinguish groups of causes, estimate their relative weight, and at some point delimit the infinite causal nexus in accordance with the meaning of its moments and in relation to our ends. Thus we articulate a system of influences in order to explain the changes in question.6

In a system of influences like the development of German literature, causation must be understood in relation to a meaning framework. An author trained and nurtured by certain schools of writing may either follow in their line of influence, or rebel. What may seem like simple causal relationships must be evaluated in light of the values of the author and his concrete life-situation. Explanation and the interpretation of relevance tend to merge.

If Dilthey was willing to grant, from the perspective of the human sciences, that the understanding of meaning cannot dispense with the explanation of fact, then in light of more recent theoretical developments we must also admit that explanation in the natural sciences cannot dispense with interpretational questions concerning a proper theoretical framework. But the response to the claim that all science is interpretive is that the human sciences are interpretive in a double sense: they interpret a subject matter which is constituted by the life and products of human beings who already interpret the meanings of their actions. An event like a revolution, however much its course is estabished by impersonal forces, is already meaningful to those who participated in it. Its meaning for today's historian will invariably prove to be different from that given it by the participants, since only by knowing its outcome and consequences can one properly define its structure and analyse it theoretically. But whatever subsequent theoretical interpretations contribute to historical knowledge, they cannot ignore the self-interpretations of the original participants.7 Interpretation in the human sciences is really a mode of reinterpretation of an already interpreted reality.

Proponents of a universal hermeneutics may be correct in observing that causal explanations in the natural sciences are not always as clear cut and determinate as Dilthey thought. As Mary Hesse points out, it is not the language of the human sciences alone that is vague. The language of natural science 'is irreducibly metaphysical and inexact.'8 But whether or not these metaphysical ambiguities in the language of the natural sciences are admitted at the general theoretical level, everyday practice of the natural sciences functions within a more controlled framework designed to forestall or minimise the ambiguous and inexact. This speaks to an important difference between the natural and the human sciences which the proponents of scientific holism tend to ignore. The human sciences proceed on the assumption that ambiguities which demand interpretation occur throughout, from the broadest theoretical level to that of everyday practice, and are not to be suppressed. Just as the philosophical aesthetician must confront the indeterminacy of human creativity in his theory of art, so must the literary critic confront it in the very text that he is analysing.

What all the sciences have in common is not the hermeneutic circle, but what Dilthey identified as a more fundamental 'classificatory circle.' All empirical inquiry involves a circularity in which we strive to integrate knowledge of details into a larger framework. To quote Dilthey:

> The formation of general methods by means of induction presupposes concepts; these are... subordinated to each other by means of classification and every classification of concepts first receives its definitive character from the entire conceptual system.'9

The strict naturalist may deny this circle by claiming that the observation of particulars leads to the formulation of a universal concept, but there must have been some vague notion of something generic which led him to consider a given group of particulars rather than another. According to Dilthey, only logico-mathematical thought can escape the 'circle of classification' - supposedly because it deals with ideal constructs. For all the empirical sciences, natural and human, classification is provisional in that we always anticipate more than is immediately given.

But it is when the process of classification is applied to our experience of human actions and objectifications rather than to our experience of natural events and objects, that interpretation begins to assume a different character. In the natural sciences the classificatory circle is refined in terms of increasingly general hypotheses; only in the human sciences does it turn into the hermeneutic circle.

In the human sciences, where experience provides an initial connectedness, the rationale for classification must lie in articulating appropriate divisions. Thus we find that the hermeneutic circle converges on the typical parts of a whole. In the natural sciences, the main goal of classification is that of overcoming any initial discontinuities and discovering similarities and hypothetical connections. Thus it is that natural description leads to inductve uniformities whereby ever more particualrs can be subsumed under universal laws.

Whereas in the natural sciences the refined universal allows us to increase the number of particulars to which it applies, in the human sciences the enlarged context of interpetation serves as a basis for a better understanding of the original material under consideration. New facts are used not merely to confirm or refine generalisations derived from old data, but to constantly reconsider the meaning of these very data. Thus, as we widen our context to that of universal history and of mankind as a whole, interpretation does not move away from the problem of individuality. Rather, we are led to compare and reflect on typical differences and thereby characterise the uniqueness or concrete meaning of a given event or life-complex. To bring the richness and scope of the historical world to the understanding of individual life is the ultimate hermeneutic task of the human sciences.

To the extent that interpretation plays a role in the natural sciences it is classificatory and not, as in the human sciences, an explication of experiential meaning. Although the two kinds of sciences share the same logical base and many of the same methods, they manifest different goals. But these differences are not of such magnitude that the two kinds of sciences cannot co-operate.

II. REFLECTIVE HOLISM

By turning now to Dilthey's theory of <u>Weltanschauungen</u> we can gain a somewhat different perspective on the relation between the sciences, which moves us from theoretical holism to what I would call philosphical or reflective holism. So far we have related the natural and human sciences by showing how the latter must make use of the results of the former. Conversely, Dilthey's reflective holism suggests that the natural sciences are in some sense dependent on the human sciences.

Thomas Kuhn, it will be recalled, has characterised basic paradigm switches in natural sciences as changes of world-view. Since this has given impetus to much of the current discussion of all science as interpretive, it seems appropriate to explore whether in Dilthey's influential <u>Weltanschauung</u> theory, a world-view is, in fact, roughly equivalent to a paradigm.

As a first step, it will be important to review Dilthey's analysis of the function and genesis of world-views.

A <u>Weltanschauung</u> is an overall perspective which integrates our different cognitive, evaluative and volitional attitudes towards the world. The idea of a unified perspective on reality has been increasingly neglected in an age marked by a tacit division of tasks: the natural sciences are prized for cognitive achievement, the humanities for evaluative discernment, and the social sciences for defining volitional goals. The possibility of such holistic perspectives is often questioned; and when considered at all, the problem is usually defined as that of combining already divergent theoretical and practical concerns. But Dilthey derives the need for a <u>Weltanschauung</u> from our everyday experiential concerns of life in which there is no theory/practice distinction as yet. Since all science grows out of this experience, it may well be a mistake to approach the problem as, for example, does Habermas, from a prior characterisation according to which the natural sciences exemplify technical interests and the human sciences practical-communicative interests. According to Dilthey, the human sciences encompass not only the evaluative concerns of the humanities and the practical concerns of the social sciences, but also the theoretical understanding of the relation among all human pursuits and results, including those of the natural sciences. This is why philosphy, for one, is a human science.

In his 1911 essay, <u>Types of World Views</u>, Dilthey has a chapter entitled 'Life and World Views' which gives an account of reflection on life prior to scientific inquiry.10 'Science' is used here by Dilthey in the singular to cover all the sciences. He shows how reflection on the meaning of life eventually comes to be articulated in religious, poetic and metaphysical world-views.

Dilthey begins by describing how the life of each individual produces his or her own world-view of life-relations. His phrase is: 'seine eigene Welt von Lebensbezüge' (here Dilthey anticipates two Husserlian ideas: that of ownness and that of a life-world or Lebenswelt.) Dilthey's life-world is constituted in lived experience - not in the special activities of thought and practice which are projective and forward looking. In lived experience I do not apprehend myself, the objects and persons about me as standing in causal relations. Rather, I find myself in meaningful life-relations to everything around me. In these life-relations I adopt neither a theoretical nor a practical, but a reflective attitude. I find that some of the things and people around me further my existence, and others restrict it. I orient myself to my world which provides the context for the meaning of my life. The result of this is called Lebenserfahrung - life-experience which sums up not only my understanding of the world, but also the understanding of those around me as embodied in a common language, customs, institutions and history.

But there is a point where this initial understanding of my world breaks down. I come upon ultimate contradictions, the riddles of life and death, which resist comprehension. Then I become estranged from my world and because I no longer understand it, I seek an explanation of its now unfamiliar features.

The procedure then is to try to explain by analogy. A world-view is an attempt to solve the riddles of life by using familiar features of ordinary experience as a basis for explaining the unfamiliar. Well-understood structures of my life-world become the basis for constructing a coherent and complete explanation of reality. The explanation may not be scientific, but merely a linguistic or metaphorical clarification. Explanation, as we see here, is no longer assumed by Dilthey to be necessarily a causal explanation.

With the admission of a non-causal kind of explanation in the context of the Weltanschauung theory, it becomes possible to reconsider the earlier distinction between explanation and understanding. Explanations become necessary whenever

9

understanding is disrupted. In pre-scientific experience this can be due to a natural event like an earthquake or to an anomaly within my familiar world, such as a hostile remark from a friend.

Within the human sciences much of the explanation for anomalies in my familiar world ultimately takes the form of reinterpretation. When a simple reason for my friend's unexpected behavior cannot be found, it may become necessary to reinterpret the pattern of his past behavior to see whether it was really as friendly as I thought. More generally, human scientists understand by articulating the implicit structures of life-experience and tradition that regulate our human activities. They also refine common sense reflection on the meaning of life: firstly by analysing the world into specific social and cultural systems and secondly by analysing world-views into distinguishable types. Explanation of anomalies will involve the reinterpretation of implicit structures in relation to the explanatory potential of specific systems and Weltanschauung types.

In the natural sciences, a natural event like an earthquake - however unusual it may be - will be explained in terms of uniform laws of nature. This is done by transforming the general riddles of life addressed by world-views into more specific problems, which are, to use Kuhn's terms, puzzles that are in principle soluble. One could claim that the natural sciences succeed in explaining natural events by deconstructing our ordinary way of looking at things. Such a deconstruction is conceived in the reductive sense of an Abbau and is not to be regarded as a reinterpretation.

A deconstruction normally serves to eliminate as much as possible the indeterminacy that characterises ordinary experience. Thus it decomposes the world by extracting or abstracting from pervasive features (such as secondary qualities) or assumptions (such as the earth being at the centre of the universe). By contrast, the kind of reinterpretation of life-experience that we have been discussing does not purposely exclude or ignore any aspects of experience, but shifts the emphasis, from aspects which were initially important, to others of current concern.

Deconstruction may, of course, occur in the human sciences, especially in those generally regarded as the social sciences where it is possible to isolate discrete systems of relations. But because human behavior involves the intersection of so many different systems, the usefulness of deconstruction is limited by the need to maintain a reference to the original whole. A psychoanalytic reading of literary works, for example, may be considered a deconstruction in so far as it exposes the underlying sexual dynamics of a text. But however interesting such a reading may be, it contributes to literary understanding only when it is referred back to the whole text and enables us to clarify aspects of it that had previously proved enigmatic or obscure. Much attention has been paid to psychoanalytic explanations of Hamlet's hesitation, which has long occupied so many critics. Here a deconstructive reading becomes a means to a literary reinterpretation which expands, rather than reduces, our original understanding.

Paradigm revolutions in science allow us to deconstruct old perspectives on nature and dismiss certain compilations of data as no longer relevant.11. As indicated by the term 'paradigm switch' such a change is often sudden, and it may be argued that shifts in world-views also involve a similarly rapid transformation. However, among the three, recurrent types of world-view that Dilthey has distinguished in the Western tradition, the transition from one to another has been a gradual, developmental process. Whichever of the world-view types may be, or is becoming, dominant in a historical epoch, the others also continue to develop to better embody the life-experiences that inform them. Thus, by the time the objective idealism of Schelling and Hegel became predominant over the subjective idealism of Kant and Fichte, it was no longer the objective idealism of Spinoza, but had incorporated the intervening advances made possible by naturalism and subjective idealism. Moreover, the process of change is inherently slow because Dilthey conceived the world-view types as expressions of life experienced in common. While natural scientists may effect revolutions by defying common sense, human scientists and philosophers must always bring their results in conformity with life-experience and its slowly developing judgements of common sense - reinterpreting the understanding attained by past generations, rather than de- or re-constructing it. The pre-scientific meanings embodied in life-experience and Weltanschauungen can never be ignored in the human sciences.

Dilthey's Weltanschauung theory has been strongly attacked by Husserl, who charges that a world-view settles fundamental questions prematurely, and thus closes off the infinite scientific quest for truth. To be sure, a world-view articulates our past and present understanding of the world, and is a way of coming to terms with what is puzzling in it. However, it presents a provisional answer to ultimate questions and need not foreclose any questions, nor compete with the kind of problem-solving that exists in natural science. This latter is the function of paradigms, which should not be confused with world-views. In point of fact, the sense of totality present in a world-view may serve as a constant reminder of the difference between partial and total solutions.

Yet Husserl's objection does speak to the point that world-views are not easily subject to change There is not in world-views the element of choice that exists in the adoption and displacement of paradigms. A world-view is arrived at on the basis of common meaning; and one usually acquires, rather than adopts, a Weltanschauung type through life-experience.

A scientific paradigm reflects a temporary consensus that establishes a program for future scientific inquiry. A consensus is a shared belief, but it may be very limited in scope and is not based on a more general, common attitude or meaning. Here we might use a distinction that Taylor has made between consensus and common meaning.12 A consensus is arrived at when different individual view-points are reconciled, when different attitudes are made to converge. A common meaning is something communal, which we accept through our participation - it is usually imbued with traditional values that are indeterminate and require interpretation. Paradoxically, the tacitly accepted common value of freedom leads to anything but a consensus when interpretation attempts to determine its meaning.

This is what happens in world-views as well. A common stock of life-experience leads different people to articulate it in different ways. A consensus is often easier to arrive at in a domain like natural science where there are no common meanings to interpret.

*   *   *

A further point concerning Dilthey's Weltanschauung theory has bearing on current discussions of the interpretive sciences. The fact that Dilthey analyses world-views as three exclusive types invites comparison with Kuhn's characterisation of paradigms as 'incommensurable ways of seeing the world and of practicing science in it.'13 Yet there are important differences. The three types of world-view are rooted in a common psychological life, although each type emphasises one of its aspects. Naturalism emphasises cognition, subjective idealism volition, and objective idealism feeling, but they do not ignore the other aspects. The world-view types are exclusive, but not incommensurable.

Kuhn's claim that scientific paradigms are incommensurable
has led to the idea of the incommensurability of
interpretations in general. Rorty has made it the basis for
his distinction between epistemological and hermeneutical
philosophy. Epistemological philosophy proceeds on the
assumption that all contributions to a given discourse are
commensurable, while heremeneutical philosophy is 'largely a
struggle against this assumption.'14 Hermeneutics, according
to Rorty, accepts the incommensurability of different
theories and cultures, and considers futile any attempt to
reduce their different claims into a neutral language of non-
interpreted facts or priviliged representations.

The thesis of this incommensurability may be taken in a
weak or a strong form. It appears acceptable enough if it is
taken in the weak sense that there are no common measures,
absolute elements or units common to all things experienced
and conceived. The only measures we can agree upon are
mathematical conventions like the meter which designate an
artifical consensus not subject to any circle of
classification or interpretation. However, the
incommensurability thesis is unacceptable if it is taken in
the strong sense of there being no common basis for
comparison. Dilthey's world-views are exclusive, but
comparable, and may be measured against a common background
of life-experience. They are even commensurable in a
figurative sense if one takes their communal context as a
measure. Different interpetations of our common meanings are
possible but they are not incommensurable when the human
sciences are called upon to understand these differences. To
the extent that the natural sciences abstract from this
common background of life-experience, different perspectives
or paradigms become incommensurable in the strong sense of
incomparability.

But we should not generalise from paradigms in the natural
sciences to interpretations in the human sciences. If we do
so, we will be led to Rorty's conclusion that interpretations
are not ways of knowing, but merely ways of coping. With
this in mind, we can turn to some final considerations on the
scope of the human sciences and their overall relations to
the natural sciences.

III. CONCLUSION

The old positivist opponents of Dilthey granted the human
sciences too little, the new holistic proponents of a
universal hermeneutics seem to grant the human sciences too
much. But to admit that all the sciences share the task of
interpretation with the human sciences is not necessarily to

grant a fundamental status to the human sciences nor to elevate its results. Many have used the interpretive parallels to show that irrational, non-scientific factors are at work in the natural sciences, just as they have always been assumed to be operative in the human sciences. All scientific theory is reduced to a kind of pragmatic coping.

Others point out that background practices may influence science without necessarily contaminating the final theoretical product. Thus Hubert Dreyfus writes:

> The holistic point that Vorhabe or pre-cognitive practical know-how is necessary even in the natural sciences does not preclude the possibility of formulating scientific theories in which the interpetive practices of the observer play no internal role.15

Background practices are involved in natural sciences but can be ignored, according to Dreyfus. He contrasts this with the human sciences where background practices cannot be ignored. For if

> the human sciences claim to study human activities then the human sciences, unlike the natural sciences, must take account of these human activities which make possible their own disciplines.16

The human sciences are inherently self-referential because they are created by man to study all that man has created. How can they avoid reflecting on their own products when claiming to study human products in general? Moreover, I would add, how can they avoid studying the activity of natural scientists and the theories they have produced? Kuhn's history of scientific revolutions and of the background practices which produced them is really a kind of sociological interpretation of science. He is analysing natural science from a human science point of view. It is therefore not too presumptuous to say that the human sciences like history, sociology and philosophy can study and even analyse the claims the scientist makes about nature, as long as we remember that they are not assuming to verify these claims.

Since nature as we see it around us is everywhere reshaped by human activities, it is only by a special act of abstraction that the natural scientist can study nature as if it existed independently of us. Thus one could modify Dreyfus' claim about the natural sciences and say that the background practices involved in them are not so much

14

ignored, as self-consciously suppressed. Yet background practices stand in need of analysis by human scientists when questions are raised about the means of discovery or about the wisdom of developing certain areas like nuclear energy or biogenetic engineering.

It has been suggested that the natural sciences can be a model for the human sciences in being able to confirm results, and that the human sciences can provide the elements of metascientific reflection about the relations between discovery, extra-scientific influences and the setting of goals in the natural sciences.17 This is based on the hope that the hermeneutic circle of the human sciences can be expanded to become the basis for a general logic of discovery. Whether or not this is possible can be left an open question. But the point that bears emphasis here is that the hermeneutic circle in the human sciences is a productive circle. The purpose of the circle is to widen our framework of interpretation and generate new meaning, so that we will not just refine our original understanding, but enrich it. The hermeneutic circle of the human sciences is vicious only if it is used to demonstrate or confirm a thesis - used, that is, as a confirmatory circle. If we appeal to the overall sense of a passage to assign a meaning to an ambiguous phrase, and use this part to confirm our original reading of the passage, then we are guilty of a petitio principii.

It is easy to view interpretation pragmatically as a useful way of discovering new ideas without worrying about verification. This is especially the case with a paradigm. It suggests avenues of inquiry which may be verifiable, but is not itself verifiable. But interpretations in the human sciences must be more than heuristic. They are expected to stand the test of life-experience and common sense. Although the hermeneutic circle does not allow us to confirm our indeterminate pre-understanding of human affairs, it must permit us to enrich it while at the same time reaffirming it.

By expanding the experiential background of the sciences to include not only practice, but also reflection on life-experience and world-views, it becomes possible to move beyond the theory/practice distinction between the natural and human sciences.

The theoretical and practical extrapolate from experience in their separate ways; theory is problem-oriented and practice task-oriented. In reflection about life-experience, however, we articulate a sphere of relations that can be expanded into a world-view including not only the everyday practices and pre-conceptions that we share with immediate contemporaries, but also theoretical interpretations of reality. When the human sciences are grounded in such a broad reflective understanding of experience they can provide the framework for the natural sciences as well.

Perhaps the best way to conceive the relations between explanation and interpretation in the sciences is to consider them in terms of the two modes of judgement Kant distinguishes in the Critique of Judgement. Explanation is like making a determinant judgement where the rule is clear and the task of judgement is to properly subsume particulars under it. Interpretation is like making a reflective judgement where there is no given rule to guide judgement. A determinant judgement characterises the particular facts of experience by some already established theoretical universal - whether this be a principle, law or concept. With reflective judgement, however, we begin with particular data in an attempt to formulate a not already available general characterisation. Reflection never accepts incommensurability as final.

Kant himself applied the concept of reflective judgement primarily to the problem of taste, and I have elsewhere tried to generalise about the role of reflection in the human sciences.18 But Kant also applied reflective judgement to the problem of discerning teleology in a nature which is constituted for us in terms of mechanistic causality, and most importantly to the problem of systematising our knowledge of nature. This suggests that reflective judgement can be a model for interpretation both in the human sciences and the natural sciences. At the same time, we can apply Kant's claim that reflective judgement functions constitutively for questions of taste and culture, but merely regulatively for question of teleology in nature, by arguing that interpretation is constitutive for the human sciences and regulative for the natural sciences.

The importance of the distincion between determinant and reflective judgement is that one deduces order, the other educes it. Determinant judgement imposes order on data from without (i.e., from a relatively and absolutely fixed context). Reflective judgement, however, finds an indeterminate order within what is given and proceeds to relate it to ever more encompassing contexts. An example of a determinant judgement is a specific hypothesis which is either confirmed or disconfirmed by being applied to particular instances. An example of a reflective judgement is a comparison in which X is claimed to be a prototype for Y. In the former the particular is subsumed under a universal - and if it diverges it disproves the hypothesis. In the latter a degree of divergence is accepted and may lead us to enrich the prototype. Determinant judgements are refined by being narrowed, reflective judgements by being broadened. Reflective judgements are adaptive to specific data of our life-experience and ultimately point to the most concrete and inclusive of all contexts: the life-world. There is no doubt then that all determinant judgements must ultimately be framed within the scope of reflective judgement. This is another way of developing the insight of the proponents of universal hermeneutics that all determinate explanations occur within the indeterminate framework of interpretation.

In all inquiry we ultimately come upon indeterminacies which require interpretation. Yet all science, whether natural or human, aims to articulate relatively stable contexts - what Dilthey called systems - in order to arrive at determinant judgements. That is, by carving out determinate subsystems within the world as a whole, data can be more readily correlated and explained. It is clear, however, that whereas in the natural sciences determinant judgements about physical processes can be for the most part abstracted from reflection on the life-world, any determinant judgements arrived at in the human sciences about human action and production must be related back to reflective judgement about life-experience.

It is in this sense that interpretation is more deeply rooted in the human sciences than in the natural sciences. It is worth reaffirming that those who have pointed to the role of interpretation in the natural sciences are historians and philosophers looking at the history of science from a human science perspective. This suggests that instead of seeing the natural and human sciences as standing side by side, and gradually becoming more alike, we could regard the human sciences as coming once again to encompass the natural sciences in their view. This potential orientational role of reflective judgement and interpretation in the human sciences is important if the natural sciences are not to be reduced to mere technological endeavours.

REFERENCES

Translations from the German text are Professor Makkreel's.

1. Charles Taylor, 'Understanding in Human Sciences,' Review of Metaphysics, vol.XXXIV, 1, 1980, p.26.

2. Wilhelm Dilthey, Gesammelte Schriften, vol.V, Vandenhoeck & Ruprecht, Göttingen, 1924, p.139.

3. Ibid., p.144.

4. Ibid., p.172.

5. Ibid., p.173.

6. Ibid., p.158.

7. Cf. Richard Bernstein's discussion of Alfred Schutz and the postulate of subjective interpetation in The Restructuring of Social and Political Theory, University of Pennsylvania Press, Philadelphia, 1980, pp.138-40.

8. See Mary Hesse, Revolutions and Reconstructions in the Philosophy of Science, Illinois University Press, Bloomington, 1980, p.173.

9. Wilhelm Dilthey, Gesammelte Schriften, vol.VIII, Vandenhoeck & Ruprecht, Göttingen, 1931, p.160.

10. Ibid., p.78ff.

11. See Thomas Kuhn, The Structure of Scientific Revolutions, University of Chicago Press, Chicago, 1975, p.129.

12. See Charles Taylor, 'Interpretation and the Sciences of Man,' reprinted in Paul Rabinow and William M. Sullivan (eds.) Interpretive Social Science: A Reader, University of California Press, Berkeley, 1979, pp.25-71.

13. Kuhn, op. cit., p.4.

14. Richard Rorty, Philosophy and the Mirror of Nature, Princeton University Press, Princeton, 1979, p.316.

15. Hubert Dreyfus, 'Holism and Hermeneutics,' Review of Metaphysics, vol.XXXIV, 1, 1980, p.16.

16. <u>Ibid.</u>, p.17.

17. See Walther Ch. Zimmerli, 'Paradigmawechsel und Streitbehebung. Einheitswissenschaft-einmal anders,' in Roland Simon-Schaeffer and Walter Ch. Zimmerli (eds.) <u>Wissenschaftsheorien der Geisteswissenschaften</u>, ed. Hoffmann und Campe Verlag, Hamburg, 1975, p.352.

18. See Rudolf Makkreel, <u>Dilthey, Philosopher of the Human Studies</u>, Princeton University Press, Princeton, 1975, pp.226-246.

2 Self-evidence or mediation in intercultural understanding? The dialectics of self and other in social anthropology

KLAUS-PETER KOEPPING

PHENOMENOLOGY AND SEMIOTICS AS OPPOSING MODES OF 'VERSTEHEN?'

It has often been suggested there is an unbridgeable chasm between the philosophical attitudes of Husserl and of Pierce, or between mediation and presuppositionlessness, between radical doubt leading to incontrovertible truth and enthusiastically held a priori prejudices, between phenomenological belief in unmediated self-evidence and the semiotic insistence of an infinite interpretational task.

 For the social scientist, particularly the social anthropologist who considers the objective to lie in the understanding and explaining of the social reality through the discovery of the invariant features behind cultural variability, it may seem necessary to choose between the above solutions to the problem of acquiring knowledge about this social reality. Considering that most modern social scientists are concerned with the task of describing and comparing the multitude of lived worlds, those many forms of legitimising (through so many different value-preferences) diverse designs for living called 'cultures,' it would seem only natural that the very awareness and admission of this multiplicity of world-views (and the awareness that researcher and researched belong to different horizons of meaning) might force the comparative scholar to come down squarely in favour of the semiological paradigm. This paradigm holds that a sign is a representation of an object, but that neither object nor meaning are directly presented to cognition, that cognition is always mediated and that the mediating agent, the sign, 'stands for that object not in all respects, but in reference to a sort of idea.'1   More importantly the sign is, as the founders of structural linguistics asserted, completely arbitrary.2 Thus, while the direct givenness of the everyday life-world 3 seems to predispose toward an epistemology of unmediated self-evidence, the bridging of diverse cultural horizons seems indeed more naturally to make the researcher prone to be a mediator par excellence, to play the role of the translator or hermeneutic agent.

THE FUSION OF TWO RESEARCH MODES IN SOCIAL ANTHROPOLOGY

However, the reality of research in the social sciences is more complex and thus the choice between two apparently opposite paradigms, the choice between interpretation and 'direct understanding,' is not by necessity mutually exclusive. Depending upon which kind of research within social anthropological work we rely on and to which element of the research process we refer, each paradigm may play its appropriate part.

   The apparent contradiction between paradigms of unmediated self-evidence and of interpretation seems reflected in and paralleled by two opposing, but mutually dependent operations, namely the collection of data which is generally referred to as ethnographic field-work, and the comparative approach of the ethnologist who looks for the commonalities between diverse cultures and societies.

   The first procedure referred to, the ethnographic data-collection, seems to find its ideal epistemological basis in the notion of direct givenness or the taken-for-granted life-world of the social actor under observations, provided the aim of the field-work is the accumulation of data about the meaning which actions have for the actors engaged in such. Underlying this notion of ethnographic field-work is the application of the procedure of participant observation which incorporates the methodological step of 'understanding,' with its Weberian implication of 'subjectively meaningful action.' If the ethnographer's work includes these parameters in his or her approach to field-work, it should remove the suspicion that participant observation entails or is understood as a misguided Diltheyan form of 'reliving' or 'empathy,' or any equally suspicious notion of a nebulous subjectivity which cannot be intersubjectively corroborated or verified (or even replicated).

By contrast, the second, or comparative, step of the procedure, works with pre-given and pre-selected terms of reference - mostly taken from the scientific orientation of generalised concepts, - which seem to fit more easily the approach of hermeneutic interpretation. The comparative procedure can of course be informed by very different theoretical presuppositions. In order to be truly a hermeneutic or interpretative, comparative science, social anthropology or any other field dealing with the establishing and maintaining of intersubjective areas of meaning have to ensure that the scientific terms of reference do not violate the categories established by ethnographic work. Otherwise, the comparative procedure could, if only relying on generalised concepts, end in a more structuralist approach which does not take cognisance of individual variation and context. While generally the ethnographer could easily be labelled an empiricist, however impure, the comparativist tends easily towards structuralist interpretations. In order to not have the two steps or procedures break apart completely in the social anthropological tradition, the reference to the horizon of the social actor, or the ethnographic paradigm within the comparative framework, becomes very important.

Yet, as I shall show in the following excurse, this dichotomy of the separation of two research methodologies or approaches to reality within social anthropology, paints a much too simplified and therefore misleading picture of the research realities. Even the ethnographer who collects 'neutrally' those data which show the meaningfulness of life-events to the actors performing those acts (in their frame of reference), is 'contaminated' by the very questions with which he or she as social anthropologist approaches this subject matter in the field, and the frame of references under which the research act itself is performed.

Though I shall in the following concentrate on the research procedure and processes as they are performed or experienced by the ethnographer (the passive voice is intentionally added here), it is clear from the start that any social anthropologist who works with the currently acknowledged requirement of the field-work approach, uses both modes of methodology: namely 'direct givenness' through understanding actions in the frame of reference of the actors, as well as interpretative mediation in the comparative phase of the work. (Actually even this directly given is already implicitly mediated by the field-worker's implicity underlying self-referential base).

I would therefore preliminarily suggest that the social anthropologist is thus executing constant shifts of emphasis of methodological paradigms, and, according to the varying demands and aims of the research orientation, will have to shift hence and forth as of logical, epistemological, even existential necessity. Phenomenological approaches as well as semiotics (in the sense of Peirce a task of interpreting signs), as modes of legitimation for the comparative methodology, have therefore to be seen as a dialectical unit which cannot easily be separated without the danger of falling either into the reductionist camp of pure positivism, (treating the social world as natural object), or into the equally indefensible position of a spurious subjective view of cultural life which, were it not for the 'material sedimentation' of meanings, (for instance in the form of mythologies or social conventions which may be recalled and recorded in symbolic form) would - disregarding for the moment the variations of those symbolic representations through the actors themselves - only be accessible to the intuitions of an individual researcher.

There are two reasons for the impossibility of opting unambiguously for one of the two supposedly opposed paradigms for deriving sense from the social world. The first is the invaluable assistance which Husserl's questions have given the social sciences' self-understanding, and the second is the rapprochement which has taken place between phenomenological and semiological (in Pierce's sense) views regarding the influence of the social sphere upon cognitive structures, about the relationships between perception and intersubjective action (of which dialogical language is the paradigm case).

PHENOMENOLOGY AS ANNIHILATION THROUGH EPOCHÉ,4   NOT AS PURE TRANSCENDENTALISM

Thus, the Husserlian return to the foundations of knowledge as anchored in a self-aware subjective consciousness, and his search for a knowledge which surpasses any contingent empiricism by concentrating on the givenness of the essence of meaning in consciousness, seemed to open the way for the social scientist to get away from what Zygmunt Bauman has called the 'sociologist's irritating habit' of objectifying meanings which are imposed upon the individual from the outside, from such nebulous entities as society or culture; norms or values that are understood as reified entities. Husserl's question, 'how do we know what things are,' seemed finally to combine the two realms of epistemology and ontology (a possibility hinted at by the pre-Socratics) which much of European philosophy had been intent on separating.

Husserl initiated the restoration of subjectivity as the only source of true knowledge about the objective world (ourselves included) whereby the act of intentionality 5 bestows meaning on the objects which we know or are conscious of. However, in order to arrive at the essence of the world of things, everything contingent has to be cleansed from consciousness, and to this end Husserl introduced the methodological device (as attitude or mental operation) of epoché or transcendental reduction, suspending all, including the individual knowing subject, which is culturally specific, or contingent in some way. What was left, Husserl maintained, was our immediate or unmediated consciousness of things.

It is clearly this kind of experience of the essential features of the object world which transcendental consciousness is supposed to provide, but it is this level of 'non-mediated givenness' which has drawn most of the attacks against the whole Husserlian enterprise: it is indeed questionable how relevant this transcendental consciousness is to the social sciences. Even if we were to admit that the social scientist who is engaged in field-work in the form of participant observation could, qua participant, become conscious of an essential or culturally unmediated or 'objectively' given world, we cannot avoid the fact that the very attempt to describe and transmit this experience (of self, of the other or of any interplay between self and other) involves a return to that form of socio-culturally relative contingency which is inherent in any symbol-using context. This is the very criticism which Bauman has in mind when he asks:

> What is the value of understanding which can remain itself only in the thinned, antiseptic atmosphere of phenomenological insight, only at the cost of its separation from daily discourse, only in so far as no attempt is made to return it to the discourse from which it has been separated.6

Bauman thus voices the scepticism of most social scientists who cannot imagine that we can really regain the world of intersubjectivity via the rarefied atmosphere of transcendental subjectivity; a problem which leads most scholars to prefer the phenomenology of the everyday life-world as modified by Alfred Schutz.7

In this light it becomes clear that for Husserl there are two levels of self-evidence, one being the self-evidence of essential structures, the product of transcendental subjectivity, the other being the self-evidence of taken-for-granted presuppositions (Selbstverständlichkeit) which are the essential features of our everyday naive experiencing of the life-world. Yet even recognising this, few of our difficulties are resolved: in both cases the primary experience remains unreflected, unexamined, non-transmittable. Instead of attempting to solve the apparent antinomies and paradoxes of consciousness and self-consciousness, which Husserl's attempt to found the sciences on transcendental or essential precepts seems to entail, I would rather like to take up other aspects of the methodological suggestions of Husserl. As we have just hinted he did not merely advocate an epoché which leaves us with the unmediated transcendentalism or absolutist perspective supposedly characteristic of 'the scientific world-view:' he also introduced the epoché as a reverse methodology a movement back from the presuppositions underlying the sciences, to the life-world of our immediate experience. In order to regain the life-world, says Husserl, we ought to bracket or suspend those beliefs and presuppositions which we derive from science itself: here lies the great promise for a genuine social science. This seminal approach is entailed by Husserl's notion of annihilation (Vernichtung) with which all phenomenological approaches must start:

> If one carries through the reduction, as the precondition for a thoroughly critical and radical philosophy, he must make it clear to himself that he has defined an artificial domain of inquiry. To disengage the thinker and his experiences from his natural and cultural setting is to introduce artificial conditions. 'Pure subjectivity' is not to be found in nature. It is a device of method, an abstraction, a falsification in fact.8

Although one may entertain the point of view that it does not matter what form of 'falsification' is imposed upon the world of objects and of human action, I think that with the attitude of epoché in reverse, with the suspension of the scientific prejudices - or, to put it into a hermeneutic frame of reference, the admission as well as the putting aside of the scientific prejudice, - we 'falsify' in a very different way than would be the case if, following Durkheim, we adopted the method of objective science. This would result in a form of naturalistic fallacy, the reifying of the social world as if it were an object, implying that it is possible to describe without effort or without inner reflection the world as it really is. For Durkheimians, as for instance Gellner, things and ideas stand apart from the researcher as items which do not need an interpretative agent, or if such is required, the scientific status of social enquiry is taken as unproblematically objective and superior to any other form of knowledge. Though sceptical about the feasibility of Husserl's programme, it was Kolakowski who pointed clearly to the naturalist and empiricist limitations to which Husserl directed our attention:

> He better than anybody, compelled us to realise the painful dilemma of knowledge: either consistent empiricism, with its relativistic, sceptical results.... or transcendental dogmatism which cannot really justify itself and remains in the end an arbitrary decision...9

The epistemological impasse has been most succinctly put by Kolakowski as follows:

> The transcendentalist compels the empiricist to renounce -for the sake of consistency - the concept of truth: the empiricist compels the transcendentalist to confess that in order to save the belief in Reason, he is in duty bound to admit a kingdom of beings he cannot justify.10

Yet, I would add, the impasse shown is not of an absolute order: it is and remains an impasse as to the truth value of statements about reality, and at that level the impasse can certainly never be resolved in a logical manner. But Husserl's very search for the essence of reality and his proposal for an adequate methodology are not touched by the critique. If we start from the premise of the relativity of world-views, including the relative truth of scientific descriptions of reality, it remains worthwhile to search for a way which most adequately takes account of the distortions which creep into those descriptions of reality. If the epoché, the bracketing or suspending of scientific prejudices,is a falsification, so be it: I think that most social scientists who work with qualitative methodologies, in particular social anthropologists, will welcome this epistemological device, this conscious application of a reverse mental reservation, because they intend to get as close as possible to social reality as it is lived by people, people who do not normally undertake the falsifying abstraction of distinguishing their natural prejudices when living and experiencing. Critics of Husserl might be correct in maintaining that the transcendental subject is speechless and therefore irrelevant to social discourse. But so is the subject who lives unreflectively. The social scientists who wants to get close to the very nature of the unreflective life-worlds of others (and his own) will be able to do so only by applying the epoché in reverse; by reflecting on the presuppositions or prejudices of their so called objective method of investigation. Before embarking on a description and analysis of the qualitative method which has become paradigmatic for a number of social sciences, of participant observation as introduced at first by social anthropologists (who did not often have even an inkling of the Neo-Kantian debate on the status of the method of 'Verstehen'), it is important to point to a perhaps surprising convergence of thought between linguistics and semiology and the self-reflective interest of Husserl. The former area has undergone several radical changes since Peirce and now comes close to many precepts of Husserl himself. A focus on language, the mediating tool par excellence, shows how Husserl's point of view evolved from a very stringent abstract search for general laws to an admission of the subjective element in communication, which taken together with recent moves in the field of semiology, enables us to become aware of, to assess and evaluate diverse forms of prejudice, even if we cannot eliminate them.

CONVERGENCE OF PHENOMENOLOGY AND SEMIOLOGY

The convergence of phenomenology with diverse schools of linguistics is of a twofold nature: phenomenology and structural linguistics start on the basis of similar premises, and paralleling Husserl's moves from his austere Logical Investigations to his Formal and Transcendental Logik, structural linguists moved from the search for invariable patterns to the investigation of the speaking subject. Peirce as well as Husserl, and independently of both, Saussure, started with similar aims in mind, and, as Roman Jakobson has convincingly shown, Husserl and Peirce both start with John Locke's science or doctrine of signs, as established in his Essay Concerning Human Understanding. Peirce took over Locke's term, semiotics, for the doctrine of signs, and he defined as his task the 'study of the doctrine of the true nature and the basic modifications of a possible semiosis.'11

Structural linguistic's development was all but based on Husserl's programmatic statement in his Logical Investigations concerning the possibility of a pure grammar, for subsequent inquiry led away from the then

fashionable empirical grammars to arrive at the so-called
structural elements, and the laws governing all language.
Anton Marty (amongst others) showed that Husserl's conception
of an a priori grammar has important forerunners in the Stoic
literature, the Cartesians of the Port-Royal as well as in
Locke and Leibniz: the leader of the Moscow circle of
linguists, Gustav Spet, also wanted, like Husserl, to
establish the science of a universal grammar. This project
meshed very well with Husserl's lecture of 1935 on the
Phenomenology of Language, and it was continued by the
founder of the Prague linguistic circle, Vilem Mathesius.12

However, it is at this time that the shift of emphasis away
from transcendental realities and from pure structural
analysis occurs in both linguistics and phenomenology. As
Merleau-Ponty has convincingly shown, 13 Husserl changed
his views on the relation of language to reflection between
his Logical Investigations (1900) and his later work
Formal and Transcendental Logic, (1929) moving away from
the search for the apodictically true and essential grammar
and the postulate of a pure universal essence (which passes
concrete language by) of which each empirical mode of speech
is only a possible instance. Husserl thus actually parallels
in his search, and in his movement from a priori linguistic
universals to an awareness of the speaking subject, the
movement of structural linguistics from invariable features
of la langue to the interdependence between langue and
parole, between form and content, between code and message,
between competence and performance, between signans and
signatum. As far as Husserl is concerned, his radical shift
toward the speaking subject can be gauged from the following
statement:

> The intention of signifying (Meinung) is not found
> outside the words or at their side. It is rather the
> case that, in speaking, I constantly achieve an
> internal fusion of the intention with the words.
> This intention, we may say, animates the words, and
> as a result all the words, and indeed each word,
> incarnate an intention; and once incarnated, they
> bear this in themselves as their meaning.14

As Merleau-Ponty rightly observed,

> We are with this statement far removed from the
> initial position of Logical Investigations, where the
> existence of a given particular language was founded
> on ideal existence, a universal grammar, the essence
> of language. Here now, the possibility of an ideal
> existence and of communication between particular

subjects is ultimately grounded in the act of speaking.15

The relevance of a phenomenological return to the speaking subject for the starting point of a modern and revised form of structural linguistics, has been expounded in great clarity by the Dutch disciple of Husserl, Hendrik Pos who showed that, if we follow Husserl, reflecting on language is no longer a departure from it: it is rather to recover an experience which is anterior to the objectifying of language and certainly anterior to the scientific observation of it.16

Pos' position is particularly relevant because he insists on the speaking subject (sujet parlant) as focus of study, in opposition to what he called behaviouristic objectification. I think that this return to the social world, the life-world of acting subjects as object of study, is in perfect accordance with the statements of Husserl on the science of linguistics. Pos extrapolates this by saying that phenomenology tries to recover the awareness of what a speaking subject really is; the phenomenological linguist (and structuralist) is, as Merleau-Ponty has also clearly noted, not like the learned observer who confronts something external to him. Pos maintains that observation from the outside leads to the result that the linguistic (speaking) subject and the scientific subject lose their common ground when the first is made over into an object of the second, and he continues:

> this form of epistemology which states that the object is constituted by scientific construction, is opposite to the phenomenological point of view... there exists no unlimited divergence between primary consciousness and science: the linguist is linguist due to the fact that he is a speaker, and not in spite of this fact... The reality per se of primary subjectivity will always remain his point of reference.17

Natanson makes the point that the domain of phenomenology is the study of the meaning social acts have for the actors who perform them and who live in a reality built out of their subjective interpretation or the study of the intentional life of actors in social reality.18 It is precisely at that point where Husserl's notion of a phenomenological linguistics as a science of the speaking subject as extended by Pos, and the study of the indubitably given life-world of social actors as posited by Natanson, mesh, and it is this point which is also corroborated by Husserl's shift to the speaker's point of view.

However, I cannot quite agree with Merleau-Ponty's view that the programme Husserl envisaged comes close to that of Saussure.19 This might be true of the Husserl who sought general rules of universal grammar, but not for the Husserl who sees intentions of actors as incarnated in words. If I can summarise the complex position of Saussure, it is in his system that we find the strongest emphasis on the clear separation between langue and parole. The proper object of linguistics was for Saussure only langue which he defined as 'that part of language which is independent of the individual,' thus permitting us to ignore the speaker.20

Husserl's programme has rather more in common with that form of structural linguistics as it was developed after Sassure under the influence of Jakobson who pointed out that the strict separation of langue and parole, or of code and message, is not possible, since the analysis of a code has to take account of the messages. Jakobson saw that Saussurian definition does not account for the existence of, for instance, a personal code that transcends the discontinuity in time between diverse speech acts and thus gives the sense of identity and continuity to the speaking subject.21

Furthermore, Husserlian phenomenological incorporation of the speaking subject into the realm of investigation, putting, as Pos would have formulated it, the scientific investigation on the level of the speaking subject, is rather close to the postulates of socio-linguistics.22

Husserl's notion that 'to speak is not at all to translate a thought into words,' but that it is rather 'to see a certain object by the word,' closely coincides with the criticism of the Saussurian programme by Benveniste.

Benveniste pointed out that the arbitrariness which Saussure postulated for the relation between signifiant (the acoustic image) and signifié (the concept) is not really true for the relation between concept and form, as this relation is inseparable, but may be true only for the relation between the sign and its substantial referent. In other words, the connection between sign and reality has been introduced underhandedly by Saussure.

When Benveniste extends the necessary connection between phonetic expression and concept to the relation between thought and language, he indeed comes to the important realisation that it is misleading to speak of container and contained, for the metaphor of the container as form and the contained as content-material cannot be broken apart. In no instance, says Benveniste, could we imagine the container (the linguistic form) as void of content (thoughts, concepts), nor the content as independent of its container.23

I hope that this short excursion into the development of linguistic approaches to reality has paved the way for an adequate understanding of the epistemological problems which are entailed in a human science which has as its objective the description of the life-worlds of others with the least possible distortion. Before discussing the qualitative tool of participant observation and its relation to the phenomenological epoché of Husserl, it might be useful to summarise the results of this excursion into the history of structural linguistics and semiotics.

Under the influence of phenomenological approaches semiotics, or semiology, as the science of the structure, interplay and social application of sign systems, grew to incorporate and perceive more clearly the importance of the speaking subject (sujet parlant) as integral part of the studied system. In an extension of this paradigm which shows through the convergence of positions of structural linguistics and phenomenology, I would contend that any science which makes the intentions of the social actor into a focus of study cannot succeed if it separates structure from its actualisation, essential form from contingent content and both from context, for it will ultimately end up with a scientific system which is utterly divorced from the life-world of social actors, the researcher included, with the deplorable consequence that we will no longer be able to recognise ourselves in the accounts which result. It is for these reasons that a narrowly Saussurean structuralism, in spite of its impressive results in discovering deep structures of the mind which are supposedly hidden from the consciousness of those individuals who carry the structures (for instance in a mythical tradition), seems almost irrelevant to a genuine methodology of field-work, and indeed avoids discussing the dialectic between researcher and researched. This shortcoming can easily be illustrated by reference to many remarks of Lévi-Strauss who, representing the structuralist method in social anthropology, eliminates the subject from the discussion altogether:

> it is immaterial... whether the thought processes of South American Indians take place through the medium of my thought, or whether mine take place through the medium of theirs.24

THE RISE OF METHODOLOGICAL AWARENESS IN SOCIAL ANTHROPOLOGY

Surveying the field of social anthropology, it seems that

follows in its initial phase the trend of other social sciences in the nineteenth century. Just as sociology, employing the canon of Durkheim, regarded social reality as a natural object in its 'thingness,' so social anthropology adopting the epistemological canon of the natural sciences also observed a reality 'out there,' as if it were of the same order as a rock or a star. This is the period of anthropological writings which led to sterile systems purporting to describe the evolution of culture by imposing classificatory schemes from the outside in much the same way as fossils were classified. It was only at the end of the nineteenth century that the natural history approach gives way to the study of cultures as individual entities, in order later to arrive through comparison at pan-human generalities. Boas expressed this clearly when he stated:

> Thus a critical examination of what is generally valid for all humanity and what is specifically valid for different cultural types comes to be a matter of great concern to students of society.25

Boas, who with his insistence on the uniqueness of each cultural entity clearly stands in the tradition of Herder, 26 already adds the pertinent note:

> Absolute systems of phenomena as complex as those of culture are impossible. They will always be reflections of our own culture.27

The indissoluble coexistence of the uniqueness of cultural systems and their presentation, with the researcher's point of view, finds ultimate expression in Kluckhohn's words:

> Anthropology holds up a great mirror to man and lets him look at himself in his infinite variety.28

Practitioners considered two questions on the theoretical level: the comparability of diverse cultural phenomena and the uniqueness of each cultural creation. It became increasingly evident to them that ultimately they were not studying a natural object out there, but that those doing research, eventually find only themselves, their prejudices, their pre-occupations, their own life-world.29 This insight was achieved through the awareness of the difficulties, initially less epistemological than existential, of applying the qualitative method of participant observation, which in its dialectic between researcher and researched and in its relation to the theoretical premises has rarely been epistemelogically clarified.30

MALINOWSKI'S DOUBLE BIND

We have indications that the practitioners of participant observation in social anthropology were torn between two modes of interpretation which are implicit in the method itself: those of participation, of grasping the inner experience of the social actors, and the outer the observational stance of the student of behaviour who comprehends the charters of institutions, not as they are understood by the social participants themselves, but as they appear to an observer. Thus we find in Malinowski the statement, made in 1922, that it is of tantamount importance to grasp the native's point of view, and he describes the result as follows:

> Perhaps through realising human nature in a shape very distant and foreign to us, we shall have some light shed on our own.31

Yet in contrast, Malinowski also insists on the prerogative of scientific construction, when he says:

> The main achievement of field-work consists, not in a passive registering of facts, but in the constructive drafting of what might be called the charters of native institutions... The principles of social organisation... have to be constructed by the observer out of a multitude of manifestations of varying significance and relevance...32

That Malinowski did not quite see the contradictory requirements of the two attitudes,and could not reconcile or rather could not logically defend the double-pronged approach which field-work entails, might account for what Leach has called the 'epistemological naivety' of his work.33 I must agree with Leach, and I think that this naivety of Malinowski shows most remarkably in the following statement:

> There is all the difference between a sporadic plunging into the company of natives, and being really in contact with them. What does the latter mean? On the ethnographer's side, it means that his life in the village, which at first is a strange,sometimes unpleasant, sometimes intensely interesting adventure, soon adopts quite a natural course very much in harmony with his surrounding.34

I would caution here and point to the epistemological and existential reserve which the method and the goal-orientation of the field-worker impose upon any complete merging with the native's mental horizon: the native awaking in the morning might think of the fields, consider the weather and assess the success of yam planting, while the ethnographer, as distinct from a permanent resident, awaking in the same surrounding is guided by a very different set of relevant questions, namely whether he or she will be successful in finding out which method of yam planting is used or which kinship relations will be mobilised to plant the fields.

What then is entailed in the method of participant observation is a double frame of relevances, that of the native's point of view, and that of the scientific value-orientation with which this native point of view is studied. The field-worker's practice certainly has the cognitive position of a double hermeneutic, or as Bauman expressed it:

> Understanding sociology... cannot help but be permanently engaged in a discourse with its own object: a discourse in which the object and the subject of study employ essentially the same resources.35

However, I think that the purely cognitive double level of interpretation which social sciences generally achieve, whether by pure observation or otherwise, is surpassed by the potential of participant observation: the field-worker is in the position which Simmel has so cogently summarised in the figure of the 'stranger.'36

THE DILEMMA OF THE STRANGER

With unsurpassed analytical insight Simmel has clarified what the position of the stranger entails and thus gives us a sophisticated epistemological underpinning of the dilemma which the method of participant observation encompasses in its existential focus on the single researcher in alien surroundings. For Simmel, the stranger is that person or type who is defined by the constant change from nearness to distance, the dialectic of changing points of view on a psychological as well as geographical plane, and in whom objectivity is guaranteed because the stranger is not bound to the onesided tendencies of the group he or she lives with.37 Yet for Simmel, the stranger is not defined by distance and disinterestedness, but is the embodiment of a particular constellation which encompasses 'disinterestedness and engagement' at the same time.38 This dialectic unity has rarely been understood correctly: the stranger has been made into a negative or marginal figure, while for Simmel he or she is a thoroughly positive figure. It is the traditional understanding of ethnology or social anthropology as a science for collecting the 'facts' of the life-world of others, of the elusive objectivity of 'the world out there' that I have labelled the naturalistic approach. What by contrast can be the only possible and defendable aim, is to find ourselves, and to learn that travelling to other cultures does not afford us the possibility of 'escaping ourselves,' as Michel Leiris once put it.39

The field-worker as participant observer is always haunted by the dilemma of trying to reconcile the modes of gaining knowledge through reflection and through commitment, through participation and observation, through engagement and distance. The social anthropologist deliberately puts him or herself into the situation of the stranger, by estranging and disentangling from his or her own life-world, including the world of the scientific community, in order to get close to a different world, the cognitive and emotional world of the other, changing from a 'stranger' to a 'friend.' Yet, the anthropologist will always be the stranger who comes today and goes tomorrow, who cannot become the native, and who does not want to become the same as the researched subject, for the anthropologist is still guided by a commitment to the ultimate goal of mediation, of transmitting his or her commitment into a written work for his or her own cultural contemporaries, thus initiating not only in themselves but also in the audience a form of e   ipation from the prejudices of superiority. The anthropologist holds the mirror up to the subject not in order to show us the bestiality or the paradisical life of others (as Hobbes or Rousseau might have done or travellers of the eighteenth century like the naturalist Forster, the companion of James Cook), but rather to show us our own virtues and vices. Through distancing themselves from their own self-understanding, from their own 'taken for granted world,' field workers try to come close to otherness, which in turn discloses to them their own uniqueness. As one moves through into the distance,one brings ones own distant world close to the native's world while participating in the latter's life-world and so also sets in motion a reflective, thus emancipatory, process in the other.40 Through participation the field-worker thus ideally climbs down from the pedestal of superiority, be it the superiority of the nineteenth century evolutionist thinkers or colonial administrators, or the superiority of the scholar's point of view.

Participation does not aim so much to validate collated knowledge as to authenticate the experience of the other as well as of the researcher, to let both find themselves, to make the other a partner (in the true sense of the word) of a dialogue, and thus let both surrender to the emancipatory force of dialogue. Through participation in the life-world of others the field-worker also acknowledges the humanity of the other, he authenticates the other's existence and in so doing also forestalls his or her (the field-worker's) dehumanisation.41 The method of participant observation thus fulfills the famous saying of Chesterton:

> Science is a grand thing when you can get it... But what do those men mean when they use it nowadays?.... They mean getting outside a man and studying him as if he were a gigantic insect; in what they would call a dry impartial light, in what I should call a dead and dehumanising light... So far from being knowledge, it's actually suppressing what we know. It's treating a friend as a stranger and pretending that something familiar is really remote and mysterious.42

The opening of a true dialogue in authentic participation thus requires from the scientist the sacrifice or surrender (to use a metaphor of Kurt Wolff's)43 of the unquestioned, unreflected, self-evident reality of scientific superiority. It may be true that for traditional social sciences the price which they have to pay for pulling down the barrier dividing the experimenter and the subjects of study, for dissolving the difference in status, which the attempt at authenticity brings with it, might, as Bauman suspects, 44 be considered exorbitant, particularly for a science which is concerned more with certainty than with the significance of its results. It is through participation that the field-worker as scientist surrenders part of him or her self, in order to gain a reflective and critical understanding of this self by incorporating it into the other and vice versa. It is thus the only possible way to fulfill the requirement of a true anthropology as Husserl, after having acquainted himself with Lévi-Bruhl's work, evisaged it:

> It is a task of the highest importance, which may be actually achieved, to feel our way into a humanity whose life is enclosed in a vital, social tradition, and to understand it in this unified social life. This is the basis of the world which is no mere representation (Weltvorstellung) but rather the world

that actually is for it (sondern die für sie wirklich seiende Welt ist).45

As far as the technical and cognitive steps are concerned which give us access to this lived world of the other, Husserl has given us one methodological suggestion of great import: reverse the phenomenological epoché and apply it to the objective sciences instead of to the natural world:

Clearly required before everything else is the epoche in respect to all objective sciences. This means not merely an abstraction from them, such as an imaginary transformation in thought of present human existence, such that no science appears in the picture. What is meant, is rather an epoché of all participation in the cognitions of the objective sciences, and epoché of any critical position-taking which is interested in their truth or falsity, even any position on their guiding idea of an objective knowledge of the world. In short, we carry out an epoché in regard to all objective theoretical interests, all aims and activities belonging to us as objective scientists or even simply as (ordinary) people desirous of (this kind of) knowledge.46

COMMUNICATION AS CRITICAL DIALOGUE AND THE PARADIGM OF PSYCHIATRY

It is not so much by re-constitution of the lived experience and life-world of the 'primitive' that the ethnographer learns: rather is it through participation that he or she is taken in, grasped by, immersed in and excited about the other's world. He or she is truly in a state of utter pre-occupation during the experiencing of the immediacy, closeness and intimacy of the other. Of this state of mind of being pre-occupied in the context of the artist's involvement in the creative process, of having not yet gained distance from the involvement through externalisation, Friedrich Schlegel wrote thus:

In order to be able to write something well, one must not be interested in it anymore...As long as the artist invents and is enthusiastic, he finds himself in a state of Unfreedom (illiberalen zustand), as far as communication is concerned.47

The requirement of experiencing otherness is entailed in the intent to understand the horizon of the other from the other's point of view, because only through disclosure by the other can I enter his or her mental and existential realm: but if I do not give, I cannot expect to receive, as the other perceives my reticence and will react accordingly: my sham-participation would be reciprocated by sham-insights, built upon sham-disclosure. The metaphorical imagery and comparison between the act of participation (in observation) during field-work and the relationship in marriage or friendship is rather apt: only by mutual surrender at least of parts of the autonomy of my personality can the fusion of body and mind occur which surpasses for a short time the discontinuity of two individuals.

It is at this point that I should like to refer to the insights of Georges Bataille who insists that erotic and religious phenomena become absurd monstrosities if observed as things from the outside.48 It is nevertheless a truism - though in the light of the quantification mania of the mainstream social sciences a truism that needs emphatic discussion - that one cannot at the same time and with the same orientation both participate in full immediacy and reflectively comprehend,49 or, to put it into the context of anthropological field-work, that there will always be a break between participation (experiencing) and communication to the outside (observation and analysis). If I maintain the double objective of social anthropology of reporting on the subjectively meaningful experience of others, on insights which can only be won by personal commitment, the researchers who put themselves and their cultural and scientific frame of reference into suspension, who surrender to experience for the sake of insight and understanding, will have to perform a great number of steps of bracketing, of epoche, in the field as well as out of it.

The first and foremost epoché which I have to perform is that of putting into suspension any belief in the claim to superiority and universality of western rationality, at least in the form which has as its main goals instrumental and technical control, a requirement already recognised in the discussion of Evans-Pritchard's work on witch-craft and magic among the African Zande.50 Most recently, Habermas, in a spirited critique of Lukes, insisted that we do not have the choice whether we want to treat a belief-system, which at first sight appears to us as irrational, either as such or to treat it 'charitably' by starting from the assumption that the irrational belief might be interpreted as rational when the context is understood.

As Habermas points out, the requirement of hermeneutic severity consists in a critical attitude to our own presuppositions, because we cannot apply criticism without self-criticism, unless we want to fall into the error of forcing other cultures into the framework of our own standard of rationality which we universalise a priori.51 However, the guiding principle for the insistence on the act of surrender, intimacy and immediacy of experience, and the concomitant effect of putting the other on the level of equality - true dialogue always requiring the admission of equal status - entails the ultimate commitment to a rationality which is guided by emancipatory interest. Emancipation should then be defined as a form of freedom, which means that every person is autonomous insofar as I take them seriously as hermeneutic agents, as an interpreter of the meanings that comprise their own social world.

Habermas was one of the first modern social theoretical thinkers to delineate the possibility and desirability of a so-called 'nondistorted form of communication' which through acknowledging the other as autonomous agent transforms the discourse of positive science into a dialogue in the realm of praxis. Habermas uses the example of the relation between patient and psychoanalyst as a pragmatic paradigm for that form of communication which is guided by emancipatory interest.52

Habermas considers the therapeutic critique, which enables and forces the patient to become aware of self-delusions, to be the prototype for the process of self-reflection.53 However, I have some doubts as to whether this example is applicable to the intersubjectivity of research into the life-world of others with which we are concerned as anthropologists. As Bauman has pointed out, the recipients of critical knowledge, for whom the therapist may be crucial, might refuse to consider themselves as patients and might instead perceive all attempts at redefining reality as a threat aimed at the foundation of their reality which they do not regard as unfree.54 It is true that the patient-therapist situation would still entail a power differential, although the implications of this depend to a large extent on whom we consider as patient. It is even doubtful whether the proposal of Habermas could be salvaged if we were to turn the whole relation around by making the field-worker the patient who through the experience of otherness finds him or her self.

This then would be more in line with the emancipatory goal of authentication of the experience, of authentication of the self of the researcher and of the change of the objectives of the social sciences, which should finally cease to search for reality as it supposedly exists, separate from the observer and participant, but rather reach for knowledge about ourselves, and ultimately about the essence of humanity, as encapsulated in different experiences, an ideal for which the Stoic term humanitas stood so long.55

EMANCIPATION THROUGH LAUGHTER AND IRONY

That this kind of emancipation may in fact be possible during field work, though occuring in a different and unexpected form of a dialogue, has been strikingly demonstrated by Elenore Bowen. Before leaving her field area, the research subjects were performing for her a pantomime in which they poked fun at the anthropologist who was shown as running around with pen and paper jotting down notes. The natives then proceeded to play a further pantomime where they showed the coming of a missionary who told them that all people are brothers. When the native who considers himself quite a specialist in kinship relations tries to sit down in order to discuss with the missionary the lineage through which all people since Adam might be brothers, the missionary, so depicted in the pantomime, tells him off, saying that he has to stand in the face of white authority.56 In both cases, Bowen admits how she was at first not sure whether she should laugh, stay solemn, or get angry. What this experience shows firstly is that the researcher's subject is distancing himself through mockery from the researcher's world, from the researchers intrusiveness, and, by presenting it to the researcher with the expectation that she as patient will laugh about herself, is pointing to the unspoken fact that the researcher has been accepted. Secondly, the pantomime points to the attitude which is required of somebody who wants to get at essential human traits and who is guided by emancipatory interest: it is the attitude of not taking oneself too seriously, of relinquishing the claim to superiority, surpassing the constraints of scientific training through laughter and irony. The Romans termed this attitude the one of perpetua festivitas as a remedy against gravitas. We might translate festivitas as that kind of humour which can find a balance between self-enjoyment and sympathy for the suffering. It is the same attitude which Friedrich Schlegel has described as irony and self-irony:

> Irony is the clear consciousness of eternal agility,
> of the infinitely full chaos. (and) Irony contains
> something of, creates a feeling for, the insoluble
> struggle between the impossibility and at the same
> time the necessity of complete dialogue. With irony
> one surpasses one's self.57

However, the encounter of self and other in the field situation is rarely as clear nor the irony as obvious (though many layered) as in the above case. Sometimes the researchers have to look beneath the obviousness of the surface in order to discover their own ridiculousness. To illustrate this, I shall refer to my own experience in Japan. When I entered a Japanese bath-house, in particular in the countryside, most Japanese present would automatically cover their private parts: it took some time of living in an area until this ceased to happen. Upon enquiry it was admitted that this behaviour was not so much a sign of shame or even bashfulness, but rather a response to the fear of being considered barbarian by Westerners. Japan and many other non-European countries are full of examples of this kind. The normal response of western visitors who encounter such activities would be to label the Japanese as 'silly,' 'ridiculous' or 'slavish imitators' (or even indeed to commend the subjects as to their standards of civilised behaviour). It is at this juncture where we should ask ourselves whether it is not our own culture which is made ridiculous, for the Japanese are not only reacting to us and fulfilling the expectations they impute to us: they are at the same time holding a mirror up to us in which we can marvel at our hypocrisy and the caricature of ourselves: our own inconsistencies and our 'superiority' are thrown back at us in grotesque distortions. Perhaps few who come across similar reactions would recognise themselves, indeed not even many professional researchers might be willing to admit to this; yet rarer is the scholar who would submit to the position of the 'patient,' for it requires not only reflective activity of the mind, which is more than a suspisio judicii of Kant, but considerable courage to admit that we actually appear as a kind of 'clown' in some other life-world. The Japanese have a particularly telling word for this figure: henna gaijin means the foreigner, who behaves oddly because he is a foreigner and therefore cannot help but violate normal behaviour, being consistently funny. It is at this point that we have to realise that the method of bracketing, the attitude of epoché, is indeed more than a purely cognitive, vicarious and technical, procedure for it entails an act of doubting and suspension, of surrender to otherness, which leaves the performer indeed 'suspended' or floating in the air. Ultimately it should lead to the knowledge of the self.58

THE FIELD-WORKER AS CONTAMINATING AGENT?

The process of finding the self through self-transcendence (irony) should not be confused with the adulation of everything exotic, foreign and strange, with the Rousseauean syndrome of the 'Nobel Savage:' it is rather unfortunate that Lévi-Strauss put the situation of the field-worker into and terms of black/white opposition instead of recognising the dialectic of the stranger. As he once stated:

> At home, the anthropologist may be a natural subversive, a convinced opponent of traditional usage: but no sooner has he in focus a society different from his own than he becomes respectful of even the most conservative practices.59

I think this uncritical attitude would be that only of an intellectual without a mind (and without a heart, one might like to add), of Max Weber's 'Fachmensch ohne Geist.' With such an uncritical attitude, no self-reflective criticism could occur either, or at least it would be inauthentic, not true to itself. It is the attitude which is the reverse of utter and extreme ethnocentrism, which Lévi-Strauss again sees only in either a black or white fashion, when he writes:

> Either the anthropologist clings to the norms of his own group, in which case the others can only inspire in him an ephemeral curiosity in which there is always an element of disapproval: or he makes himself over completely to the objects of his studies, in which case he can never be perfectly objective, because in giving himself to all societies, he cannot but refuse himself... to one among them.60

This perception of opposing dichotomy of either ethnocentrism or total alienation forgets the dialectic or complementarity of both attitudes within the research act. In both cases, in that of extreme ethnocentrism as well as that of total alienation from one's own society, the other is actually made inhuman, in one instance as close to a paradisical state, in the other as the dirty barbarian! In one case the other becomes 'superhuman,' in the other 'subhuman,' in both cases 'inhuman.'

Without realising it, we would thereby deny our own humanity. I think that the search for the 'uncontaminated' native is very telling (as is the German word 'Naturvolk') it is as if we have realised all along, possibly subconsciously, that our own way of life could be the 'contaminating' agent. Could it be that in both cases, either in praising the inhabitants of 'paradise' or cursing the 'barbarian,' we are in reality exhibiting a fear and trepidation about the otherness in ourselves?

REFERENCES

Translations from German and French texts are Professor Koepping's.

1. Charles S. Peirce, Collected Papers (1931-38), (ed.) C. I. Hartshorne and P. Weiss, Harvard University Press, Cambridge, Mass., 1971, vol.2, p.228.

2. Ferdinand de Sassure (1916) in Roman Jakobson, Aufsätze zur Linguistik und Poetik, Ullstein, Frankfurt, 1979, p.160f.

3. The term 'life-world' or 'Lebenswelt' was employed by Edmund Husserl in recognition of the fact that different individuals and groups each perceive 'the world' and their existence in it from a different historico-socio-cultural perspective or point of view, and that consequently the members of any particular such group may be seen as sharing a common 'life-world' with other members of the same group, but a 'life-world' that is different from the one inhabited by members of another group.

4. The epoché or phenomenological reduction is the suspension of all previously taken for granted presuppositions.

5. As Husserl points out, we cannot have direct experience of the existence of a (Noumenal) world of objects and meanings existing outside or beyond our conscious experience. The objects and meanings we do experience are therefore clearly present to or, to use his terminology, Intended by, acts of conscious experience.

6. Zygmunt Bauman, Towards a Critical Sociology, Routledge and Kegan Paul, London, 1976, p.172.

7. The concept of the 'life-world' (see 3 above) as introduced by the later Husserl and taken up by Schutz and others, recognises the historico-socio-culturally mediated nature of our everyday experience.

8. Marvin Farber, The Aims of Phenomenology, New York, 1966, p.156.

9. Leszek Kolakowski, Husserl and the Search for Certitude, Yale U.P., New Haven, 1975, p.85.

10. Ibid., p.29.

11. Roman Jakobson, op. cit., p.170.

12. See Ibid., p.154.

13. Maurice Merleau-Ponty, 'Husserl and the Problem of Language' in J. O'Neil (ed.) Maurice Merleau-Ponty: Phenomenology Language and Sociology, London, 1974.

14. Edmund Husserl, Formale und Transzendentale Logik, (1929), translated by Dorian Cairns as Formal and Transcendental Logic, Nijhoff, The Hague, 1969, p.22.

15. Maurice Merleau-Ponty, op. cit.

16. See Roman Jackobson, op. cit., p.155.

17. Hendrik Pos, (1898-1955) A dutch disciple of Husserl, in his work of 1939 'Perspective du Structuralisme' in Travaux du cecle Lingustique de Prague, 8.

18. See Maurice Natanson (ed.) Essays in Phenomenology, Nijohff, The Hague, 1966, p.157 and 165.

19. Maurice Merleau-Ponty, op. cit.

20. See Roman Jakobson, op. cit., pp.161-2.

21. Ibid., p.162.

22. Basil Bernstein, Class, Codes and Controll, Routledge and Kegan Paul, London, 1971.

23. Emile Benveniste, Probleme der Allgemeinen Sprachwissenschaft, Syndikat, Frankfurt, 1977, p.p.77-8, Originally in Les Etudes philosophiques, No. 4, Oct-Dec., 1958.

24. Claude Lévi-Strauss, Tristes Tropiques, Atheneum, New York, 1971.

25. Franz Boas, Race, Language and Culture, Macmillan, New York, 1948, p.261, reprinted 1968, p.261.

26. See Klaus-Peter Koepping, Adolf Bastian and the Psychic Unity of Mankind, University of Queensland Press, Brisbane, 1983.

27. Franz Boas, op. cit., p.311, my emphasis.

28. Clyde Kluckhohn, Mirror for Man, MacGraw-Hill, New York, 1949, reprinted 1967, p.19.

29. Kalus-Peter Koepping, 'Leib und Leben, Sprache und Speil Schweigen und Scham' in Hans-Peter Duerr (ed.) Der Wissenshaftler und des Irrationale, Syndikat, Frankfurt, 1981, vol.2.

30. See Klaus-Peter Koepping Ibid., and 'Phenomenological Reduction in Ethnographic Field-Work' in Proceedings of the Phenomenology Conference, ed. M. Harney, Canberra, Austrailian National U.P., 1977, and 'Ist die Ethnoligie auf dem Wize zur Mündigkeit?' Paideuma, 26, 1980.

31. Branislaw Malinowski, Argonauts of the Western Pacific, Dutton, New York, 1922, p.25.

32. Branislaw Malinowski, The Coral Gardens and Their Magic, Allen and Unwin, London, 1935, 2 Volumes.

33. Edmund Leach, 'The Epistemological Background to Malinowski's Empiricism' in R. Firth (ed.) Man and Culture: An Evaluation of the Work of Branislaw Malinowski, Routledge and Kegan Paul, London, 1957, p.p.119-23.

34. Malinowski, Argonauts of the Western Pacific, p.7.

35. Zygmunt Bauman, Hermeneutics of the Social Sciences, Hutchinson, London, 1978, p.234.

36. Georg Simmel, Grundfragen der Soziologie, (1917), Walter de Grugter and Co., Berlin, 1970.

37. Ibid, p.65.

38. Ibid., my emphasis.

39. Michel Leiris, L'Age d'homme, Gallimard, Paris, 1939, p.202f.

40. Klaus-Peter Koepping 'Leib und Liben, Spreche un Speil, Schwigen und Scham,' op. cit.

41. See Klaus-Peter Koepping, 'Ist die Ethnologie auf dem Wege zur Mundigkeit,' op. cit.

42. G. K. Chesterton, The Secret of Father Brown, Penguin, Harmondsworth, 1975, p.p.12-13. See also Koepping 'On the Epistemology of Participant Observation and the

Generating of Paradigmes' in <u>Occasional Papers in Anthropology</u>, No.6, Brisbane, 1976, p.159.

43. Kurt Wolff, <u>Surrender and Catch</u>, Dordrecht, 1976.

44. Zygmunt Bauman, <u>Towards a Critical Sociology</u>, p.109.

45. Edmund Husserl quoted by Maurice Merleau-Ponty in <u>Les Science de l'homme et la Phénoménologie</u>, (1961) translated by John Wild as <u>Phenomenology and the Sciences of Man</u>, New York, 1977, p.275.

46. Edmund Husserl, <u>The Crisis of European Sciences and Transcendental Phenomenology</u>, translated by David Carr, Northwestern University Press, Evanston Ill., 1970, p.135.

47. This is part of a critical fragment, which appeared first in Berlin in 1797, cited here Friedrich Schlegel, <u>Schriften zur Literatur</u>, W. Rasch (ed.), Deutscher Taschenbuch-Verlag, Munich, 1972, p.11.

48. Georges Bataille, L'Erotisme, Paris, 1957. German translation as <u>Der Heilige Eros</u>, Ullstein, Frankfurt, 1979, p.33.

49. <u>Ibid.</u>, p.250.

50. See Peter Winch, <u>The Idea of a Social Science</u>, Routledge and Kegan Paul, London, 1958.

51. Jürgen Habermas, <u>Theorie des Kommunikativen Handelns</u>, 2 vols., Suhrkamp, Frankfurt, 1981.

52. See Jürgen Habermas, <u>Theorie und Praxis</u>, Suhrkamp, 3rd ed., 1974, reasserted in <u>Ibid.</u>, vol.1, pp.42-3.

53. Jürgen Habermas, <u>Theorie des Kommunikativen Handelns</u>, vol.1, p.43.

54. Zugmunt Bauman <u>Toward a Critical Sociology</u>, p.105.

55. See Kalus-Peter Koepping, <u>Adolf Bastian and the Psychic Unity of Mankind</u>, <u>op. cit.</u>

56. Elenor Smith Bowen, (Laura Bohannan) <u>Return to Laughter</u>, The Natural History Press, New York, 1964, p.265.

57. Freidrick Schlegel, Lyzeum-Fragment No.108, cited by Ernst Behler, <u>Freidrich Schlegel</u>, Rowohlt, Hamburg,

1967, p.78.

58. See Klaus-Peter Koepping 'Leib und Leben, Spreche und Speil, Schweigen und Scham,' op. cit., for the relation of this attitude to the proposals of Erasmus of Rotterdam in his 'Encomium Moriae,' ('In Praise of Folly'), of 1509.

59. Claude Lévi-Strauss, op.cit., p.381.

60. Ibid., p.382.

3 Radical reflection and the human sciences*

WOLFE MAYS

In his book, Radical Reflection and the Origin of the Human Sciences,1 Calvin Schrag proposes a radical version of Husserl's epoché 2 as a methodological foundation for the human sciences. This radical reflection, which Professor Schrag contrasts with the self-reflection of traditional philosophy, makes possible, so he argues, the deconstruction of a number of traditional philosophical dichotomies: for example, those of transcendental/empirical,theory/praxis, fact/value and subject/object. It is through such a process of deconstruction that we are enabled to arrive at an originative experience, which has both a socio-historical cast and a physical horizon, and is prior to the very distinction of man and the world.

When Schrag describes radical reflection as an inquiry into the original setting of world experience, we are given the impression that there is something like a common pool of authentic experience, open to us all: the person in the street, philosopher and scientist, if we only have the wit to

*This article was first published in The Journal of the British Society for Phenomenology, vol.14, no.1 (Jan. 1983), and appears with the permission of the editor, who is the author.

make it out. And, further, that the various kinds of knowledge, philosophic and scientific may be extracted from this experience.

But before we can embark on the path of radical reflection, we must at least know what we are after and possess the necessary skill to perform the radical epoché. And this initially presupposes the acceptance of a specific philosophical theory, one which reflects the doctrines of phenomenology and hermeneutics. As the radical epoché is thus carried out within a framework of philosophical interpretation, it is doubtful whether we can completely suspend our beliefs about ourselves and the world we live in. The most we are able to do is to replace one set of beliefs about the nature of things, which we consider to be inauthentic, by another set which we take as being more authentic, as judged by certain criteria implicit in the hermeneutic framework. Because of this one might say the process of deconstruction involves something like a reinterpretation of the more sophisticated experience from which it started.

It is also clear that the dichotomy subject/object must already be in existence before we can dismantle the philosophical dichotomies. As the process of deconstruction starts from a reflective level, it involves the activity of a subject. The attempt to eliminate the reflective subject by means of the radical epoché, reminds one somewhat of Hume's demonstration that all our experience is made up of sensations, and that the self is but a bundle of sensations. But this does not prevent Hume from using such phrases as, 'Whenever I look into myself, I cannot discover a self.' In any case deconstructed experience does involve a subject, even if it is not a conscious reflective one, but one rather acting within the world and not isolated from its socio-historical context. Heidegger who is concerned to break down the Cartesian dualism of subject and object, posits being-in-the-world as fundamental, where being-in-the-world refers to Dasein as involved in the world.

Perhaps this is the point Schrag wishes to make when he says, 'It will be a reflexivity upon originative experience rather than a self-reflexivity of an epistemological subject.'3 But it is evident that radical reflection is not an anonymous one. Schrag does talk about the need to base such experience on the Merleau-Pontyian conception of the 'lived-body,' and in this respect he emphasises human performance. It would therefore seem that radical reflection has much in common with the kind of performative acts Sartre puts under the head of the pre-reflective cogito.

One wonders, however, whether the performative activities or pre-reflective behaviour of the 20th century Western town-dweller are similar to those of the mediaeval one, and to those of the inhabitant of Athens in Pericles' day. Apart from anything else, modern humanity is living in a different social and economic environment, one possessed of an advanced technology, and if we are to believe Marx this will influence our behaviour, both rational and irrational. But can we assume that in all these cases the individual's pre-reflective behaviour will be identical: that no matter what culture he or she belongs to the individual will arrive at the same originative experience if able to perform the radical epoché? If this were so, it would no doubt be easier for primitives to achieve this, since they have less cognitive furniture than we have to discard.

Schrag makes the further point, 'that there is a genesis and development of meaning already at work in the life-world.'4 However, such achievement is not entirely a depersonalised matter. It is individual human beings who carry out meaningful activities even if they do not consciously reflect upon them. In such cases individuals probably have at least some dim awareness of the rationale underlying their actions, insofar as they are directed towards certain ends. Perhaps this is what Schrag has in mind when he says that, 'Understanding is seen as a pre-categorial deployment of meaning in the interpretation of self and the world.'5 The notion of reason is then widened to include intentional behaviour before the division of self and world occurs. Reason, as it manifests itself in our everyday life, is hence conceived by him to be 'more like a "performance" than like an entity or a faculty.'6 This extended definition of reason therefore covers behaviour, whose underlying motivation we may not always comprehend.

Schrag regards our everyday life as:

>   a context of connections and conjunctions which
>   surface not only in the intentionality of thought but
>   also in the circumspection of practical engagements
>   within an economic and social order.7

The model here would seem to be James' radical empiricism, which assumes that the logical connections and relations (between things) are actually implicit in the stream of consciousness, and are experienced as such, rather than being imposed upon it in the shape of Kantian categories. As James puts it when talking of language, 'We ought to say a feeling of and, a feeling of if, a feeling of but, and a feeling of by quite as readily as we say a feeling of blue or a feeling of cold.' James states that the relationships implicit in experience 'are numberless, and no existing language is capable of doing justice to all their shades.'8 Russell too believed that relations subsisted independently of our knowledge of them, although he gave them an independent existence as universals.

When James says, we can have direct feeling of if's, and's and but's, and of relations, sequences and tendencies, just as we have feelings of blue and cold, he can only at the most be describing adult experience. The child at first (if we are to believe Piaget's findings) has neither a feeling of contradiction nor is he or she able to grasp the notion of the excluded middle, a point already made by Locke. Indeed one of the most frequent fallacies met with in the reasoning of young children is that of the fallacy of the undistributed middle, since they have difficulty in distinguishing between part and whole relations. The child cannot have any feeling for logical relations before being initiated into their use. Children would, for example, have to learn to understand the significance of hypothetical situations which involve the contemplation of future possibilities, before they could use 'if then' expressions or conditionals. Since such understanding is not present at an early age, and without subscribing to James' conception of a big, buzzing, booming confusion, as far as the child's experience is concerned, are we to assume that the radical empiricism of James' account of the stream of consciousness only applies to the Western adult?

The view that we may by a process of hermeneutical analysis uncover (in our experience) hidden intentional meanings, is also a feature of Freud's psychoanalytical theory. In discussing the analyst's attempt to get back to the repressed memories of the patient, he contrasts the work of the psychoanalyst with that of the archeologist, who has to make reconstructions from material much of which has been lost or destroyed. 'But it is different,' Freud says:

> with the psychic object whose early history the analyst is seeking to recover.... All of the essentials are preserved even things that seem completely forgotten are present somehow and somewhere, and have been merely buried and made inaccessible to the subject.

Indeed, he doubts whether any psychical structure can really be the victim of total destruction. 'It depends,' he says, 'only upon analytic technique whether we shall succeed in bringing what is concealed completely to light.'9

Freud's views that we can arrive at our repressed memories simply by, as it were, uncovering what is already there hidden in our unconscious, has not gone unchallenged. It has been argued that although our present affective experience is determined by the past, we are continually reconstructing or interpreting the past in terms of our present experience. In remembering past events, we reconstruct them, much as a historian does when interpreting history in terms of the incomplete data available at any particular time.

Schrag's position regarding the tradition would seem to resemble Freud's vis a vis our repressed memories. There appears to be the suggestion that the variety of possible experiential structures is in some way embedded in our originative experience, and that we can separate them out without these structures being radically changed in the process. Although I see no reason to disagree with Schrag that certain basic structures are immediately given in this way, they are, however, reconstructed by us in accordance with our particular aims and interest. We also imaginatively generate new structures which become part of the subject matter of specialised branches of knowledge. Thus the basic structures of space, time and causality are variously interpreted by the human and natural sciences. For example, the time of history is differently conceived by the historian, than is the time of physical science by the physicist, as Heidegger has pointed out.

In this connection, consider Schrag's statement that 'constellations of sense and significance are already established and already understood in the workaday world of practical projects and everyday discourse.'10 But this would seem to imply that something like a process of intersubjective understanding between individuals is already at work there. Schrag appears to hold this view when he talks of 'the taken-for-granted shared meanings and activities within the originary stream of experience,'11 from which the specialised worlds and sub-worlds of science are constituted.

Constructive activity is taken into account by Schrag in the shape of constitution which he gives a central role in the development of the various branches of knowledge. But, he considers it to be the work of communities of investigators rather than due to some ego, transcendental or otherwise. Although the communal aspect of knowledge is of considerable importance, communities are, however, made up of individuals among whom is to be found a leavening of

innovators and creative thinkers. In the scientific
community one can name Archimedes, Galileo, Newton and Darwin
among others. In religion, art and literature a host of
creative individuals could also be named. Without wishing to
embrace the 'great man' theory of history, there were
certainly in our cultural past, saints, scholars, scientists
and artists who by their example, pointed the way forward to
their fellows. Even in biological evolution, sports (random
or otherwise) play an essential role in evolutionary
development.

One ought then to take account of the role played by the
individual in history, even although Marxist's and Hegelian's
may think otherwise, the one emphasising historical
determinism, the other the cunning of reason. I do
recognise, however, that individuals cannot be isolated from
their cultural context. Although each is a child of their
times, it would, nevertheless, be equally mistaken to
overlook those seminal thinkers and innovators who have
played an important part in the past history of our culture.

Schrag then believes that such shared meanings play an
essential role in our lived world. But can we not further
analyse their nature and their taken-for-granted character?
Schrag gives us a hint as to how we might proceed in this
matter, when he recommends us to understand constitution as
'the work of the various communities of investigators
(scientists, philosophers, artists and theologians) seeking
agreement on common topics of concern.'12 But this in turn
raises the question of how intersubjective agreement itself
comes about. It is clear that before this can be achieved,
the individuals in these communities, need to share certain
objective meaning criteria with their fellows. Communication
within each such community, let alone between different
communities would not be possible otherwise: there would be
no way of reaching agreements as to the truth of the
propositions we hold. We would not, for example, be able to
say that Laplace's nebular hypothesis was more veridical than
the Babylonian creation myths.

Gadamer's hermeneutics has recently been criticised by Roy
Bhaskar on the grounds that Gadamer does not take adequate
account of the speaker's intentions or meanings. As a
consequence, Bhaskar says:

> Gadamer lapses into a (judgemental) relativism, in
> which the notion of the corrigibility of
> interpretations cannot be maintained or can only be
> maintained by appeal to the practices of tradition
> within which the interpretation is circumscribed.13

But this move, Bhaskar claims, only displaces the problem of interpretation of meaning on to practice. He believes that without some notion of the meaningful object for a subject in a culture that produced it, it becomes difficult to maintain any notion of adequacy (or correctness) for interpretations at all. What Bhaskar seems to be saying here is that we must postulate objective judgemental criteria for validating the truth of the meaning of the propositions we hold about things. It is not good enough, he thinks, simply to appeal to the practices of the tradition as this leads to conventionalism. He believes that our only way of testing the adequacy of these practices is by justifying them in terms of criteria or norms standing outside the tradition.

Bhaskar has also argued that in this respect there are certain similarities between positivism (of the Humean sort) and hermeneutics. They both, he tells us, accept a norm rooted in the constitutive character of lay accounts, namely our common sense experience. And they both assume that technical scientific knowledge is based on this account. Bhaskar, however, contends that lay accounts are corrigible and subject to critique.14 Believing, as he does, that there is an objective social world independent of our knowledge of it, he claims that the social sciences in their constitution are not simply restricted to the data given by common sense. Gadamer might, however, reply by pointing out that as we have to engage in interpretation to make the tradition clear to us his own approach differs from that of the lay account, since the latter, firstly does not appeal to the tradition with its socio-historical content, and secondly believes that common sense is self-sufficient and requires no interpretation.

Bhaskar's critique of the lay account seems much more applicable to the doctrines of linguistic philosophy, which finds its holy writ in The New English Dictionary. Austin, for example, believed that everyday language had built into it all the subtle distinctions man has found it necessary to draw in the past. And as it had stood up to the test of time in all ordinary and reasonable matters, we ought not, he argued, to interfere with it, unless we had good reasons for doing so.15 Against this view it might be said that knowing how to use our language will not answer our philosophical questions unless we arbitrarily assume that one specified language gives us a privileged insight into reality. But, on the other hand, if instead of appealing to common sense we appealed to the tradition, we would still be assuming, perhaps with more justification, that the latter gives us a privileged insight into reality.

To return to Schrag's discussion, he postulates two levels

of interpretive understanding, one precategorial, the other categorial. These would seem to resemble Sartre's prereflective and reflective cogito.16 The first level, Schrag tells us:

> is the primordial level of interpretive understanding which is an on-going process in the precategorial meaning-formation and meaning-establishment... of daily affairs.17

But if there is meaning-establishment, do not these meanings possess some sort of structure. As Kant remarked, 'intuitions without concepts are blind.' Even our supposedly irrational affective behaviour usually has something like a logic about it as Pascal and Max Scheler have noted. As Pascal put it, 'le coeur a ses raisons.' It would seem that the difference between these two levels is that in one case we live out the meanings involved through our actions in the world, in the other we consciously reflect upon them.

For Schrag on the originary level the performing act of reason is as much the work of the community as it is of any particular self. Although the tradition weighs heavily upon us, following it is not always rational if rationality is identified with the possibility of having to choose between alternatives. Indeed, Sartre believes that choice can occur on the prereflective level, which would seem to come under the head of Schrag's extended notion of reason as a performative act. Although the performative act in the shape of 'knowing how' may antedate the mental act (or the 'knowing that') of an epistemological subject, they are still the acts of a subject, whether it be a social one or the 'lived body.' Schrag tells us that the meanings which social subjects express in their motivations bear the marks of co-authorship. But he would also seem to give a role to the individual (albeit a social one) in the origination of meaning, since it takes account of our unconscious motivations - motivations which shape the significance of the present for us as well as others.

Although Schrag is in agreement with the views of Heidegger and Gadamer, he does not think that they fully grasped the significance of the new hermeneutic for dealing with the irrational positive feature of the texture of world experience.18 As I have already noted, so-called irrational behaviour has often a definite rationale about it, and if we are to believe the reports of psychiatrists, is usually directed to certain meaningful ends of which the subject may not always be conscious. Schrag also seems to be of this opinion when he, for example, refers to 'segments of both personal and social life that remain "irrational" in the sense that rational motivation is repressed.'19 It is precisely the task of the psychoanalyst to display these reasons to patients, so that they are now able to discern the motives behind their actions. The disjunction rational/irrational would therefore appear to be a somewhat artificial one. What we are rather dealing with here are polar concepts.

An important feature of Schrag's book is his critique of the Enlightenment concept of reason, with its postulation of an isolated human subject.20 But this does not mean that the concept of reason is necessarily flawed in itself, nor for that matter is the Greek concept of reason, which is closely linked with the attempt to arrive at metaphysical foundations as well as deductive thought. What it does mean is that we ought to take account of the fact that reason as it occurs in our everyday life cannot be divorced from our social context. But it does not mean that we cannot in the case of such formal disciplines like logic and mathematics, bracket, as it were, the social situation in which we as subjects study these disciplines.

Following Gadamer, Schrag emphasises the importance of the tradition, and tells us that one of the

more pressing demands of a hermeneutic of everyday life is to retrieve the thought and praxis of the world of predecessors as it impinges on the world of contemporaries through a discernment of the role played by myth and symbol.21

He continues by stating that 'the logos of scientific-technical reason blends with the logos of mythos.'22 And by this I take it he means that the rationality of science has its origins in that of myth. At the same time Schrag is critical of the anthropologist's attempt to study myths in evolutionary terms, where myth is prejudged 'as a relic of primitive societies which was superseded by the development of man's rational consciousness and the introduction of logico-scientific modes of thought.'23 Although the evolutionary method has a legitimate function when correctly used, I cannot but be sympathetic with Schrag here. There is a profound difference between the totemic practices anthropologists usually expatiate on, namely, those belonging, for example, to the totemic practices of the natives of the South Pacific, and the myths which form part of our contemporary culture.

The myths of our tradition might be classified under two

heads: (a) creation myths and (b) those concerned with
socio-personal relations, particularly family ones. But in
practice it is often difficult to distinguish the two. In
the myth natural phenomena are usually seen in terms of human
experience, and the destinies of human beings are usually
taken as controlled by external forces. Thus the Oedipus
legend, though exhibiting a somewhat basic family pattern in
our culture, presupposes the working out of something like an
inexorable fate.

Further, even if the Oedipus story as used by Freud as a
hermeneutic device enables us to understand more clearly the
modern family situation, this may be because the family
situation and human nature have not radically changed since
Greek and biblical times. We still appreciate Greek tragedy
and comedy, as these concern themselves with what might be
described as universal human relationships. However, it is
possible to interpret certain aspects of the family situation
by means of another tradition than the Greek. Adler tried to
do this in terms of the biblical story of the conflict
between Cain and Abel. On the other hand, we could explain
the same kinds of behaviour in a more scientific way by
transactional analysis as R. D. Laing does.

Schrag speaks, for example, of a precategorial
understanding of the self and the world informed by mythico-
poetic interpretation. However, in some ways, mythico-poetic
thought is as much an individual product as it is a
collective one. It is the imaginative product of individual
story tellers (or legend makers) of these earlier cultures,
handed down from one generation to another, and in the
process undergoing change and development. Earlier legends
are thus collected, reshaped and put into a new form. No
doubt the Illiad and Odyssey of Homer and the Mort d'Arthur
of Malory originated in this sort of way. J. R. R. Tolkien's
Lord of the Rings is an example of a modern set of legends,
based upon Tolkien's scholarly studies of English tradition
and language.

Schrag speaks of 'the concrete multivalence of
significations that lay embedded in myth,'24 and goes on to
state that 'this expanded notion of reason allows the
disclosure of a precategorial self-understanding within the
drama of everyday life.'25 It would therefore seem that the
basic structures of both the human and natural sciences are
inextricably intertwined in our orginative experience. And
as a consequence Schrag believes that the separate worlds and
paradigms of these sciences can no longer be regarded as the
categorial constructs of a transcendental subject, nor as
resulting from an independently existing world. The end-

result of the radical reflection is our originative experience, where the notions of an isolated subject and an external world no longer occur. Realists like Bhaskar would, of course, not accept this position as giving us a true picture of what they take to be the real world which for them is made up of both subjects and objects.

As we have noted Schrag's position has certain similarities with James' radical empiricism. But there is also a family resemblance to the doctrines of structuralism, since we are told that the various sciences result from structural distinctions and modes inherent in the fabric of lived experience itself. The structuralist position as exemplified in the writings of Lévi-Strauss, has been criticised by Piaget on the ground that experiential structures are not just given synchronically, but also have a history.26 This may not, however, be very evident in the case of the totemic practices of the primitive peoples studied by Levi-Strauss, since they regard these practices as having been with them from time immemorial. On the other hand, the myths of our culture certainly do exhibit a history - they show a continuity with our present day cultural practices.

Piaget therefore argues that if we are interested in origins, we ought to study the genetic development of our categorial structures. This may be a more viable approach than the stratographic one, which holds that the complex later structures in our cultural and intellectual development, are, as it were, sedimented on to the simpler earlier ones, much as geological strata are laid down. If Piaget is correct here, and for that matter Aron Gurwitsch, no such sedimentation occurs. There is rather a reconstruction of the simpler more basic categorisations both in the history of our culture and in that of the individual. Over a period of time they become transformed into the more sophisticated structures exemplified in our contemporary culture, and into those of the adult individual who belongs to it.

Piaget's criticism of Lévi-Strauss' ahistorical approach would not apply to Schrag, who manifestly takes account of socio-historical factors. But what might be questioned is the apparent assumption that the diversity of meaning of the whole range of our knowledge is embedded in this originative experience. If this were so, how would we account for the imaginative creation of novelty, both in the arts and the sciences? Kronecker's statement, that God made the natural numbers, and all the rest is the work of man, although undoubtedly allegorical, does make a significant point. On the other hand, Mach, good positivist that he was, thought that all physical science could be based on the data given in sense-perception, thereby overlooking the part played by creative imagination in the construction of physical theory.

The originative experience described by Schrag which has a mytho-poetic as well as a socio-historic content does seem to be that belonging to the adult. However, it might be worth while when speaking of origins to refer not only to myth and tradition, but also to the undeveloped thought of the young child. In a somewhat different but relevant connection Sartre argued that the Marxists ought to take into account the child's reaction to the family situation on which adult experience was founded:

> Today's Marxists, (he says), are concerned only with adults; reading them, one would believe that we were born at the age when we earn our first wages. They have forgotten their childhoods... The family in fact is constituted by and in the general movement of History, but is experienced on the other hand, as an absolute in the depth and opaqueness of childhood.27

Sartre does bring out here the need to refer to the experience of the child if we wish to obtain a fuller understanding of that of the adult. In any case, the child's experience of the tradition would be different from that of our own. Apart from the fact that the distinction between subjective and objective may not have been clearly made by the child, children have not yet been adequately initiated into the tradition and may have little understanding of its rules and conventions, moral or otherwise. Further, children are not at first in possession of biblical stories or Greek legends. Such stories and legends have to be learned and they usually are in a simplified form either from the parents or in the class-room.

It is Schrag's contention that radical reflection brings into view a world, which antedates the constructs of pure theory (science and philosophy), functioning within the context of an expanded form of reason. What we may ask, however, is: how do we know at what point to cease the process of radical reflection or deconstruction? It might not be difficult to stop thinking about the world in Galilean terms, which Aristotle never did; and it is doubtful whether the ordinary person in the street does either. If we accept the view that mental acts such as perceiving, feeling and imagining involve interpretation, it might be difficult to arrive at presuppositionless experience. In any case it would not be feasible to deconstruct the more basic spatial, temporal and causal structures which are to be found in any form of mythological thought. To deconstruct them could only render experience meaningless, 'a tale told by an idiot full of sound and fury, signifying nothing.'

There is, however, a form of deconstruction of our basic conceptual structures, which occurs in certain pathological conditions. I refer here to the amnesiac aphasias described by Goldstein,28 where owing to brain damage there is a breakdown of the categorial structures by which patients order their world. The patient is unable to name familiar objects and colours, although he or she can recognise them and handle such objects perfectly well. Thus the patient who has been a carpenter will be able effectively to demonstrate the use of a tool like a chisel; but the patient is unable to name it, since he or she has lost the capacity to use words to symbolise things. In other psychopathological conditions like schizophrenia, there may be a breakdown in the linguistic categories in terms of which we order words, so that the patient is incapable of producing coherent speech.

As a result of his neurological studies Goldstein came to the conclusion that language is not merely a tool by means of which we name objects. As he saw it, it rather expressed a particular conceptual way of building up the world through abstraction. The capacity to organise our experience categorially Goldstein termed the abstract attitude. The word-finding disturbances of aphasic patients, are symptomatic of an impairment of this attitude, although the patient's concrete performances remain unimpaired.

As opposed to such pathological deconstruction, the radical epoché must presuppose that the language in which descriptions of originative experience occur, has not been deconstructed or decategorised. If it were, we would be left with a disorganised jumble of words, a word salad, with little descriptive value. The position here is similar to that of Descartes, when he engages in his method of systematic doubt. He needs language to express his new found certainty that he exists in terms of the cogito ergo sum.

Ross Harrison has argued that if we are to talk intelligibly about experience, the structures of our language must reflect those of experience. He has criticised what he claims to be Husserl's view that an analysis of the structure of prepredicative experience could be completely independent of the structure of predicative thought as expressed in language. Such a distinction, Harrison argues, is artificial. One has, he tells us, to work within the limits of one's language. What we are concerned with when we report on our prepredicative experience is really a composite structure - an amalgam of language and experience.29

He continues:

> There have, of course, been many famous attempts to
> assert that the really important things in life lie
> outside the boundaries of language and attempts made
> to show, suggest, or indicate their nature; for
> example, Bradley on experience or Wittgenstein on the
> mystical. However Wittgenstein's magnificent
> tautology on this subject that 'whereof we cannot
> speak, thereof we must be silent,' is as true for
> Wittgenstein himself as it is for anyone else. As F.
> P. Ramsey remarked 'if you can't say it, you can't
> say it, and you can't whistle it either.'30

What Harrison does not point out is that this situation may
be somewhat mitigated, since one can construct different
varieties of language and terminology to describe different
aspects of experience. We are not restricted in this to
everyday linguistic usage. Everyday language insofar as it
is impregnated with the natural attitude may be ill-fitted
not only to handle the concepts of advanced science and
technology, but also poetic and mystical experience. We may
perhaps have to use the more symbolic, imaginative language
of the poet to do this - to use, as Schrag suggests, the
language of myth and metaphor.

There is also a dramatic or expressive use of language,
which Harrison only hints at. This may exhibit itself in
mime, song or dance, and give rise in the performer or
spectator to certain meaningful experiences of both a
cognitive and emotional kind. Religious or other kinds of
ritual employ language in this sort of way, as did, for
example, early Greek tragedy and comedy. Greek tragedy we
are told, grew from the ritual connection with the mysteries
of suffering; those concerning the great issues of life and
death and our relation to the gods. On the other hand, Greek
comedy grew from rites concerned with the mysteries of
fertility and procreation.31

I would therefore disagree with Ramsey's punchline, 'If you
can't say it, you can't say it, and you can't whistle it
either.' Not only might we be able to whistle it, we might
also be able to mime and dance it as well. Ramsey's error
lies in assuming that we can only communicate meaningful
experience by a process of descriptive naming, thereby
overlooking that we can also do this through concrete
performance. And on this point my sympathies lie squarely
with Schrag. On a somewhat different level, although it has

been denied by some philosophers that the dance of the bees indicating the location of nectar exhibits rationality on their part, it is nevertheless a kind of language since it does convey information to the rest of the swarm. Similarly one can refer to other sorts of animal performance which seem meaningful, the marking out of territories and ritualistic courting behaviour. Among human beings 'the language of the eyes' is often more eloquent than words.

If we are able to dismantle the categorial attitude so that we arrive at our originative experience, we will still need to describe this experience. And our language may have to be refashioned for this purpose. Sartre's account of the root in Nausea, appears to be an attempt to give a description of a basic experience in which categorisation has partly broken down. The language Sartre employs there seems to be guided by some perceptual experience he had had, perhaps when under the influence of a psychedelic drug. As Sartre expresses it, 'The root, with its colour, shape, its congealed movement, was ... below all explanation. Each of its qualities escaped it a little, flowed out of it, half solidified, almost became a thing; each one was in the way in the root and the whole stump now gave me the impression of unwinding itself a little, denying its existence to lose itself in a frenzied excess.'32 The mystic and the poet may also attain such basic experiences, but they will need a language in which complex symbolism and metaphor play an important role in expressing their revelations.

The capacity to convey suitable emotional experience is an essential element in poetry. To take a specific example, in his poem The Eve of St. Agnes, Keats writes:

>   Full on this casement shone the wintry moon,
>   And threw warm gules on Madeline's fair breast.

If we now try the experiment of replacing the emotionally coloured words in these lines by more neutral ones, we might arrive at the following:

>   Full on this window shone the wintry moon,
>   Making red marks on Jane's uncoloured chest.

Although the objective meaning of these lines is roughly similar to Keats', their beauty and dramatic quality has been completely lost.33

On the other hand, we are told, that if Keats had been giving a scientific description, he might have instead spoken of the selective transmission of homogeneous light by pigmented glass. Whereas the scientific description largely obtains its meaning from the conceptual susperstructure of the laws of optical physics, Keats' lines describe a very different sort of reality, one more akin to what Heidegger takes Being to be. Perhaps this was also the point Goethe was trying to make in his Theory of Colours, when he discussed the nature of light. For Goethe, light was 'the bright, white radiance of a sunny day, not that ray distilled by Newton.'34

In his later work Heidegger thought that the linguistic expressions of the Western philosophical tradition were inadequate for articulating his conception of truth. In abandoning them he appealed instead to poetry and especially to the work of the mystical poets. His aim in doing this, was to bring out the limitations of both philosophic and scientific language. By investigating the concretely richer language of the poet, we may, he believed, be able to attain an insight into the nature of ultimate reality. But Heidegger does not seek to go beyond language: he wishes to locate his experience of Being within the limits of language itself. He contends that through a study of the writings of the poets, we may achieve an understanding of the nature of human existence and our relation to Being, and of Being itself.

Heidegger, however, is specifically interested in certain kinds of poetic writing. An example of this may be seen in the following lines by Silesius, a mystical poet and a contemporary of Leibniz:

The rose is without why; it blooms because it blooms;
It cares not for itself; asks not if it is seen.

The aim of the poet here, so we are told, is to give us a direct insight into the world of the rose - what the rose is in itself.35

There are, of course, a variety of kinds of poetry, some restrict themselves to the dramatic content of the human situation, others of a more cerebral sort, express a well-articulated meaning. Poets of a philosophical cast of mind, such as the mystical poets, attempt in their verse to convey certain insights into the nature of humanity and the world. What would seem to be the case, is that these poets already possess a degree of philosophical understanding which is distilled out in their poetry. And it is these kinds of poetry which serve Heidegger's purpose, rather than, say, love lyrics. The truths Silesius wishes to convey are perhaps closer to those the pre-Socratic philosophers were seeking in their more rational approach to the nature of things, rather than anything to be found in the life-world of the primitive as described by Lēvi-Bruhl. Robert Burns' lines 'When a body meets a body coming through the rye,' perhaps gives a fairer picture, of at least, one aspect of the primitive's life-world than do Silesius' lines. What this comes to is that though Heidegger is now interested in poetic writing, he has not abandoned philosophy for literary criticism, nor for that matter, anthropology.

Nevertheless, even if we accept the view that poetic writing truly reflects experience of a basic cognitive and emotive kind, it might be difficult to claim that a poetic description of our present social situation exhausts all that we can know about human existence and society. Social phenomena usually have a law-like character, and to state these laws or rules, we need general principles, which a more technical language seems better equipped to deal with than is poetic or ordinary language.

*   *   *

We have earlier on noted that Schrag in his discussion of myth is primarily concerned with those myths which form the basis of our contemporary culture, and not with say the totemic practices of the Trobriand Islanders. Ricoeur has looked at this question in some detail in his discussion of the role of myth in Lēvi-Strauss' <u>Savage Mind</u>. He notes that all the examples in this book are taken from a geographical area which is that of totemic thought. It happens, he says, that a part of our civilisation, precisely that part from which our culture does not proceed, lends itself better than any other to the application of the structural methods transposed from linguistics. But this does not prove, he goes on, that structural comprehension is just as enlightening elsewhere. There exists another pole of mythical thought, where the structural element is less evident, but the meaning content is much richer, and he draws our attention to Hebrew Biblical thought.36

An interesting account of the mythical thought of the ancient civilisations of Egypt and the Near East has been given in <u>Before Philosophy</u>.37 The authors note that earlier peoples regularly conceived nature in terms of human experience as a <u>Thou</u> rather than as an <u>It</u>. Such people did, however, they tell us, recognise certain problems which transcend the phenomena. For example, the aim and purpose of being, and the order of justice. The difference between

mythical and modern thought is rather to be found, they
claim, in the emotional attitude and intention. For example,
the modern distinction between subjective and objective, was
meaningless for the primitive. So was also the distinction
between appearance and reality; the Egyptians of the Middle
Kingdom, for example, depicted dragons, griffins and chimeras
among gazelles, foxes and other desert animals, as belonging
to the same natural order.39

Although the reason referred to here is not the reason of
the Englightenment, since it does not necessarily postulate
an isolated ego, it is none the less a rational approach to
philosophical and scientific questions. I doubt whether one
would wish to strip away the philosophic insights of the
early Greek thinkers from which modern philosophy and
science proceed, and accept in their place, say the
Babylonian creation myths. Even in the socio-political
field, the Greek concept of rationality plays an important
role. Plato's Republic is an attempt to base society on the
rational principles developed by the early Greek thinkers,
and so for that matter are Aristotle's Ethics and Politics,
together with the whole concept of law concerned with the
notions of equity and justice. I would not myself, and I may
be wrong here, wish to deconstruct them in favour of the
Homeric myths, even if they may be already embedded there in
a rudimentary form.

The question I wish to ask is: is there a place for the
Greek concept of reason and the autonomy of thought in the
modern social sciences? I would have thought that the
hermeneutical method and the distinction between erklären and
verstehen are examples of the application of rationality to
this field. True they may omit the seminal insights of Freud
as far as the irrational is concerned, but these insights do
depend on rational procedures and on an acceptance of the
notion of causal laws. Merleau-Ponty at the end of his
Les aventures de la dialectique,40 seems to emphasise the
part reason ought to play in politics, when he contrasts the
liberal approach to politics with that of Marxism. His
approach to the political scene is now a cool reflective
one,41 one manifestly sympathetic to Husserl's goal of a
'rational liberal society guided by philosophical
principles.'

This leads me to my final point which is concerned with one
of the basic questions dealt with in Schrag's book, namely
that of origins. We ought, I think, to put on one side
quasi-archeological analyses of our experience in terms of a
fictional stratification of conceptual structure and take up
a considered genetic approach, as Aron Gurwitsch advocated.

I have the impression that despite his approach to this question through the radical epoché, Schrag is not entirely unsympathetic to this kind of position. Does he not after all talk of the 'genesis and development of meaning in the life-world?'

Some years ago I gave a talk at a conference on Piaget's genetic epistemology. When I had finished a distinguished philosopher drew me on one side and asked, 'What on earth has child thought to do with philosophy?' I replied that a genetic enquiry is of some value if we are concerned with the origins of the categorial structures we use in ordinary thought and scientific theory. The simpler structures of child thought may throw light on the more sophisticated adult ones, especially if we cannot completely deconstruct adult experience. Husserl in his later years moved away from static structural analysis to a more genetic analysis. I think he was moving in the right direction.

REFERENCES

1. Calvin O. Schrag, Radical Reflection and the Origin of the Human Sciences, Purdue University Press, West Lafayette, 1980, (hereinafter referred to as R.R.)

2. The phenomenological Epoche is the suspension of all previously taken for granted presuppositions.

3. R.R., p.55.

4. R.R., p.63.

5. R.R., p.104.

6. R.R., p.105.

7. R.R., p.98. See also pp.63-4.

8. Cf. Lester Embree, 'The Phenomenology of Speech in the Early William James,' in Journal of the British Society for Phenomenology, vol. 10, no.2, May 1979, p.106.

9. Cf. Sigmund Freud, 'Construction in Analysis,' in The Standard Edition of the Complete Psychological Works of Sigmund Freud, vol.v, Hogarth Press for Institute of Psychoanalysis, London, 1950.

10. R.R., p.65.

11. Ibid.

12. R.R., p.66.

13. Roy Bhaskar, The Possibility of Naturalism: A Philosophical Critique of the Contemporary Human Sciences, The Harvester Press, Brighton, 1979, p.198.

14. Ibid, p.195.

15. J. L. Austin, 'A Plea for Excuses,' Proceedings of the Aristotelian Society, vol. LVII. 1956-7.

16. Sartre distinguishes the prereflective cogito, a conciousness of the self which is implicit in our everyday, cognitive, evaluative and active relationships to the world, and the reflective cogito in which consciousness becomes explicitly self-conscious, making of itself an object of its own conscious awareness. It is this latter or reflective cogito with which Descartes

was exclusively concerned.

17. R.R., p.99.

18. R.R., cf. p.107.

19. R.R., p.112.

20. R.R., cf. pp.112-14.

21. R.R., p.118.

22. Ibid.

23. Ibid., pp.118-19.

24. R.R., p.125.

25. R.R., p.126.

26. Jean Piaget, Structuralism, Routledge Kegan Paul, London, 1971, cf. pp.106-19.

27. Jean-Paul Sartre, Search for a Method, Vintage Books, New York, 1968. p.62.

28. Cf. Kurt Goldstein, Human Nature in the Light of Psychopathology, Harvard University Press, Cambridge, Mass., 1940, and Language and Language Disturbances, Grune & Stratton, New York, 1948.

29. Ross Harrison, 'The Concept of Prepredicative Experience,' in Edo Pivcevic (ed.) Phenomenology and Philosophical Understanding, Cambridge University Press, Cambridge, 1975.

30. Ibid., p.107.

31. Cf. C. M. Bowra, Ancient Greek Literature, Oxford University Press, Oxford, 1945, Chs. III and V.

32. Jean-Paul Sartre, Nausea, New Directions Publishing Corp., New York, 1964, pp.74-5.

33. Robert H. Thouless, Straight and Crooked Thinking, English Universities Press Ltd., London, 1946, pp.15-17. Thouless belongs to the Ogden and Richards school and identifies straight thinking with unemotive thinking, a view which some may regard as being too restrictive.

34. Cf. Erich Heller, The Disinherited Mind, Penguin Books Ltd., Harmondsworth, 1961, p.20.

35. Cf. A. G. Pleydell-Pearce, 'Philosophy, Poetry and Mysticism,' in Journal of the British Society for Phenomenology, vol. 10, no.2, May 1979, pp.122-9, and especially p.124.

36. Paul Ricoeur, The Conflict of Interpretations Northwestern University Press, Evanston, Ill., 1974, Cf. 'Structure and Hermeneutics,' pp.40-1.

37. Henri Frankfort, Mrs. Henri Frankfort, John A. Wilson and Thorkild Jacobsen, Before Philosophy, Penguin Press Ltd., Harmondsworth, 1949.

38. Cf. H. and H. A. Frankfort, 'Myth and Reality,' in Ibid.

39. Cf. H. and H. A. Frankfort, 'The Emancipation of Thought from Myth,' in Ibid.

40. Maurice Merleau-Ponty, Les aventures de la dialectique, Gallimard, 1955, especially the 'Epilogue,' Cf. pp.273-313, translated by J. Bien as The Adventures of the Dialectic, Northwestern University Press, Evanston, Ill., 1973.

41. Maurice Merleau-Ponty, Signes, Gallimard 1960, Cf. p.20, translated by R. C. McCleary as Signes, Northwestern University Press, Evanston, Ill., 1964.

4 Practical reasoning and social science: from the phenomenology of the social world to a radical hermeneutics [1]

DIETER MISGELD

INTRODUCTION

This paper attempts to inquire into the role of social science in the investigation of society which commonly takes place in social life. It participates in the questioning of social science influenced by phenomenology and ethnomethodolgy, by hermeneutics and critical social theory. Nevertheless, the inquiry which I propose differs from them. I have chosen to call this form of inquiry 'radical hermeneutics.' I mean by radical hermeneutics a reflection on the relation between social science and the organisation of social relations in everyday life. This reflection includes studies of the actual organisation of social processes in those areas which already are subject to the influence of social science. These are areas in which knowledge has become professionalised and has been influenced or become dependent upon a growing body of social scientific information. One only has to think of education, and the changes in it since 1945 (in the United States since the end of the first world war). The more professionalisation increases, the more old distinctions are subverted. The differences between what is public and what is private, between common cultural knowledge and professional managerial or organisational knowledge, have either become abiguous, or they do not hold at all. Whole areas of practical discourse may lose their appeal and cogency, from the discussion of educational aims and of family life, to the interpretation of sexuality and personal relations.

Radically hermeneutical reflection is no antidote to these developments, nor a comprehensive critique. It is merely an attempt to come to terms with these developments by reflecting on their actual organisation and by inquiring into what they entail practically. It shares the scepticism of the hermeneutical tradition with respect to comprehensive theories of the society and of history, and with respect to the possibility of cogent non-alternative explanations of social phenomena. On the positive side, radical hermeneutical reflection means to permit oneself to be drawn into the conflict between the professionalisation of social knowledge and the ordinary communicative understanding a society has of its social situations and social practices, which still exists as a cultural resource.

My introductory remarks are to indicate that the traditions I draw upon for a formulation of this project are frequently too concerned with theory to seriously take up the study of the actual organisation of social practices. This is true, in my view, of phenomenology and of critical social theory in particular. Indirectly, therefore, I aim at an argument against the preoccupation with theory in critical studies of social scientific knowledge. I shall address this topic in Section One entitled, 'Scientific Sociology and the Topic of the Life World: A Basis for Studies of Practical Reasoning or for Metatheory?'

I shall offer a first statement of the problems mainly by referring to sociological theory as a theory of sociology as science, and by addressing the alternative traditions I draw upon, from phenomenology to critical social theory. Here I build on their common reference to the theme of the 'life-world'2 and consider some of the implications of this conceptual metaphor for what I mean by 'radical hermeneutics.'

In Section Two entitled, 'Common Sense Reasoning and the Scientific Interpretation of Social Action: An Examination of Alfred Schutz,' I single out phenomenological sociology. Schutz's work is important because in some of his work he employed phenomenology for the purpose of examining and redesigning social science. The formulation of the concept of the 'life-world' has been of the utmost consequence for sociology. But because foundational concerns prevailed with Schutz, there is no questioning of the practices of reasoning in social science. Schutz aimed at a philosophical social science, not at an explication of the place of social science in the world of everyday life.

In Section Three entitled 'Practical Reasoning and Social Science in the Perspective of Radically Hermeneutical Reflection,' I address the project of radical hermeneutics. I use some examples from socialisation theory in sociology and try to show what kind of reasoning is employed in it and how it differs from reasoning in everyday life. Radical hermeneutics is considered as a reflection relying on the lay knowledge of everyday life. For radical hermeneutics this knowledge is the major cultural resource.3

I   SCIENTIFIC SOCIOLOGY AND THE TOPIC OF THE LIFE WORLD: A BASIS FOR STUDIES OF PRACTICAL REASONING OR FOR METATHEORY?

The argument in this section shall proceed from two assumptions.

1.   There is a common belief that there are forms of social inquiry which can be called scientific. Among these sociology is usually included. In its most basic sense, for social science to be scientific means that concepts and techniques can be developed which explain and describe social phenomena and the society more adequately, correctly, more objectively and cogently than commonsense reasoning would.

2.   There is now a developed body of research and theory which has made this belief problematic, at least among groups of people trained in the social sciences and in sociology. Phenomenology and hermeneutics, ethnomethodology and ordinary language philosophy, and, of course, critical social theory, belong here. Their influence has led to a reconsideration of the foundations of social science and sociology. New forms of social research have arisen from it which do not fit under any of the familiar conceptions of scientific knowledge. They frequently look more like an empirical documentation of philosophical claims or documentations of the self-organising properties of social settings reminding us of the practical knowledge we ordinarily rely on.

I now turn to the first assumption.

Consider a definition of scientific theory in sociology by Talcott Parsons: 'Scientific theory is a body of interrelated generalised propositions about empirical

73

phenomena within a frame of reference.'4 Jürgen Habermas has commented upon this conception and the action theoretic frame of reference (Parsons' theory) which it alludes to. He says that it was meant to <u>constitute</u> the object domain of social science, not to describe or explain it.5 This so-called 'analytic realism' establishes a hierarchy of problems which reaches from a categorical frame to empirical theories, scientific predictions and finally to facts.

An edifice of theory is introduced in which every theme of a possible discourse about the society becomes a theme internal to the organisation of scientific theory. Thus sociology can become a science (scientific theory) by removing the very network of everyday concepts and terms with reference to which one would ordinarily explain what is meant by action or interaction, by system and role. The use of these concepts becomes accountable to a system of rules internal to the organisation of scientific theory in sociology. Our common understanding of the society which we regularly employ in order to be able to act together and to speak with one another enters into the system of sociological theory only insofar as sociology cannot avoid terms of the common language. It cannot replace them entirely with more abstract symbols. But it constructs its own order of the relation of terms, without any reference to how we ordinarily use them.

Consider an example. Sociological systems theory states in one case that all so-called action systems (biological and social, individual and collective) including the society, can functionally be defined as 'relations of meaning between actions, which reduce complexity by means of the stabilisation of an internal/external differentiation.'6 Clearly the language of everyday life does not suggest these formulations. Mostly people just do not speak this way, at least not yet.

This is, of course, not an argument against the theory. For normally there is no reason in everyday life for speaking of action systems in general. But it is significant that the theory ignores the relation of the concepts which it employs to the concepts used in the interpretation of social action under conditions not determined by formal theories. In other words, sociological systems theory reduces complexity by describing relations of meaning between actions in terms of procedures which have the reduction of complexity as their aim. It organises the very conditions, - the relations of meanings between actions - which might otherwise raise the question of the adequacy of its concepts to its subject matter. It will permit no explication of these relations other than the one required by it. The question of adequacy of its concepts is reduced to another question: Does the functionalist systems-postulate, that action-systems reduce complexity, indeed permit the reduction of complexity in the theory of action systems?

Consider what it means to think of actions and their meanings as reducing complexity. There are many circumstances in which we feel warranted to think of an action (including actions for which we use words) or an event as simplifying matters. An introduction to someone we have frequently met, but whose name we do not know, makes it easier to exchange greetings on future occasions. An uncertainty in interaction is removed. Thus we have 'reduced complexity.' But thinking of this action as a reduction of complexity in simple interaction (Luhmann calls interaction the simplest action system), seems like adopting a very artificial view of the event. It seems to be inadequate to what we take the situation to be as we experience it. The phrase 'reduction of complexity' seems to be more appropriate when used in instances such as that when a set of complicated traffic lights is rearranged or channels of communication in an office hierarchy are changed. Thus there are classes of actions to which Luhmann's theory may apply quite naturally. They belong in the field called sociology of formal organisations. But not all our actions are controlled by them, although Luhmann's analysis makes them appear that way. Thus one would not know what could be meant by Luhmann's phrase were one not to think of particular classes of action as being interpreted within a framework of organisational knowledge. It is hard to conceive, from the perspective of everyday experience and everyday knowledge, how the function of reducing complexity could be attributed to all social actions, at least from the perspective of what people really do and how they appraise their actions. Most of us don't regard ourselves as systems engineers or organisation specialists when we go about our affairs. But it is, of course, the point of a functionalist theory perspective to search for mechanisms which underlie overt performances, as they are believed to be unknown to their performers. By doing so the theory does not describe the actions in question. It reformulates them to fit into a systems-perspective so that all actions appear to have the same sense as long as they are regarded from the overall perspective of the theory. By endorsing the result of its analyses of social action as the maxim of its procedure, Luhmann's theory refashions the phenomena it lays hold of. Thus, systems theory becomes plausible as a general theoretical perspective upon the society. Its conceptual accounts are not measured by their adequacy to the phenomena, or by their explanatory force. For the criterion for the adequacy of their theory is simply its capacity for reducing complexity. It cannot do this once it recognises different social perspectives as productive of different accounts of the society and of its organisational forms, unless these accounts and these organisational forms can be analysed in terms of one overriding mechanism. The systems requirement of reducing complexity is sufficiently abstract, yet also sufficiently situation specific, for Luhmann to provide the general rationale for the systems analyses of all types of organisational forms.

Parsons and Luhmann both believe that scientific explanations require theory. A scientific theory of the society must be able to grasp society and social action directly as its object, through the use of theoretical constructs, without indicating the social location from which it arises. In this sense sociology is like any science. The sociologist has no other identity than that furnished by the professional activity he or she engages in.

Luhmann's understanding of sociology as a science is more radical, however, than Parson's. For he interprets social systems as posing problems of technical mastery.[7] Just like any action system, science, including sociology, also engages in the reduction of complexity, the stabilisation of an external/internal differentiation. Thus sociology is not merely theory construction for explanatory purposes. It has a position of practical consequence in the society, just like any action system. Insofar as it is conscious of this task (the reduction of complexity by means of increasing differentiation) it has the particular role of guiding social action systems toward the acceptance of these tasks. This is equivalent to sociology assuming the conscious formulation or planning of tasks, indicating possibilities for more actions which reduce complexity and produce further differentiations, (i.e., more organised sub-systems of the society). Clearly, then, sociological reasoning is placed above everyday reasoning. It can claim to have access to a perspective from which all social activities can become visible in their co-ordination. This is not, I repeat, the same perspective from which one understands the society in one's everyday activities.

Could it therefore be that sociological theory is more like ideology than scientific theory? But even if it is, one needs to understand what is entailed by this account of the society. It is my hypothesis that such sociological theory places managerial conceptions of social intervention at the centre of what now clearly becomes an instrumental knowledge of the society, and it provides a mandate for the increasing professionalisation of social knowledge, the creation of a technical intelligentsia for the furthering of increasing organisational power. In this sense, I think, those - including Marxists - are right who argue that authors such as Parsons and Luhmann can be linked with the emergence of corporate structures in business, and the growth of government administrations. Sociology together with those structures makes up one complex of relations. Perhaps, one may call it, with one critic, a 'ruling apparatus.'8   This, at least is an interesting phrase which can serve as a guide for further analysis.

It follows that it may be adviseable to analyse social science and sociological theory from the perspective of its application, as applied social science, for these reasons:

(a) By claiming to be scientific sociological theory can appropriate the meaning of ordinary terms such as action and society, without feeling obliged to explicate their sense with reference to their ordinary use. It can therefore establish a dominant position vis a vis everyday discourse.

(b) Applied social science, such as management theory, borrows from social scientific theories in the strict sense and derives programmes for the rationalisation of social action from them. It thus either subordinates pre-scientific modes of reasoning to itself, or integrates them. Or it tries to exclude them, thus possibly provoking a clash of interpretations, a confrontation between differently organised understandings of social reality.

(c) This field of potentially conflicting interpretations is the area in which it can be determined, by inspecting the practices of social scientific theories as they are applied, to what extent they are instrumental in the reorganisation of practical action and/or communication. I locate what I call radically hermeneutical reflection in this field.

I now turn to the second assumption I mentioned at the beginning of this section. I mentioned that there is now much theory and research which makes it increasingly problematic to regard the social sciences as positive sciences in the classical sense. Much of this criticism has been inspired by the discovery, in phenomenology, of the difference between the world of science and of daily life. Even critical social theory has, as a result of Jürgen Habermas's recent work,9 now recognised the compelling character of the conceptual metaphor 'Lebenswelt.'

I refer to this term 'Lebenswelt' or 'life-world' in order to invoke all the perspectives already mentioned, from phenomenology to critical social theory. They all propose that the technical formulations of social scientific discourse, (from forms of cognitive psychology to sociological theory and back to the use of systematic techniques for the assessment of social and cognitive competences) restrict the scope of interpretations, thereby imposing limits on what could be meant by living in the society and acting socially.

From the perspective of phenomenology and of ordinary language philosophy, the practices of social scientific theorising seem narrower and more restricting than those of everyday communication (commonsense reasoning).

From the perspective of ethnomethodology the practices of formal sociological discourse acquire the character of policy statements, which prescribe how to understand the society prior to our encountering the actual contingencies of social organisation. The actualities of the social organisation of particular areas of social activity are treated as arising from the reasoning that is internal to these areas, and thus they are differentiated from conceptions of the society which rest on the general premises mentioned.

From the perspective of philosophical hermeneutics, social scientific explanations of the orientation of action are seen as failing to acknowledge the cultural foundations for understanding the society, and for failing to become aware of the tradition context of language, and the role of history, in understanding social situations.

From the perspective of critical social theory, finally, the social sciences and even sociological theory, are seen largely as operating with a conception of the rationality of social actions which is restricted to purposive or instrumental action. They have failed to take account of, or explicate, a concept of rationality that in any way does justice to the organisation of the social life-world in communication, and to the conflictual development of rationalisation processes in industrialised societies.

For two of the first three approaches mentioned, (phenomenology and ethnomethodology), the structures of the 'life-world,' the invariant features of making sense of social situations and of the particulars of socially organised settings become the topics of analysis. A descriptive attitude prevails which resists the reduction of the objects of sociological study (the field of social action and communication), to systemic constructions and comprehensive explanatory schemata.

Studies of attempts to understand the society based on ordinary language philosophy deny the universal validity of scientific concepts and turn to the comparison of a plurality of language games, which in the end serves to demonstrate the dependency of socially constructed meaning on language. They introduce the study of language as a kind of metatheory for social inquiry, sometimes debunking social scientific concepts as non-sensical reconstructions of everyday terms.

Philosophical hermeneutics gives rise to accounts of the generation of meaning and sense in the society which take the interpretive competence realised in reflecting on one's culture as their model. They construe societal communication as a thoughtful and open-minded dialogue with cultural traditions, supported by a reading of culturally significant documents or texts which shows little regard for popular culture. Philosophical hermeneutics thus encourages a meta-reflection on the self-constitution of tradition, in a discourse which cannot objectify its own limits.

Critical social theory, in its recent form, has explicitly cultivated the development of metatheoretical discourse in order to compare various concepts of social action, from instrumental action to communicative action. It has also proposed a two-fold approach toward understanding the society. One is based on the perspective of the interacting participant who encounters the rational basis of social interaction in the use of language for communication. Here the society is conceived as equivalent to the social cultural life-world. The other form of social theory is based on the perspective of an observer who can analyse functional relationship as they are required, for example, by a market-economy. These relationships are not themselves explicit in everyday actions oriented toward reaching understanding, which rely on the interactive use of natural language. The market as a set of functional relations is not visible in everyday practice.10 Critical social theory is a metatheory because it combines both perspectives and establishes one framework for the anlaysis of two types of rationality, the rationality of purposive action and the rationality of communicative action. Systems of purposive action co-ordinate social action by means of the refinement of abstract mechanisms of control (steering mechanisms). The rationality of communicative action depends on the ability of identifiable social actors (i.e., persons) to respond to claims to validity built into the use of natural language.

With the exception of ethnomethodology, the positions addressed will attempt to ground social science in a more comprehensive understanding of the society and of social action than the social sciences usually possess. They also include metatheories or metareflections on the logic of the understanding of social phenomena themselves.

Thus, they do not take up the problem of social science in its societal actuality. They do not begin with it having become a form of policy studies or with it having produced policies, procedures and techniques for the reorganisation of social life. Techniques for the managerial control of education, for example, have already been introduced and are used to monitor and reform school education. They entail the reformulation of education as a process of instruction which is geared toward the application of detailed assessment procedures.11 The latter are aligned with an organised system of social relations including assessment specialists, consultants, supervisors and public authorities in charge of education. Developments like these represent the practical intrusion of applied social science into the 'life-world' and into tradition based modes of cultural understanding. They may have the capacity to suppress a host of cultural resources on which people working in the field of education have so far relied. These resources had furnished them definite, even if controversial, identities as teachers and students reciprocally engaged in the daily activity of teaching and learning.

A comprehensive theoretical reflection on these developments grounded in an examination of the history of sociological theory 12 for example, is certainly useful in order to draw attention to the implications of these developments. But it falls short of the actualities which are already there. It already is the case that teaching and learning as daily activities are made systematically accountable to authorities external to these activities. It already is the case that family life is accountable to perceptions, images, rules, which emanate from the media or public and commercial organisations. In all such cases techniques of applied social science research are used in order to refashion cultural understanding.

The conflict between organisationally controllable formulations of social experience and the interpretations of personal and collective experience generated in everyday life with reference to cultural traditions, may give rise to the radical reflection I call radical hermeneutics. Radically hermeneutical reflection is the basis of a practical critique, and thus of actions of resistance. It seizes upon the possibilities contained in the situation, as they are defined by the conflicts mentioned. It does not proceed from an overriding rationale, a general epistemological or metaethical and metapolitical framework. What is at issue for radically hermeneutical reflection is the politics of the actual situation.

Radically hermeneutical reflection recognises practically constructed situations as the horizon for understanding the society. It will therefore attempt to keep the technical reorganisation of social action and discourse open to interpretations which resonate with the full set of considerations belonging to a reflective appraisal of any topic. The kind of thoughtfulness which it pursues wants to address what, for example, teaching and learning really mean, or personal relations, or work, as opposed to what an organised process of formal and abstract procedures derived from the systematic objectification and categorisation of social action and discourse tell us they mean. Thus, conflicts between different accounts of practically constructed situations are of major concern to it. Thoughtfulness in the hermeneutical sense requires this weighing of what is opposite to one's beliefs in relation to one's beliefs. This was already Gadamer's conception. Practicing attentiveness to the situation and to different account or interpretations of it, accounts which depend on the different social positions of those giving them (e.g., the 'instructional objectives' specialist versus the teacher) gives rise to the recognition of possibly conflicting lines of action. Radically hermeneutical reflection attempts to explicate these differences in the situation without either referring to more comprehensive strategies of rationalisation, or assuming a continuity of cultural tradition.13 It is no more nor less than an effort to recognise the actualities of cultural life on the basis of the experience of antagonistic perspectives on social life. The respective merits or otherwise of such perspectives are to be appraised solely in terms of the demands of the situation. One might also describe radically hermeneutical reflection as a radical pedagogy.14 It is radical insofar as it is primarily self-education and insofar as it interprets general theoretical ideas and conceptions in the light of practical orientations to the situation. It is also radical for seriously engaging in a reasoning which recognises conflicts of interpretation as its element.

I am proposing this reformulation of the hermeneutical enterprise in order to ground practical reflection as the appropriate way to approach the topic of the life-world. Instead of remaining a theme of descriptive explication it becomes what the 'life-world' has always been described as: The constantly receding, yet constantly available resource for understanding. A radical hermeneutics is no more than a proposal to employ this resource, rather than to attempt to explicate how it functions as a resource. One engages in a co-operative process of reflection which, rather than taking as its object of analysis and interpretation the social world itself, focuses instead upon the creation of social meaning, and its employment in social policy.

By foregoing a comprehensive theory of social reality one also foregoes metatheory. The world of social life and the common grounds for understanding the society built into the use of natural language are no longer the object to be explained by social science and sociology, but themselves become the resources to be relied upon and used for the interpretation of social science. Nor is there any need for a general theoretical explanation of what we mean by social reality and the world of everyday life.

Radically hermeneutical reflection heeds Wittgenstein's observation that the search for general theoretical frameworks and general conceptual explanations of cultural and linguistic resources fails adequately to capture its culturally grounded and therefore pre-theoretical use. No theory can do justice to the depth and cogency of this practical recognition. The early Heidegger and even Gadamer, (in spite of his pre-occupation with the high culture of the tradition), have recognised this. They have interpreted knowledge with reference to practical application. We only know something when we know how to apply it practically to a situation and ourselves. Had this recognition of the practical grounds of social and cultural knowledge been incorporated into the phenomenological reflection on social science and sociology, a practice of critical reflection on social science and sociology could have emerged from phenomenological sociology. What actually happens in the society could have become its guide for a reflection on the foundations of social science and sociology.

II   COMMON SENSE REASONING AND THE SCIENTIFIC INTERPRETATION OF SOCIAL ACTION: PHILOSOPHY AND SOCIOLOGY (AN EXAMINATION OF SCHUTZ)

So far I have argued that social science is to be examined in terms of the reasoning commonly employed in everyday life. The influence of social science upon action and communication is to be accounted for in terms of this reasoning rather than by a metatheory of the philosophical foundations of social science.

One may think of this suggestion for analysis and reflection as somewhat analogous to the later Wittgenstein's critique of philosophy. Wittgenstein didn't merely make this or that idea <u>in</u> philosophy problematic. He questioned philosophy as <u>such</u>, at least insofar as it is believed to consist of a distinctive practice of reasoning, the employment of which would let the philosopher acquire ultimate clarity about the relation between mind, world and language. To feel driven to search for such clarity - that was the problem.

In some cases ordinary language philosophers have discussed social scientific concept formation, as if it resulted from a similar compulsion.15 They might think it odd for sociologists to believe, for example, that the society can be treated as a 'subject' and talked about in the singular, as the 'action system' of the society. They might find it still stranger that sociologists such as Luhmann and Parsons compare the action system of society to action systems in general. For would one not need to rely on concepts such as society, action, systems, which already have a social use, in order to explain this social use as a function of an action system? Should sociologists not consider the functions of the terms they use in the language, before they proceed to generate their conceptual constructions? Otherwise, their failure to explore the logic of terms used in natural language obstructs the conceptual delineation of the object domain appropriate for sociology. The conditions for the intelligibility of sociological statements are not brought into view.

However, it would be mistaken to think that the technical language of sociology and its formal theories could be corrected or proven to be wrong on this basis. There are reasons for sociology and the social sciences to refrain from the analysis of rules for the use of terms in natural language. For if sociology had proceeded on this basis from its beginnings it would have located the society on the level of the most commonly occurring reasoning about the society, as the rules of language are themselves social rules. The reasoning in which these rules are identified and applied to the explication and characterisation of social phenomena in the context of ordinary activities would have been all that such a sociology could have concerned itself with. Sociology and the social sciences attempted to be sciences, however, because commonsense reasoning could not be trusted to give a correct view of the society. They have followed Durkheim who believed that non-scientific reasoning about the society was unreliable, geared to particular interests, and simply not objective. He treated common sense knowledge of the society as representing a fleeting reality. If it was to be a topic for sociology at all, it could only be the explanandum for sociology, not the explanans.

The stability of social action, which was and is a major topic of sociology from Durkheim to Parsons and Luhmann, is thought to depend on conditions not ordinarily known to social actors: They do not perceive their actions in their systematic co-ordination, even if they do the co-ordinating. Classical sociology assumed that there are real underlying factors, which do not ordinarily come into view. One can see how a critique of sociology that was simply based on ordinary language analysis could take up this view and refute it in the manner discussed. And this has indeed occurred, in the critique of ethnomethodology.

But one must also grant that the technical discourse of sociology is not simply based on a mistake or on a conceptual error. Sociology as a discipline grew simultaneously with developments in modern societies, such as industrialisation, which indeed pose new problems of social stability and social organisation.16 They seemed to warrant a more technical treatment of questions pertaining to the conditions of the stability of social action, the co-ordination of expectations and the complexities of social organisation. Sociology arose together with the need to recognise social planning as a task. Therefore a critical appraisal of sociology cannot merely be concerned with the correction of conceptual mistakes. One needs to address it as an enterprise in which the critical tasks go along with practical ones. The correct theory of the society also is a theory which has an effect on the rationalisation (and scientisation) of social practice. When I considered the sociological systems theory of Luhmann I tried to show that systems theory had made the unity of theory and practice the basis of its conceptual reductions. Common sense reasoning, and the knowledge people have of the society as implicit in their ability to organise their affairs, is entirely subjected to the primacy of this reasoning.

However, one may also give an account of sociology as a continuation and development of our ordinary knowledge of the society. While not forgetting that it also obstructs common sense knowledge (as discussed). Phenomenology has failed to illuminate this obstruction; but it has recognised the continuity between sociology and common sense knowledge.

It is important therefore to show that phenomenological sociology is a turning point in the critical/interpretive appraisal of social science. In addressing this topic I shall also show, once again, the importance of foundational deliberations. They were the central topic of Schutz's work, at least insofar as he addressed the social sciences which were not phenomenological.

Phenomenology, since the later Husserl 17 and the early Heidegger, has interpreted the specialised activities of scientific reasoning in terms of a wider set of considerations. The term 'Lebenswelt' gains its significance in this context. It signifies a ground, or a horizon of knowledge and communicative understanding, which reaches beyond, yet also encompasses the special knowledge of the sciences, as well as the special knowledge connected with any particular activity. It signifies the idea of a world held in common. Phenomenology perceives this world as a common background of understanding. Alfred Schutz has captured the sense of this background of social understanding by calling it the common sense knowledge of the society. Common sense knowledge of the society, common sense interpretations of social action, occur against the background of or in terms of the world of everyday life and are therefore also constitutive of it. Schutz recognises therefore that a description of the life world is needed if sociology is to grasp its own potential. He says:

> The Sciences that would interpret and explain human action and thought must begin with a description of the foundational structures of what is pre-scientific, the reality which seems self-evident to men remaining within the natural attitude. This reality is the everyday life-world.18

The everyday world is the paramount reality for Schutz because any possibility of understanding the society is grounded in it. The everyday world has this primacy not so much for methodological reasons, but because it has real or ontological primacy for the members of the society. It is through daily life that a common, communicative world can be constituted. People's everyday activities, as they are regularly carried out, provide the sense of this world as a world held in common and taken for granted in this commonality. They provide the good sense, to use a phrase of Antonio Gramsci's, of our common sense understanding of social structure and social process. The argument of phenomenology therefore is that sociology cannot account for the sense of its categorisations and explanations unless it first recognises the commonsense understanding societal members have of the society as constitutive of the subject matter of sociology itself. Insofar as sociological categories are to resemble the common sense concepts actually employed by people, their understanding of these concepts and the rules they follow when they use them must be explicated. The meaning constitutive activities of common sense reasoning become the objects of inquiry. Of concern are the <u>essential</u> features of common sense reasoning.

Description as a method is thematic throughout Schutz's work. Description must have primacy for Schutz, because the interpretation and explanation of social action are activities specifically allocated to social scientific reasoning. Description is the method of phenomenological sociology because it secures the phenomenal first foundation of the social sciences, the phenomenon of the social world in its entire range. By description we mean a procedure not prejudiced by explanatory or interpretive interests, or a reflective and constructivist concern. Description makes us aware of the constitutive activities of social actors acting in concert in an everyday world, as well as of the meaning constituted in and by their activities. It uncovers a field of phenomena which claim the attention of the investigator beyond his or her method-directed and theory-dependent interests.

Phenomenology is the method for bringing taken-for-granted pre-occupations and theoretical conceptions of the objects to be investigated under control. It can show in what way explanations are explanations of an object prior to the object functioning as a variable in an explanatory construction. Therefore, phenomenology constantly expands its reflective as well as descriptive analyses both of the subject-pole and of the object-pole of inquiry. Reflective analysis in phenomenology reflects on the inquirer's procedures for constituting the object of inquiry (analysis of intentional acts as meaning constitutive, analysis of horizon intentionalities,19 etc.). Descriptive analysis shows what the objects (to which these procedures refer and which they constitute) are and what they mean.

All in all, both sides of phenomenological analysis always aim at the removal of insubstantiable prejudices in favour of objects really existing in and of themselves in a realm beyond experience, which prevent our analysing the acts which are constitutive of the meaning of something as 'really existing.' Phenomenology, therefore, is a method for the clarification of the intentional meaning of methods in general. It needs to uncover the field of the social as the ground of the possibility of rich and varied description, in order to elucidate the particular manner in which the constructions derived from the methods of the natural and social sciences are themselves modifications of ordinary knowledge of the society.

Explanation and interpretation are secondary to phenomenological description. Their use in social science (for example, in terms of Weber's programmatic methodological statements) relegates to a secondary status the crucial analysis of the modes in which the social world is present to the activities of societal members and how it receives its sense from them. Schutz asks how, or in what sense, courses of action can be regarded as rational, and how they are regarded as rational if we examine them in their normal context, (in the world of everyday social relations). He identifies social action as the phenomenon giving rise to social scientific study, as what it attempts to explain and interpret. But he describes social action as it appears when it is not yet subjugated to the procedures of social science. He is looking for standards by which one can determine whether in fact social scientific procedures are adequate to their object.

Thus, phenomenological analysis and description furnish the social sciences with their realm of investigation, without permitting these sciences to proceed as if their own methods alone could determine the sense, meaning and significance of their object. This has the consequence that one may become clearer about the telos of the social sciences. Are the social sciences theoretical sciences, like physics is? Or are they practical sciences, like engineering is? Are they forms of craft knowledge or of art? For Schutz they clearly are not the latter. Literature cannot take the place of science. Folk-knowledge of customs and conventions is not social science, it is the object of social science. Finally, social science is not as theoretical as philosophy, but not as practical as engineering either.

Social science can benefit from phenomenology insofar as it can become more theoretical, more conscious of its explanatory and interpretive claims. It can also become more practical by being committed to the telos of universal rationality. For Husserl, phenomenology, as philosophy, was committed to this goal. Phenomenology, as philosophy, was to pursue this goal by means of an encompassing reflection penetrating the constitutive achievements of science as well as of practical reasoning in the world of everyday life, or of praxis.20 Phenomenology, according to Schutz's conception, inspired by Husserl, could help the social sciences achieve clarity about basic assumptions regarding their object domain. It could thus help them establish the conditions of their applicability to the social world by outlining the conditions which must be fulfilled by their methodical constructions if they are to be adequate for the comprehension of this object domain. It could also clarify the place of the social sciences in the praxis of life. Phenomenology, for Schutz, would render the constructive achievements of the social sciences visible as partial rationalisations of the social world ('regional-ontologien'), which themselves belong to the totality of rationalisation. The latter was to be the aim of a critical praxis based on ultimate foundations in pursuit of the ideal of universal rationality.

While Schutz hardly ever expressed the interest in the ideal of 'Letztbegruendung,' and in a universal critical praxis, that Husserl did, it is clear that for him the social sciences belong to the sphere of culture and human thought just as do the natural sciences. They contribute to the realisation of rationality in particular spheres of the constitution of meaning and sense. They thus add a necessary diversity to the phenomenological concept of rationality (reason). This phenomenological concept of rationality is to be understood as descriptive of the rationalities internal to particular spheres of activity if it is to avoid functioning as a prescriptive construction.

Schutz's deliberations arise from these problems and specifically address the relation of social science concepts to those of everyday reasoning. They also deal with the place of social science theorising in the sphere of culture. Undeniably, Schutz recognises restrictions with respect to the possibility of rationalisation which Husserl could not acknowledge. Coming from Weber, Schutz at times is closer to the sociology of knowledge than to Husserl. But for him description remains the method of phenomenological analysis of the world of everyday life because, for this world to be acknowledged in its ontological primacy (as 'the paramount reality'), there cannot be any prejudgement as to its validity. The theorist of social science must become conscious of the forms in which the recognition of the world of everyday life is accomplished. These forms are the typical, (i.e. generally pervasive) features of commonsense reasoning whose validity can be as little in question in sociology as they are for us in our everyday life. The basic assumptions of social science are the very assumptions without which there could not be everyday life nor a world constituted in these practices of commonsense reasoning. These assumptions are the practically acknowledged necessities of commonsense reasoning.

Schutz employs the method of phenomenological description in order to open up the field of everyday life as the domain of the 'common sense interpretation'21 of social reality. The social life world, or the everyday life world is the objective correlate, the universal horizon, of the common sense constructs and typified courses-of-action employed in everyday reasoning. It is the ever present, yet receding background to the organisation of action in everyday situations. In these situations we do not seek theoretical certainty, we look for practical knowledge.

Schutz claims that the practically interested point of view which characterises one's daily attitude toward events and states of affairs, requires the 'building up of the perspective structure in which our social world appears to us in daily life.'22 Because the organisation of perspectives is practically motivated, whatever knowledge satisfies the practical interest at work in them will be all that is needed. 'As we normally have to act and not to reflect in order to satisfy the demands of the moment, which it is our task to master, we are not interested in the 'quest for certainty.' We are satisfied if we have a fair chance of realising our purposes.'23 This is why the ideal of knowledge in everyday life is 'likelihood,' an ideal of practically applied and practically applicable 'cookbook knowledge' which provides rules and recipes for proceeding in particular ways for a purpose at hand.

Everyone of us, insofar as we all remain human beings in our daily life orient to this idea of knowledge; we know it to be the common idea of knowledge. This itself is part of our commonsense knowledge. Common sense knowledge is knowledge of others, and is shared with others through 'the normal, self-evident routines of daily life.'24 One may also call these routines the 'thought objects of common sense, formed by men in everyday life in order to come to terms with social reality.'25 I recognise that this Schutzian formulation is 'mentalistic.' It reflects the origins of his thought in Husserl's philosophy of consciousness and in his critical discussions, based on Husserl, of Weber's distinction between an observational understanding of the subjective meaning of an action and a motivational (explanatory) understanding of the meaning of an action. The basic concern is, of course, to clarify by means of an analysis of the constituting process 26 what could be meant by Weber's statement that 'the actor attaches a meaning to his action.' In his later work Schutz therefore never relinquishes the belief that the adequacy of social scientific explanations must always be judged by the postulate of subjective interpretation.27 Explanations of human action require models of an individual human mind and reference to the activities of such a mind which are productive of the facts observed by the scientist. However, rather than criticise Schutz's mentalistic vocabulary, I merely note how Schutz proposes to make social science adequate to social reality, thus securing the conditions of its applicability to the latter. On the whole, his postulate of adequacy stands out among the list of three postulates 'for scientific model constructs of the social world.'28 According to Schutz:

> Each term in a scientific model of human action must be constructed in such a way that a human act performed within the life world by an individual actor in the way indicated by the typical construct would be understandable for the actor himself as well as for his fellow-men in terms of common sense interpretations of everyday life. Compliance with this postulate warrants the consistency of the constructs of the social scientist with the constructs of commonsense experience of the social reality.29

This statement indicates how, for Schutz, the social sciences can secure their object for themselves. The postulates of logical consistency, of subjective interpretation, and of adequacy establish the canons of social scientific inquiry. They help it achieve objective validity for its thought objects, constructed according to the rules of formal logic. And they are meant to ensure the adequacy of these constructions to their object domain. But this means that the social sciences are treated entirely as theoretical sciences. Their involvement with the world of everyday life is exclusively confined to examining the relation of their 'thought objects' to common sense reasoning.

On Schutz's view social scientific explanations, if they are to have any content, must be applicable to the everyday world of common sense, and it is with the conditions of applicability that phenomenology is concerned. However, as Schutz admits, social scientific explanations work only at the level of typification of courses of action and with models of actors which are emptied of all the particular characteristics attributable to them in life-world contexts.

They are constructions of a homunculus that may only be animated by reimplanting the features of actors and action known through the commonsense reasoning of everyday life. Thus, phenomenology, at least in its Schutzian and Husserlian form, is incapable of critically examining the proximity of sociology to the formation of social policy that's so much a feature of the social sciences. It is also incapable of using its own discovery, of the construction of social reality in common sense reasoning, in order to indicate what practical relation the reasoning of everyday life can have toward sociology and the social sciences.

Phenomenology (based on Husserl's ideal of a comprehensive theory clarifying all hidden horizon intentionalities 30 of any particular meaning intention in universal reflection) asks more of social science than social science can give: that it be thoroughly adequate, (i.e. emphatically correct) in its depiction of social reality. In order to meet such a demand sociology would have to become a theoretical science similar to phenomenological logic. Phenomenology thus fails to address how the rise of sociological theorising itself has meant a historical innovation, a break with the epistemological tradition of classical philosophy. Sociology is always faced with self-reflexive questions about the meaning of sociological reasoning as an intervention in social reality. One expects of sociology that it have a sense of its own contribution to the rational organisation of social activity. Schutz either ignores this or he gives peculiarly idealist answers, which reveal a naive belief that the realm of intellectual culture is self-sufficient and self-justifying.31

But this is not to say that phenomenology has not made important discoveries, although it may have misunderstood sociology. By applying the method of eidetic or intellectual intuition 32 to the production of systematic descriptions, phenomenology reflects on the origins of the canons of adequacy regarding social scientific concept formation. It establishes criteria of adequacy by consulting common sense reasoning. Following phenomenology one can therefore begin to understand that the formation of concepts in social scientific discourse is nothing more than a peculiar reorganisation of the common sense knowledge of everyday life. However, common sense knowledge of everyday life appears paradoxically enough to have been obliterated by social science, to have lost any claim to validity. It is no longer recognisable as reasonable.33

Schutz however establishes a distinction between the practical attitude of everyday life and the theoretical attitude required for the scientific study of social action. Indeed he treats common sense knowledge of social action as a basis for social scientific knowledge, to which the latter must therefore be adequate. This makes it possible to claim that social science does, after all, deal with the same reality which is known in everyday life. Phenomenological description shows how different interpretations really are interpretations of the same object. It mediates between the radically practical perspective of daily life and the theoretical knowledge of social science. There can be objective theoretical knowledge of the society after all, even if, or indeed precisely because, social science arises from common sense knowledge.

Schutz, I believe, is not interested in a critique of social scientific knowledge, or in the insight that it is a degenerate, somewhat empty form of everyday knowledge. Nor does he want to show that social scientific interpretations of social actions are themselves based on practical grounds or reflect a practical interest, which we, following Habermas, tentatively call a technical interest. Schutz simply wants to secure the foundations for social science which are appropriate for it. For him the issue is the delineation of the object domain appropriate for social science, not a critical interpretive account of it as a mode of reasoning not readily compatible with the reasoning of daily life. The conceptual metaphor of the 'life-world' loses its suggestive force in the end and simply becomes a term for a field open to infinitely refined and detailed description.

III   PRACTICAL REASONING AND SOCIAL SCIENCE IN THE PERSPECTIVE OF RADICALLY HERMENEUTICAL REFLECTION

When Schutz thought of social science, he thought of it as an exclusively theoretical enterprise. He could say that 'as scientific observers of the social world, we are not practically but only cognitively interested in it.' He added: 'This means we are not acting in it with full responsibility for the consequences, but rather contemplating it with the same detached equanimity as physicists.'34 Schutz did not consider to what extent the social sciences are applied sciences or to what extent they contribute to policy deliberation. He never addressed the social sciences as aiming at intervention in social life, as deeply implicated in those very processes of societal rationlisation which they themselves describe and analyse.

Thus he could not address the conditions for the stability

of social action, the possibility of social order, or of the self-differentiation of society through the division of labour, as practical questions. He could not inquire into the historical development and the historical fate of modern societies or into the conflicts which occur in them. Most importantly of all he did not recognise that his 'discovery' of the common sense reasoning that was involved in construction of course of action types, typical motives and typical interests, could be seen as exemplifying the reasoning which takes place when social knowledge becomes professionalised.

I regard it as a task of a radical hermeneutics to address these questions. It addresses the formulations of social action and of the concepts of the society in professionalised social science discourse, as emerging from a reasoning which makes common interpretive conceptions of the society and of social action subservient to special interests. By special interests I mean an interest in specific ways of rationalising social action, for example, or of reasoning about the society. One might say: Social science discourse aims at a formal validity, it proceeds in an 'abstracted conceptual mode'35 which permits uniform and comprehensive treatment of the multiplicity of interpretations which are generated and considered in everyday life.

I turn to an example, in order to illustrate the point. In a standard work of sociology functionalism entitled Socialisation and Society, 36 one of the authors aptly observes that 'the verb socialise and its cognate "socialisation" were current in the language well before they were used as concepts by sociologists, psychologists, or other behavioural scientists.' He refers to The Oxford Dictionary of the English Language and mentions a usage dating back to 1828. Then 'to socialise' simply meant 'to render social, to make fit for living in society.' He compares this with two later formulations, coming from sociologists. 'What does the society expect, demand or require of the typical member of the system when he comes to play the adult social roles he either will select, or to which society will assign him by virtue of his age, sex, colour, occupation and the like?' Or, 'There is adequate socialisation in a society if there is a sufficient number of adequately socialised individuals for the structural requisites of a society to operate.'

Going back to the formulation from The Oxford Dictionary; to make someone fit for living in society is an adequate characterisation, indeed, a description of what anyone does who is engaged in work with people growing up, with those who are newcomers to a society or people who have been ill, etc. Given that the formulation is a dictionary entry, we readily understand that it is a gloss of many descriptions we might employ were we to describe what we are doing when we try to put someone in a position of living more fully with others.

The formulation has the plausibility of a common sense description, of an ordinary maxim, even of a moral exhortation, ('You are to be fit for society, boy, dress accordingly'). Not so the social scientific formulations: The first formulation purports to be an explication of a particular conception of socialisation which places emphasis on societal expectations regarding adults as competent performers of social roles and how these societal expectations build upon general characteristics attributable to these same adult persons. But as an explication and description of societal expectations it does not seem to emanate from any particular practical concern. It arises out of the attempt to organise a research programme, to systematise findings, to bring about a shift in explanatory perspective, etc. It also places the sociologist into a position of authority. He or she can determine what the society needs, requires, etc., better than others. One may note how society becomes a subject in this formulation. It is not merely an abstract noun glossing a multiplicty of accounts which express what it means to live together with others, or to live in organised groups, to share common cultural traditions, to be a party to organised settings. A general vantage point is established, similar to a planning perspective. One proceeds as if manpower requirements are catalogued, in order to properly plan for a steady supply of labour.

The second formulation is even more revealing. It suggests the possibility of a deductive procedure which identifies the conditions under which a society can maintain stability and identity over time. Again, this conception is put forward without any reference at all to the many possible ways in which what counts as stable in social life can be determined in the course of everyday life.

The sociologist who proceeds like this acts as if all the practical concerns yet to be confronted by the societal members could be brushed aside in favour of one requirement; that social actors conform to conditions which state once and for all when adequate socialisation has been achieved in the society.

The sociologist puts aside or suppresses all those ordinary interests or values which underly a description or evaluation

94

of someone's being fit to live in society. Alternative possible uses of this description in common discourse no longer count; indeed are no longer countenanced. By turning the verb 'to socialise' into an abstract category of theoretical discourse, and treating it as an 'objective' matter to be explained through the accumulation of research findings, the sociologist can now influence the process of socialisation. He or she can consider methods of practical treatment for making people more fit to live in society, but on the terms provided by sociology. The primary social locations for the use of the term 'socialise' can be ignored and the ordinary uses of the verb 'socialise' are put aside. It is no longer even a cause for comment that 'making people fit to live in society' would have been, in the times predating sociological socialisation theory and its use in the society, the exclusive task of certain categories of people (parents, teachers, governesses, etc.). One would have had categories of definite individuals in mind, not abstract processes. Definite rights and obligations would have been circumscribed by these categories.

But in socialisation theory the educational efforts of parents, for example, become primary socialisation. School education becomes secondary socialisation. The relation between the two is one of anonymous and comprehensive processes, attributable to the society and its reproduction, or to its general requirements for self-maintenance. Society itself becomes the instrument of 'making people fit to live in society.' It is no longer what actual people do and say, in particular settings that matters, but abstract mechanisms of a general kind, which function as the organising procedures in bringing about adequate socialisation.

One may note that as a consequence psychiatrists, social workers, psychologists may be called upon in certain circumstances to comment on people's proper socialisation. The assessment of socialisation can become the object of professional judgement. This is a process of assessing the behaviour of a person or of a group, which largely ignores the features of practical evaluation which are present in non-professional, everyday reasoning about such matters. It is conceiveable, for example, that someone could have said to someone else, in 1828: 'You just are not fit to live in society.' One could have meant by this: 'You just don't know how to behave.' It would have been clear that such a remark could only be made under certain specific circumstances. It could only be addressed to some people, not to all. It would have been obvious that most people in most situations would not be spoken to in this manner. One would not dare assume, ordinarily, that one's friends, for example, or one's superiors did not know how to live in society (there are exceptions, of course).

But sociology or social psychology as socialisation theory no longer recognise such limits, which ordinary practical judgements respect. They make it possible in principle, to ask in general, if anyone is properly socialised. They make it possible to think that no one is, thus generating infinite planning tasks. For socialisation theory establishes general conditions and requirements for the assessment of social integration in a society, for example, which seems to separate the criteria for adequate socialisation from practical judgements made in situations.

By contrasting technical sociological discourse with a more common form of practical reasoning, and noting how our common conceptions are translated into the technical vocabulary of sociological science, we have done what hermeneutics always does; faced the problem of translation from one communicative mode into another. Thus, the problem of multiple and often conflicting realities is posed. Thus the explication of the social dimension can no longer be conceived, as it was by Schutz, as a task that may be accomplished by phenomenological description. It has become a practical task. It raises the issue of where we are located, as people inhabiting an everyday world, vis a vis the discourse of social science. By raising this issue however, one moves beyond hermeneutical reflection. One no longer asks in what way someone inquiring into the meaning and significance of a cultural situation is already claimed by or is a part of it (this is the basic conception of the hermeneutical circle from Heidegger to Gadamer). One asks how ordinary conceptions of the significance of events and actions, as well as the practical judgements everyone frequently makes, are transformed by the sociologist into ideas no longer responsive to the exigencies of the situations in which these conceptions are formed and these judgements made? We are inquiring into forms of cultural invasion and of alienation. We are facing the possible speechlessness of everyday life. Because there are conflicts between everyday reasoning in its common form and the technical discourse of social science, hermeneutics needs to be radicalised, in order to help render the consciousness of conflict explicit. There is no longer a reason which unites us all, as Gadamer sometimes says. There is only conflict between the communicative practices of everyday life and the claims to reasonableness built into it on the one hand, and the pressure toward the increasing rationalisation of social action and discourse on the other hand.

The theme of the 'life-world' has become a topic for practical deliberation and for a struggle to secure commonalities of meaning and sense (common convictions) against the overwhelming power of a technical apparatus taking its cognitive form from social science discourse. It is no longer merely something to be described, but something to be reconstituted. In an attempt to aid this process one should try to identify commonalities between phenomenology and ethnomethodological studies of practical reasoning, between critical social theory and hermeneutics. In my view such commanalities are best established by examining particular social locations in which the confrontations mentioned are already taking place. (Consider education, professional health care, regulation of consumer behaviour, urban planning, psychological testing and assessment). Studies of this kind reveal more than general theories of communicative action 37 which have the entire history of Western European rationalisation as their object, for such theories of communicative action can only correct onesided theories of rationalisation (such as Weber's, Parson's and Luhmann's).

I have argued for a position which entails that practical decision is a necessary element of our knowledge of the society. We only understand the society insofar as we know what courses of action we are able to choose. Society and history become the domain of practical knowledge and deliberation. Interpretive approaches to the study of social action and critical social theory can join forces in an exploration of this domain. By leaving the epistemological and metaphysical assumptions of phenomenology behind, they can understand themselves as contributing to the reflective power of common sense reasoning and to its practical force.38

REFERENCES

1. This paper has been completed with the assistance of a Social Sciences and Humanities Council of Canada Negotiated Grant (431-770006). The author is one of five principal investigators. His part of the project is entitled: 'Critical Social Theory, Communicative Competence, and Practical Reasoning.'

2. Edmund Husserl, the founder of phenomenology, introduced the term 'Lebenswelt' around the 1930's. He may have chosen the term in response to Martin Heidegger's and Max Scheler's revisions of phenomenology. He meant by it the world as it is known in lived experience, as it is familiar to us in the context of pretheoretical conduct. It was not a major part of his work to consider how the meaning of the 'life-world' might differ for different individuals and groups, depending on their location in society and history. But these differences, of course, are a major theme for the social sciences. Their findings may warrant speaking of many 'life worlds' or 'multiple realites' (Alfred Schutz) rather than of one 'life world'. It must remain an open question, whether the (transcendentally) reflecting philosopher can penetrate from the multiple realities of social life to one reality, or the meaning of 'one world', as something which is present - as meaning - in those multiple realities.

    See Edmund Husserl, Die Krisis der europäischen Wissenchaften und die transzendental phänomenologie, (ed.) W. Bimel, 1936, translated by D. Carr as The Crisis of European Sciences and Transcendental Phenomenology, Northwestern University Press, Evanston, Ill. 1970. (Hereinafter Krisis).

3. The topic of 'lay knowledge' and of its communicative organisation has acquired prominence in ethonomethodological sociology. H. Garfinkel's reformulation and elaboration [a] of A. Schutz's distincting between common sense and scientific rationality [b] has helped me articulate the post-phenomenological orientation adopted in this paper. However, I differ from ethonomethodology, because I do not give primacy to descriptive inquiries, while it does. Thus my position derives from the tension between it and Habermas' critical social theory.[c] On the whole, I am concerned to find a more direct way to address some of the problems Habermas has put before us than he has shown us so far. This entails, that I am

less concerned with a correct and comprehensive theory of society than he is and place more weight on the situated organisation of critical reflection. But this is not to deny that my suggestions are dependent, in the end, on the turn given to social theory by Habermas.

[a] Harold Garfinkel, Studies in Ethnomethodology, Prentice Hall, Englewood Chiffs. N.J., 1967, pp.262-84.

[b] Alfred Schutz, Collected Papers, Vol.1, Martinus Nijhoff, the Hague, 1962-1973. See also Vol.2, 1964-1971.

[c] Jürgen Habermas, Theorie des Kommunikativen Handelns, 2 volumes, Suhrkamp, Frankfurt, 1981. The first volume has been published in English. See J. Habermas, Theory of Communicative Action, vol.1, 'Reason and Rationalization' translated by Thomas McCarthy, Beacon Press, Boston, 1984.

4. See Talcott Parsons' introduction to 'Culture and the Social System', Part Four of Theories of Society, 2 volumes, edited by Talcott Parsons, Edward Shils, Kaspar D. Naegele, Jesse R. Pitts, Vol. 2, the Free Press of Glencoe, New York, 1961, p.965.

5. See J. Habermas' critical discussion in Jürgen Habermas, op. cit., vol.2, p.355 and subsequent pages.

6. N. Luhmann in J.Habermas and N. Luhmann, Theorie der Gesellschaft Oder Socialtechnolgie, Suhrkamp, Frankfurt, 1971, p.15. See also N. Luhmann, The Differentiation of Society, Columbia University Press, New York, 1982.

7. Here I follow J. Habermas' critique of systems-theory, especially in his debate with Luhmann. See Ibid. See also, J. Habermas, Theorie des Kommunikativen Handelns, Vol.2, p.p.432-488.

8. Dorothy E. Smith, 'A Sociology of Women' in J. A. Sherman and E. Torton Beck (eds.), The Prism of Sex: Essays in the Sociology of Knowledge, University of Wisconsin Press, Madison, WI., 1979.

Smith's notion is a reformulation of the Marxian concept of superstructure. It takes account of changes in liberal capitalist societies since Marx. They largely consist of the development and refinement of organisational knowledge and power in the service of economic and political power. I am indebted to her with respect to my understanding of the place of social science in these developments. Contrary to Habermas, for example, her analyses suggests that changes in social scientific theorising are not primarily due to intra-theoretic concerns.

9. See J. Habermas, Theorie des Kommunikativen Handelns, Vol.2, p.p.171-294.

10. Ibid, vol.2, p.225-6.

11. I mean by this that certain proposals for the reorganisation of education entail the 'cognitive' supremacy of testing specialists over classroom teachers. This is due to the fact that the social situation of work in classrooms makes it impossible for teachers to gear this work to the fragmented conceptions of instructional objectives which most systematic formats for the assessment of the achievement of learning objectives require. Classroom teachers are turned into mere 'deliverers' of programme plans formulated without regard for the manner in which teachers normally make sense of their work situation.

An example for such behaviourist technologies is discussed in R. J. Kibler et al, Objectives for Instruction and Evaluation, Allyn and Beacon, Boston 1981. I have subjected this position to a determined critique, with critical social theory as the backgroud to the critique. See Dieter Misgeld, 'Education and Cultural Invasion: Critical Social Theory Education as Instruction, and the Pedagogy of the Oppressed,' John Forester (ed.) Critical Theory and Public Life, The MIT Press, London, 1985, p.p.77-120.

12. This is part of Habermas' project in his Theorie des Kommunikativen Handelns.

13. In my view Gadamer relies too much on this assumed continuity of cultural tradition whenever he points to the limits of technique in modern culture. This gives his hermeneutics a conservative bent. See Hans-Georg Gadamer, Truth and Method, Seabury Press, New York, 1975.

14. I have developed some basic conceptions for it in my essay cited in note 11. But see especially Paulo Frere, Pedagogy of the Oppressed, Herder and Herder, New York, 1971.

15. See A. R. Louch, _Explanation and Human Action_, University of Caliornia Press, Berkeley, 1966.

16. Therefore Habermas refers to sociology as the 'Science of crisis par excellence.'[a] By this he means: Sociology is _the_ science of 'bourgeois' or liberal capitalist society, because it analyses the consequences of its emergence for the cultural tradition predating liberalism and capitalism. Therefore terms such as 'anomie' (Durkheim) and 'rationalisation' (Weber) are central.

[a] See Jürgen Habermas, _Theorie des Kommunikativen Handelns_, vol.1, p.19.

17. Later Husserl is usually associated with the _Krisis_ in which he develops the concept of the 'Lebenswelt' or life-world.

18. Alfred Schutz, _Op. cit._, vol. 1, p.3.

19. Having 'bracketed' or suspended judgement upon the question of whether there is or is not a world of 'objects-in-themselves,' existing beyond or outside our experience, which are supposedly responsible for causing our experiences of them, Husserl, (in contrast to 'Naive Idealism') recognises that it is nevertheless still possible, - on the basis of experience and experience alone, - to distinguish within experience between the multiplicity of experiences or _acts_ of experience, and the unity of the objects experienced in or through such experiences or acts. The _acts_ or experiences are therefore said to be _intentional_ or to _constitute_ the object which exists as the object of experience, intentionally constituted in, or given wholly on the basis of, experience.

20. See Edmund Husserl, _The Krisis_, and Dieter Misgeld, 'Ultimate Self-Responsibility, Practical Reasoning and Practical Action. Habermas, Husserl and Ethnomethodology on Discourse and Action,' in _Human Studies_, 3, pp. 255-78, (1980).

21. Alfred Schutz, _op. cit_, vol. 1, p.34

22. _Ibid_, vol. 2, p.72.

23. _Ibid_, p.73.

24. _Ibid._, p.69.

25. Alfred Schutz, op. cit. vol. 1, p.43.

26. In his first study, Schutz analysed Weber's distinction between observational understanding and explanatory understanding. See Alfred Schutz, The Phenomenology of the Social World, Northwestern University Press, Evanston, Ill., p.p.3-44.

27. See A. Schutz, Op. cit., vol.1, p.43.

28. Ibid,

29. Ibid, p.44.

30. The term 'horizon' refers to implicit backgrounds of meaning, to what is noticed for example in perception, but not identified as perceived in focal awareness. In the context of this paper 'Horizon-intentionalities' refer to the background of socially shared conceptions, which people acting in the society take for granted, but also 'mean'while focussing on matters at hand.

31. A. Schutz, op. cit., vol.2, p.88.

32. Eidetic intuition is the process by which by fixing upon an individual, and varying it imagination to the point where the imaginatively conceived entity is no longer a member of the same essential class or type as the original, it is possible to recognise the essence of the individual in question. Thus for example I may vary say a table in my imagination, changing its colour, the number of legs, the material composition, etc. etc.,yet recognise that through such variations it continues to be a member of the self same essential class or type, table. I may however continue by imagining people sitting on it, (in which case it may well continue to be a table which is being sat upon), and giving it a back rest, at which point I may not unreasonably conclude that what I now have before me in my imagination is no longer a table, but is a chair. By a number of such exercises I will eventually be able to explicitly delineate the essence 'table' while it is clear that such a process may in principle be applied to the delineation of any and all esences, and certainly to the delineation of the essential features of concepts employed by the social sciences as is here suggested.

33. See Harold Garfinkel, Loc. cit.

34. Alfred Schutz, op. cit., vol.2, p.69.

35. Cf. Dorothy E. Smith op. cit., p.155 and 172.

36. John A. Clausen (ed.), Socialisation and Society, Little, Brown & Co., Boston 1968.

37. See J. Habermas, Theorie des Kommunikativen Handelns, vol.2.

38. See Dieter Misgeld, 'Common Sense and Common Convictions: Sociology as a Science, Phenomenological Sociology and the Hermeneutical Point of View', in Human Studies 6, p.p.109-139 (1983) especially p.p. 126-139.

5 Modern European philosophy and the critique of reductionism in the human and social sciences

SIMON GLYNN

> There were troublesome tensions between the
> (different) tasks which descended historically from
> Descartes: on the one hand, that of methodically
> treating souls in exactly the same way as bodies and
> as being connected with bodies as spatiotemporal
> realities; i.e. the task of investigating in a
> physicalist way the whole life-world as 'nature' in a
> broadened sense; and on the other hand, investigating
> souls in their being-in-themselves and for themselves
> by way of inner experience... (E. Husserl, Krisis,
> p.214)

INTRODUCTION

Einstein's Theory of Relativity, together with Quantum
Mechanics and developments in atomic and particle theory have
raised anew fundamental questions concerning for example the
nature and scope of objectivity, the relation of theories to
facts, the nature of causality and the relation of
explanation to interpretation and understanding. Indeed some
recent works in the philosophy of science go as far as to
argue, not only that 'facts' are theory laden, [1] but that
theories are nothing other than analogues or metaphors, [2]
that consequently all explanation, (even the causal
explanation usually associated with the physical sciences),

is to be subsumed under interpretation, 3 (more usually associated with the human and social sciences), and that far from being derived inductively, theories/metaphors may be derived by intuition.4 It has even been suggested that the truth of scientific theories depends upon their coherence (or harmony,) simplicity and universality, 5 qualities more usually associated in popular thought with aesthetic rather than scientific judgements.6 And as if all this did not constitute a sufficient attack on the self-image of the physical sciences, historians of science have amassed evidence to support the view of some sociologists of science, that the physical sciences' claim to objectivity rests ultimately upon a subjective or inter-subjective consensus within a particular community of practitioners of science.7

In light of all this it is surely one of the ironies of our age that a large number of those in the human and social sciences, engaged in the earnest pursuit of academic respectability, are still struggling to emulate the positivistic or neo-positivistic epistemologies and methodologies of the physical sciences, or of Newtonian Mechanics to be more precise, and to employ them in the study of human subjects and their social relations, at a time when many of the most successful practitioners of physical science have long recognised this paradigm to be wholly indadequate even to the study of physical phenomena.

If the conceptions and methods traditionally associated with the physical sciences are largely confused and inadequate even to the tasks for which they were originally supposed to be employed, we shall argue that they are in addition at best irrelevant and at worst misleading when employed by the human and social sciences. Before doing so however let us first examine in brief outline the claims of those, who I shall refer to as reductionists, 8 who attempt to import the positivistic epistemologies and methodologies of the physical sciences into the human and social sciences.

REDUCTIONISM OUTLINED

The two major forms of reductionism in the human and social sciences are, broadly speaking, physiological and behavioural reductionism. Physiological, sometimes called micro-reductionism, attempts to understand and explain all human experience and behaviour as 'responses' to physiological 'causes' or micro 'stimuli' as they are sometimes called, while behavioural, sometimes called macro-reductionism, arguing that we have no direct empirical evidence of others' minds or experiences, conceives humans purely in terms of the

behaviour they exhibit; behaviour which is typically
conceived as a 'response' to macro phenomena or 'stimuli.'
Furthermore, while both are undoubtedly deterministic,
conceiving human experience and/or behaviour as a reaction or
response to 'stimuli,' those who conceive human experience
and behaviour as determined by 'human nature' or genetics
tend to be physical or micro-reductionists, while those who
conceive human behaviour as determined by 'nurture' or socio-
cultural factors - conceived objectivistically of course
(from the 'outside' or third person extrospective
perspective) - will tend to be behavioural or macro-
reductionists.

All this however needs to be qualified, for while some
regard these two paradigms as mutually exclusive, and while,
in view of the exclusion of first person or so called
'private' human experience from the behaviourist repertoire,
strict behaviourism obviously excludes those elements of
physiology that deal with experience, it is clear that some
behaviourists actually regard physiological accounts of
experience as supplementing their accounts of behaviour.
Moreover regarding the specific task of trying to understand
human behaviour, some see behaviourism and physiology as
complementary, and some see them as contradictory, while
still others see them as simply incommensurable. The point
then is that, while we have outlined the 'ideal types' of
these two paradigms, in practice the boundary between them is
often far from clear. Additionally, under increasing
pressure from their continuing inability to give anything
approaching an adequate account of human experience and
behaviour, reductionists are increasingly driven to employ
more sophisticated paradigms that erode the boundary between
reductionist and anti-reductionist paradigms to the point of
capitulation, as we shall see.

THE CRITIQUE: THE SUBJECTIVE VALUE OF VALUE-FREE OBJECTIVITY

The first point that needs to made is that, despite its claim
to a value free objectivity, positivism itself is obviously
grounded upon implicit values. As Scheler has put it 'To
conceive the world as value-free is a task which men set
themselves on account of a value..., 9 a presumably
subjective belief in the value of value-free objective facts.
As Gadamer therefore concludes '...there is one prejudice of
the Enlightenment that is essential to it: the
fundamental...prejudice against prejudice itself,' 10 a fact
that should give the reductionists at least some pause for
thought before they embark upon a crusade to conquer the
human and social sciences in the name of 'value-free

objectivity'.

THE OBJECTIVE STUDY OF THE SUBJECT

Secondly, in their attempt to stamp out metaphysics by importing positivism into the human and social sciences, the reductionists ironically fail to recognise that they themselves are invoking a metaphysical belief; that humans and their societies may be effectively and adequately studied and understood by employing the same epistemology and methods that they fondly but wrongly suppose to be employed in the study of physical objects.11   Thus, far from being neutral as it claims, such 'objectivism' implicitly supposes what it purports to show: that humans exist solely in the manner of things; a view strongly contested by phenomenologists and existentialists.

'It has always been noted,' Husserl has pointed out, 'that psychic being (by which he means what we would today call consciousness) in and for itself has no spatial extension and no location.'12 Indeed following Heidegger who tells us that 'A person is not a Thing, not a substance, not an object,'13 Sartre insists that we are 'no-thing' at all. 'Human reality,' he tells us, 'is itself a nothingness.'14

Furthermore, while phenomenology distinguishes those experiences which we have through the five senses, our so called sensory experience of the physical world, from non-sensory or 'introspective' experience so called, it nevertheless recognises that both are, qua experiences, empirical. In this phenomenology stands in marked contrast to reductionism which, following the epistemology and methods counselled by positivism, simply refuses to accept the evidence of all non-sensory experience; a decision for which there can be no strictly 'empirical' justification as such.

J. B. Watson, one of the founders of behaviourism informs us that:

> the time has come when psychology must discard all references to consciousness... Its sole task   is the prediction   and   control   of   behaviour,   and introspection can form no part of its method.

(Indeed the behaviourist must exclude) from his scientific vocabulary all subjective terms such as sensation, perception, image, desire, purpose, and even thinking and emotions as they are subjectively defined.15

Now in the first place it is something of a paradox that Watson's injunction to exclude subjective terms like 'desire' and 'purpose' clearly has as its undisclosed 'purpose' the fulfillment of his subjective 'desire' to make an objective study of the subject. Secondly, and this is by far the most important point, while it <u>may</u> be quite reasonable for those who wish to study physical objects to ignore introspective experience in favour of sensory experience, it seems quite extraordinary that those who wish to study human subjects and their social relations should willfully ignore the major source of direct 'empirical' evidence for the existence of such subjects. Like the fishermen who, presupposing that there are only large fish in the sea, employ large mesh nets that render them necessarily incapable of catching those small fish that would falsify their unwarranted presuppositon, we can perhaps now begin to see that the metaphysical and epistemological presuppositions of the positivists and their reductionist cohorts result in their relying on a method, (sensory empiricism), which renders them necessarily incapable of finding any evidence of the existence of a conscious subject, or of social relations as lived by each and every one of us.

It is therefore clear then, that as Husserl recognised, 'In no way...can a science of souls (by which he means, consciousness or mind) be modelled on natural science or seek methodological council from it.'16 As G. K. Chesterton explained , those who counsel adopting 'objective' methods in the study of human subjects:

> mean getting <u>outside</u> a man and studying him as if he were a gigantic insect: (Kafka's beetle perhaps, or maybe on second thoughts Skinner's rats and pigeons), in what they call a dry impartial light, in what I should call a dead and dehumanising light. They mean getting a long way off....I don't deny the dry light may sometimes do good; though in one sense it's the very reverse of science. So far from being knowledge, it's actual suppression of what we know. It's treating a friend as a stranger, and pretending that someone familiar is really remote and mysterious. It's like saying that a man...falls down in a fit of insensibility once every twenty-four hours. Well, what we call 'the secret' is exactly the opposite. I don't try to get outside the man. I try to get inside...17

The key to reductionism then, as Chesterton so accurately perceives, is a 'getting outside' and adopting the third person or reflective perspective upon the subject afforded by the five senses rather than the 'inside' perspective of first person introspection. It is to elevate to the status of a methodology the schizophrenic attempt of the self to stand outside itself and to withdraw from or deny its immediate experience of itself as a human being involved in social interaction, and concomitantly to fall victim to the psychotic belief that the self is an object or thing; a reification of the subject that Sartre has analysed under the heading of 'impure reflection.'18

As R. D. Laing sums up:

It seems extraordinary that whereas the physical and biological sciences...have generally won the day against tendencies to personalise the world of things or to read human emotion into the animal world, an authentic science of persons has hardly got started by reason of the inveterate tendency to depersonalise or reify persons. ....people who experience themselves as automata, as robots, as bits of machinery, or even as animals...are rightly regarded as crazy. Yet why do we not regard a theory that seeks to transmute persons into automata or animals as equally crazy? The experience of oneself and others as persons is primary and self validating. It exists prior to...scientific or philosophical difficulties...19

And just as from the 'outside' a football match, for example, becomes twenty people chasing an inflated animal skin around a field, a description that tells us almost everything about the game except that which is essential to the significance it has for so many, so from the reflective perspective of the reductionist we learn almost everything about human existence or social interaction except what is essential to it.

NO MIND BUT CONSCIOUS CAPACITIES

The reductionist response would be that we have absolutely no experience of a mind. That therefore we have no empirical evidence of the existence of mind which must consequently be a metaphysical hypothesis or theory that was, Skinner tells us, '...invented for the sole purpose of providing spurious explanation...'.20 As Lundberg elaborates:

Today...a considerable numer of students of social phenomena are still firmly convinced that the phenomena with which they have to deal cannot be adequately described or explained without, for example, a category called 'mind' which carries with it...(thought, experience, feeling, judgement, choice, will, value, emotion, etc., etc.). 'We forget that these nouns are merely substitutes for verbs and go hunting for the things denoted by the nouns; but there are no such things; there are only the activities that we started with...' Any attempt to deal in other words with the behaviour which these words are used to represent meets with the most determined resistance on the ground that 'something has been left out.' And what has been left out? Why, 'will,' 'feeling,' 'ends,' 'motives,' 'values,' etc. These are the phlogiston of the social sciences...I have no doubt that a considerale part of the present content of the social sciences will turn out to be pure phlogiston.21

Phenomenology perhaps somewhat surprisingly finds itself largely in agreement with what is being claimed here. We have after all already seen that Husserl, Heidegger and Sartre,22 like Skinner and Lundberg, recognise that there is no experience of a mind as such. Indeed Sartre in particular has argued at great length and in considerable detail in both The Transcendence of the Ego and Being and Nothingness, that consciousness, being in and of itself inexperienceable, is No-thing or Nothingness; empirically indistinguishable from those capacities (to think, feel, judge, choose, will, value, posit ends etc.) for which it is supposed to account. Thus, following Husserl's insistence that consciousness is not some Cartesian realm of closed interiority in which feelings are 'contained' (like, say, objects in a box) but is 'intentional,' - which is to say essentially related to its object, 23 (as experiencer to experienced in experience), 24 - Sartre argues that emotions in particular,25 and by extension all the so called 'introspective states,' 26 of which we have spoken above, far from being reified things (or nouns to use our reductionist's terminology) are rather ways of 'intending' or perceiving objects or events etc. Attitudes I actively constitute rather than something I already possess, (verbs rather than nouns as our reductionist puts it). For 'human reality' Sartre affirms, 'being is reduced to doing,' 27 consciousness being conceived therefore as a process rather than a thing, a point which we shall have occasion to return to later.

However, while the reductionists are hamstrung by a positivistic epistemology which refuses to accept the evidence of non-sensory experience, and can in consequence only acknowledge those activities of thinking, feeling, judging, choosing, willing, valuing, positing ends or goals etc. if and in so far as they manifest themselves to sensory or third person experience as physical behaviour, phenomenologists, who are not restricted to sensory experience and can consequently grant significance to what is given to non-sensory 'introspective' or first person experience, have no doubt that they feel, think, judge, choose, will, value, posit ends, etc., irrespective of whether or not these capacities manifest themselves to sensory experience via behaviour.

THE METAPHYSICS OF OBJECTIVE SCIENCE

Now it is of course to be admitted that strictly speaking behaviour cannot, at least within the terms of the rigid positivism with which the reductionists have bridled themselves, directly manifest first person 'private' experiences, and that consequently no strict reductionist, qua reductionist, can ever regard behaviour, no matter how complex, as a direct empirical manifestation of first person private experiences (of thinking, feeling, judging, choosing, etc).28

However, under increasing pressure from the realisation of their inability to give anything like a credible account of human experience and behaviour in purely positivistic terms, the reductionists either fail to recognise or choose to ignore this point, and, in an effort to make at least some attempt to come to terms with human and social experience, import inferences regarding first person private experience into what are supposed to be descriptions of third person, or publically observable events; evidence, if evidence were needed, of their failure to purge the human and social science in the name of positivism.

Indeed before embarking on their crusade the reductionists might have done well to ask how the physical sciences themselves, of whose epistemology and methods they are so enamoured, would have fared in the face of a similar purge. Schutz, for instance, has noted that:

> molecules, atoms and electrons have shed all qualities capable of direct sense perception in our consciousness and are known only to us by the series of events in which they are implicated.29

Thus a chemical reaction, the tracks across a cloud chamber or bubble chamber, or the working of an electric motor, nowhere render to us any _direct_ experience of molecules, atoms or electrons. Like anti-matter and curved space etc. they are all hypothetical inferences, inexperienceable in themselves and consequently empirically indistinguishable from those phenomena for which they are supposed to account. Therefore, in respect of their epistemological status they are, as we shall see, no different from consciousness (in contradistinction to conscious capacities) to which Watson and other reductionists object so strongly, and consequently all must stand condemned, or reprieved, together. Like consciousness then, molecules, atoms and electrons together with other such key elements of the physical sciences must be distinguished from 'introspective' activities (e.g. thinking, choosing, feeling, judging, willing, valuing etc.), of which the positivists are so suspicious, on the somewhat surprising grounds that it is the latter alone, which are directly experienced and therefore truly empirical.

We may therefore now be able to see that as Husserl has noted:

> The contrast between the subjectivity of the life-world 30 and the 'objective,' the 'true,' world lies in the fact that the latter is a theoretical-logical substruction, the structure of something that is in principle not perceivable, in principle not experienceable in its own proper being, whereas the subjective in the life-world, is distinguished in all respects precisely by its being actually experienceable.31

MORE SOPHISTICATED REDUCTIONISM

While it may be easy enough to spot the more unsophisticated reductionist illicitly importing inferences concerning first person or subjective experiences under cover of what purport to be third person descriptions of 'objectively' observable events, some forms of reductionism can be more sophisticated. However, in so far as all reductionism is grounded ultimately upon positivistic or neo-positivistic epistemology, and largely limited to the methodology employed by the physical sciences, even these more sophisticated forms, employing as they do a judicious mixture of micro and macro reductionism, must ultimately fall to our already articulated analysis, as we shall now see.

Now obviously an exposition and critique of various reductionistic positions could proceed almost endlessly and therefore, in order to forestall this possibility, I shall take as a 'test-case' what I hope the reader will agree is a sophisticated, yet succinct formulation of a number of the key elements in the reductionist position:

It is possible (we are told) to interpret the event of a stone rolling down a hill into a brook as a striving or a need of the stone for the brook...But in the scientific frame of reference we have adopted or defined operationally such terms as 'mass,' 'gravity' and 'field of force,' as more suitable for our own purpose...we adopt here the viewpoint of modern psychology that the behaviour of nervous tissue and organisms is explicable in the same basic terms as the behaviour of other matter. In this orientation 'needs' become merely biophysical or biochemical inbalances in an organ or between it and its environment...That organisms behave with reference to the anticipated results of behaviour is, of course, admitted...in our frame of reference such 'ends'...exist in the form of symbols of some kind and organisms respond to the symbols just as they respond to stimuli.[32]

Here then we have what may appear to be an altogether reasonable point of view. There is an appeal against anthropomorphism, and a call to adopt a scientific outlook. Furthermore, as if in response to the main thrust of our argument immediately above, first person experiences such as those we have of 'needs' or 'desires,' and 'ends' or goals are admitted, but, and this is most important, only in an attempt to reduce them to, or explain them in terms of, such publicly experienceable phenomena as biological inbalances, or as symbols that evoke macro or behavioural responses, in much the same way as do stimuli.

THE CRITIQUE

Turning to our critique, perhaps the most obvious point is that much like atoms, molecules and electrons discussed above, even such mundane concepts as the 'force fields,' 'mass' and 'gravity' of Newtonian mechanics, not to mention the more esoteric curved space and anti-matter of recent times, are in and of themselves inexperienceable apart from the series of events in which they are implicated; a fact that helps account for the initial furore with which the Royal Society rejected Newton's theory, and for the charges of occultism levelled against him. By way of contrast human 'needs' and 'ends' are, as we have already argued, actually experienceable.

Our second point is eloquently put by Sartre who quite rightly insists that while:

> It was legitimate for the natural sciences to free themselves from the anthropomorphism which consisted in bestowing human properties on inanimate objects...it is perfectly absurd to assume by analogy the same scorn for anthropomorphism where anthropology is concerned.33

Further, the 'scientific frame of reference' is not nearly as monolithic or restrictive as implied by our 'test-case' reductionist, and one may certainly be 'scientific' without necessarily adopting Newtonian mechanics as one's paradigm of science; a paradigm which, in addition to being clearly inappropriate to the study of human experience and social relations, has, in any event, been largely superseded even where mechanics is concerned. Physicist Evan H. Walker for instance is quite happy to suggest that:

> Consciousness may be associated with all quantum mechanical processes...since everything that occurs is ultimately the result of one or more quantum mechanical events, the universe is 'inhabited' by an almost unlimited number of rather discrete conscious, usually non-thinking (but presumably aware) entities that are responsible for the detailed working of the universe.34

Strange therefore that in the name of scientific objectivity the reductionists are unprepared to grant human beings what physicists have shown themselves quite prepared to grant to matter.

With regard to the claim that many modern 'psychologists' would explain human behaviour as they would explain the behaviour of matter, in micro-reductionist of physiological terms, this merely reflects the fact that many who currently pass as psychologists are in reality physiologists who have nothing to say about such human capacities as thinking, remembering, evaluating, judging, choosing, etc., which are the essential subject matter of any human psychology worthy of the name.

As for the claim that the behaviour of nervous tissue is explainable in terms of physiology, if what is meant is that the biophysical or biochemical micro behaviour of tissue can be explained in this manner, then the phenomenologists would not argue;35 although it is worth bearing in mind that some of these physiological events can in turn be explained in terms of the socio-cultural significance or meaning of an event. (For example, confronted with apparently hostile behaviour from others, my pulse rate and my adrenaline flow will increase in preparation for 'fight or flight.') But while some of the more basic, and therefore less quintessentially human behaviour of our 'organisms,' such as eating and sleeping, may be adequately explained in purely physiological terms, it seems clear that the same cannot be said of more complex behaviour in which, although physiology undeniably plays a role, it is in the service of socio-cultural significance and meaning. In other words just as water displays properties (it is a liquid, boils at one hundred degrees centigrade, and will float wood, etc.) that are not displayed by the hydrogen and oxygen from which it is exclusively constituted, so complex cultured objects and events, such as football matches for example, appear to possess meanings and significance that is not to be found in their component parts, and human beings display capacities (to perceive/constitute such meanings and significance, as well as the capacity for autonomous action etc.) that are irreducible to the physiology from which they are exclusively constituted. Building upon the insights of Gestalt, it is clear that in this sense also the whole is irreducible to its parts.

For example a hunger striker who, after weeks without food, presumably has a far greater physiological 'need' for food than I, may continue to refuse to eat while I hungrily devour my dinner. Thus while there is no denying that from the physiological perspective the hunger striker 'needs' food, he or she may also feel the 'need' to make a political or social point, and it is in such cases clear that it is the socio-cultural context of meaning and significance that has the upper hand over brute physiology, while the less basic or more complex the 'needs' in question the more evident the subservience of the physiological and the consequent failure of the reductionist programme.

It is, for example, difficult to see how the art collectors' 'need' to own a work by Warhol can be explained in purely physiological terms, while we may ask those who stubbornly insist that it can whether Aristotle, for instance, would have responded to the same physiological 'imbalances' in the same way. The dilemma that then confronts our reductionist is obvious. Either to make the altogether absurd claim that Aristotle would, under such circumstances, have had a 'need' to possess a work of art by an artist who would not be born for over two millenia, or to claim that for this very reason Aristotle could not, under any circumstances, have the same physiological imbalances as our twentieth century art collector; and consequently to concede, at least implicitly, that historico-socio-culturally embedded meanings, values or significances are irreducible to brain physiology.

Moreover even if we could establish, (which it is far from clear we can), a constant conjunction between 'objective' physiology and 'subjective' needs, then, following Hume 36 it is clear that, in the absence of necessary connection and spatio-temporal contiguity - impossible to establish when, as we have just now shown, mind, and consequently mental needs are spatially unextended - we could not justifiably infer that they were causally related, and still less that the physiological was primary.

As Husserl sums up:

> For the ego, space and time are not principles of individuation; it knows no natural causality, the latter being, in accordance with its meaning, inseparable from spatiotemporality.37

Having demonstrably failed to give an adequate account of all but the most rudimentary experiences and behaviour, our reductionist nevertheless plays one last card. Faced with the overwhelming phenomenological evidence that we, each and every one of us, have of positing goals and ends and acting in anticipation of them, our reductionist switches tack and attempts to account for such phenomena, not as before in terms of micro-physiological stimuli, of which only physiologists are aware, but in terms of 'responses' to symbols, consciously perceived as such by those who respond to them. In other words, while the overwhelming first person experience of such ends or goals has to be admitted, our reductionist attempts to reduce the teleological 'pull' of such goals to a Newtonian mechanistic 'push' by implicitly suggesting that we 'respond' to such 'ends' or goals in much the same way as a reflex leg movement responds to a reflex hammer, for instance.

However in talking of symbols our reductionist has already conceded too much, because despite claims to the contrary, we simply do not 'respond' to symbols in the same way as we are supposed to respond to 'stimuli,' for unlike 'stimuli,' symbols are imbued with precisely those historico-socio-cultural significances and meanings that escape purely sensory empiricism; meanings to which we 'respond' in a very different way than does the leg reflex to a reflex hammer, and meanings furthermore, which we ourselves, as members of a historico-socio-culturally situated community help to constitute.

In face of such objections reductionism can only jettison
all reference to symbols and retrench around the more modest
claim that we respond to stimuli pure and simple. But even
this defence is doomed, and for two reasons. Firstly if it
is to avoid the objections that we raised against talk of
symbols then stimuli must be conceived of as devoid of all
significance or meaning, which in light of the experiences we
all have of initiating meaningful actions in pursuit of
significant goals etc., would render such a conception
incredible. Secondly, even if this were not so, as
phenomenologists have pointed out in considerable detail, we
have no direct experience, either sensory or non-sensory, of
stimuli, and therefore no direct empirical evidence for their
existence.

Husserl for instance, insisting that 'all consciousness is
consciousness of an object' reports that:

> I do not see colour sensations, but coloured things,
> I do not hear sensations of sound but the song a
> woman is singing etc.38

> ...in immediate givenness one finds anything but
> colour data, tone data, other 'sense'
> data...etc...Instead...I see a tree which is green; I
> hear the rustling of leaves; I smell its blossoms
> etc.39

PERCEPTION, CONCEPTION AND INTERPRETATION

It is clear then that, as a moment's reflection will confirm,
none of us have any direct experience of stimuli per se;
rather we experience objects, events etc. However, not
content merely to note this fact, Husserl offers an
explanation.

> objects of experience (he tells us) point to a hidden
> mental accomplishment...40

> sense-contents are given and interpreted... actually
> given sense... contents serve as a basis for...
> 'conception' or 'interpretation' in which the
> appearance of the object with the properties
> presented by these contents is constituted for us.41

Thus like Heidegger who, following the hermeneuticists, was
subsequently to claim that all description is already

interpretation, Husserl is claiming that all perception is already conception. As Merleau-Ponty points out:

> perception is just that art which creates at a stroke, along with the cluster of data, the meaning which unites them - indeed which not only discovers the meaning which they have, but moreover sees to it that they have a meaning.42

However:

> Once perception is understood as interpretation, sensation, which has provided a starting point, is finally superseded, for all perceptual consciousness is already beyond it. The sensation is not experienced and consciousness is always consciousness of an object.... pure sensation, defined as the action of stimuli on our body... is an illusion...43

In other words, Merleau-Ponty is pointing out that if all perception is interpretive and consequently we have no experience of stimuli but only of objects, then this raises a question as to how we can come to know this. To put it another way, it is only if we presuppose in the first place that there are stimuli that our perception of objects may be taken as evidence of an interpretive synthesis - for after all an alternative explanation is that we simply perceive objects that already exist as such in the world - while if as claimed, simply all perception already interpretively synthesises stimuli into objects, then there can for this very reason be no experience of, and consequently no empirical evidence for, the existence of stimuli. For this reason then stimuli, sense-data etc. are, and must in principle remain, a purely theoretical speculation, something of an embarrassment to those, such a reductionists, whose overiding concern is to be empirical.

But in spite of the demise of stimuli there nevertheless remains much direct empirical evidence that perception involves some form of interpretation. Kuhn for example, drawing upon cognitive psychology informs us that:

> The duck-rabbit shows that two men with the same retinal impressions can see different things; the inverting lenses show that two men with different retinal impressions can see the same thing.44

Similarly Ames has shown that a ball set against a featureless background and inflated silently and rapidly is perceived as retaining its size and coming nearer, 45 while having familiarised a subject with this situation we may refrain from inflating the ball and instead move it rapidly towards the subject who will, within a certain range, perceive it as being inflated. Clearly then we can conclude from such experiments that even our most basic perception is indeed interpretive, and that even the elementary significance or meaning of what we perceive depends on our conceptual framework. As Heidegger puts it '...there are no facts...a fact is only what it is in light of the fundamental conception.46

FROM STIMULUS/RESPONSE TO MEANING/CHOICE

All this being so we can now see that far from reacting to stimuli as the behaviourists would have us believe, we respond, at least at more complex levels, to contextually dependent meanings and significances which we ourselves play an active role in constituting.

Thus mountaineers, for example, who are themselves falling or whose companions are falling, will hold onto the rope joining them together despite severe friction burns which would under other circumstances lead them to let go, while drivers who under normal circumstances would jam on the brakes if confronted by a dog that had just run into the road, will refrain from doing so if driving a car full of people in icy conditions. Clearly then, at all but the most simple or 'primitive' levels we respond, not to isolated 'stimuli', but to perceived meanings; meanings which, as these examples demonstrate, are ambiguous and are shaped by the context within which they appear.47 As Merleau-Ponty, drawing on the same hermeneutic foundation as the Gestaltists, puts it:

> It is the global presence of the situation which gives a meaning to the partial stimuli and causes them to acquire importance, value or existence for the organism. The reflex does not arise from the objective stimuli but moves back towards them and invests them with meaning which they do not possess taken singly as psychological agents, but only when taken as a situation.48

Further, as our examples equally demonstrate, the projects or goals that we are pursuing (e.g. the saving of our own or our companion's or passengers' life or lives) contribute to the situation or context, which as we have just agreed gives our experiences (e.g. friction burn and choices between braking and hitting the dog) the significance (e.g. pain of friction vs death of self or companion, and death of dog vs death of passengers) to which we respond. Thus far from our experiences determining our behaviour in the unilateral way that many reductionists claim, rather, as our examples demonstrate and Sartre has argued in detail, not only are we ourselves actively engaged in the constitution of our experiences as such, but further it is our projects or goals which determine the significance of these experiences to us, while it is on the basis of such significance that we choose our particular actions.49 Moreover far from our projects or goals being determined by our perception of the world, the converse is the case. Indeed, not only do such projects or goals determine the significance of what we perceive, in the manner already demonstrated by our examples, but they even determine what we perceive, and in extreme cases whether we perceive or not; facts that conflict with our projects being actively suppressed, as demonstrated for example in the case of both psychotics and of those soldiers who remain oblivious to wounds received in battle until the immediate danger has passed.50

While, as Sartre therefore argues, our choices of action are informed by our perception of our material conditions, and of their significance - a circumstance which far from demonstrating that we are unfree is, despite much misinformed opinion to the contrary, the necessary condition of freedom51 these perceptions are in turn informed by our overall projects or goal. Our actions, far from being determined by our environment are therefore, like our very perception of that environment, a product of a process of 'negotiation' between our aspirations or enterprise and our circumstances. Sarte gives us an example:

> If my companion suddenly starts towards the window, I understand his gesture in terms of the material situation...for example...the room is too warm. He is going 'to let in some air.' This action is not inscribed in the temperature; it is not 'set in motion' by the warmth of a 'stimulus' provoking chain reaction...the perceived settings are abstract motivating schemes and insufficiently determined; they are determined within the unity of the enterprise.52

This is obviously correct for had Sartre and his companion been engaged in the enterprise of taking a sauna for example, rather than in academic collaboration, the same heat would not have produced or 'caused' any reaction in his companion. As he observes: '...the cause, far from determining the action appears only in and through the project of an action.'53 Moreover the choice of project itself, so far from being unilaterally determined by the environment is, rather, informed by a perception of the environment and its significance which reflects an original or primary choice which, Sartre insists, is beyond reason, 54 and is that by which I first define myself.55

GENETIC DETERMINISM

In face of the demonstrable inability to reduce human behaviour to the status of a reaction to stimuli, or even to the environment as such, reductionism has one last card to play in its attempt to provide a mechanistic or quasi-mechanistic causal account of human behaviour, and that is to claim that such behaviour is genetically determined by heredity.

   Now while it may indeed be possible to suggest that the behaviour of an object or thing is in some sense dependent upon its physical make-up, we have already noted that, despite the tendency of impure or reifying reflection 56 to make of consciousness a thing, it is not in fact a thing but a process, 57 and as such indistinguishable from those activities (e.g. feeling, valuing, thinking, choosing, acting, projecting goals, etc.) for which it is usually supposed to account. As process then, 'consciousness' is, in Sartre's words 'impossible to define...as coincidence with itself,' 58 a feature it shares with Heraclitus' river, and indeed with any other process. Thus like a river which is distinct both from all that is not the river and, - as a process in a perpetual state of change, - at any moment distinct from itself a moment earlier, consciousness is both distinct from its environment and, - as a process, - distinct at any moment from itself a moment earlier. In other words, not only as we have just now argued, is consciousness a surpassing or negation, to use Sartre's terminology, of its environment, but in addition, and this is what now concerns us, it is, as a process, a constant surpassing at any moment of what it was a moment earlier; '...a double nihilation of the being which it is; and the being in the midst of which it is' 59 as Sarte expresses it. But unlike Heraclitus' river which, though in process, is also a thing or body of water, albeit a forever changing body of water, consciousness, as we have see Sartre argue, is not in any way a thing, but rather Nothing, 60 or pure process as such and, consequently, unlike the river which passes on or 'inherits' from moment to moment much of the water that composed it a moment earlier, consciousness, lacking such a 'medium' to inherit, has no necessary continuity. Accordingly, Sartre tells us consciousness '...must perpetually...leave itself behind it as a datum which it already no longer is.'61

This translates, somewhat more prosaically to the claim that if consciousness is indeed nothing other than those capacities to feel, value, think, choose, act, project goals, etc., if there is no direct experience either third person sensory or first person 'introspective' of a 'thing' in which such capacities subsist, then there is clearly no way in which the exercise of such capacities at any moment can be caused or determined by, or more precisely, genetically indebted to, the past exercise of such capacities, for there is simply no medium of transmission. It is in this sense then that Sartre tells us that consciousness 'nihilates itself,' 62 that it is a 'cleavage in being,' 63 while the capacity to choose, for example, _qua_ capacity, is a given. Thus while we are therefore, in Sartres enigmatic phrase, 'condemned to be free,' 64 far from this being a limit on our choice of projects, or the actions which we have argued flow from them, it is on the contrary not merely the sufficient but the necessary condition of our freedom.65

One last point before leaving the problem of freedom and determinism that we should perhaps note is that, in addition to the attempts to argue for environmental and genetic determinism criticised above, some may try to argue that the unconscious can determine our projects and actions etc. However, if reductionists are, as we have seen, unprepared to admit to the existence of consciousness, they are even less prepared to recognise the unconscious, and therefore being concerned here to simply provide a critique of reductionism it falls outside of the scope of our task to defend human freedom against the spectre of unconscious determinism. I would however simply like to indicate in passing that Sartre is again able to provide a defence by showing that the unconscious is no more a reified thing than consciousness, 66 and therefore is no more able to cause or determine our project and behaviour than is consciousness.

OBJECTIVITY AS INTERSUBJECTIVITY

Having argued in detail, and I hope convincingly, against some of the more specific claims and consequences of reductionism, I should like in this final part of my paper to return to an issue arising from our earlier, and more general, criticism of the positivist epistemology and methodology adopted by the reductionists. I have left it until now because, unlike the other points that we have raised so far which have been concerned with fairly specific epistemological issues and their methodological implications, this is a meta-epistemological issue, and as such may prove to be of a maximally broad and general significance. The point I should like to take up is that concerning the positivists' refusal to accept the evidence of non-sensory introspective or first person experience as we have subsequently christened it; a refusal which, as we pointed out earlier, can have no truly 'empirical' justification as such. In this sense then, it is, as I have already indicated, arbitrary; but there is of course a sense, albeit one that as we shall now argue is ultimately paradoxical and inconsistent, in which those who make such a distinction between sensory and non-sensory experience feel it to be anything but arbitrary. They would argue that what makes it reasonable to separate sensory from non-sensory experience, and to discriminate against the latter and in favour of the former, is that sensory experience is verifiable by others in a way in which non-sensory or first person experience is not.

Now this is a fact that some of the positivists' critics would dispute. Rothbard sums up the views of many of these critics when he points out that just as for the positivists:

> the laboratory experiment is evidence because the sensory experience involved in it is available to each observer;...the experience becomes evident to all...who care to follow the demonstration...In the same way, the fact of human action and purposive choice, (and by the same token all other subjective experiences) also become evident to each person who bothers to contemplate it, it is just as evident as the...sense experience of the laboratory.67

Reasonable as this may appear it cannot be expected to satisfy the positivists who will surely object that, while it may be true that we can in this manner all have first person experiences of our own subjective states, we are nevertheless unable to experience others subjective states which are therefore private and thus, despite the protestations of phenomenologists, 'unverifiable' in the positivistic sense of that term. That is to say that, in contrast to physical objects and events which are publicly accessible, my introspective states are only directly accessible, if at all, to me, yours to you, etc. This contrast however, and the discrimination against introspection or first person experience grounded upon it is fatally flawed as we shall now see.

In the first place it is a truism, but, as Husserl and the phenomenologists have recognised, nonetheless compelling that we can have no direct experience of a (Noumenal) world of objects-in-themselves (as they are sometimes called) existing outside or beyond our private experiences.68 Consequently, the claim that physical objects and events are publicly accessible can only be demonstrated, if at all, by an appeal to others' experiences, which, even if they are, as in this case, experiences of supposedly 'public' objects are, qua experiences, ultimately private. This being so, the verification of the existence of so called 'public' objects, relying, as we have just shown it ultimately must, on reports of 'private' experience, is therefore essentially no different from the verification of 'private' or first person introspective states. 'Objectivity' in this sense is, in a word, merely 'intersubjective' consensus.

Moreover, and here we come to an objection that strikes right to the heart of the positivists' pretentions, even if this were not so, even if sensory objects were indeed, unlike my private states, experienceable by others, the very insistance that verification therefore be restricted to the evidence of the five senses paradoxically renders the positivists incapable of verifying the existence of these others, qua experiencing subjects, whose existence supposedly justifies such a restriction. To put it differently, the positivist objection to 'introspection' rests upon the claim that unlike physical objects given to sensory experience, introspective states, or first person experiences as we have called them, are not publicly accessible, a claim which invokes a public of other experiencing subjects, who, qua experiencing subjects are, as the reductionists have argued throughout, inexperienceable through the five senses. As Schutz succinctly expresses it:

> it is not...understandable that the same actors who are convinced that no verification is possible for the intelligence of other human beings have such confidence in the principle of verifiability itself, which can be realised only through co-operation with others...69

It is not understandable unless of course one acknowledges what the positivists precisely refuse to, that the positivistic and objectivistic sciences implicitly presuppose not only, (as we earlier argued) those very subjective experiences, goals and values that it purports to deny, but that they further presuppose intersubjective experiences, goals and values. As Husserl recognised:

> Objective nature...as a subject matter of science...is the correlate of an infinite

accomplishment...of the personal community which is called the community of scientists.70

Schutz elaborates:

> For a situation to exist, as it must in the natural sciences by which scientist B controls and verifies the observational findings of scientist A and the conclusions drawn by him...B has to know what A has observed, what the goal of his enquiry is, why he thought the observed fact worthy of being observed, i.e. relevant to the scientific problem at hand etc. (Clearly then, Schutz concludes, science presupposes) ... intersubjective understanding.71

Furthermore, Schutz tells us elsewhere, those such as behaviourists, who import such objectivistic methods into the human and social sciences:

> feel no inhibition about starting all their deliberations with the dogma that language exists, that speech reactions and verbal reporting are legitimate methods of behaviouristic psychology (for example), that propositions in a given language are able to make sense, without considering that language, speech, verbal report, proposition and sense already presuppose intelligent alter egos (or at least intelligent others) capable of understanding the language, of interpreting the proposition and of verifying the sense.72

In short then as Husserl sums up:

> Natural science is a culture (and) it belongs only within the cultural world of that human civilisation which has developed this culture.73

In conclusion then it becomes apparent that a 'Copernican revolution' must be effected; that as Husserl argued half a century ago, 74 far from it being possible to apply the supposedly 'objective' epistemology and methodology of the physical sciences to the study of the human and social sciences as the positivists suggest, it is, on the contrary, only by employing the epistemology and methods of the human and social sciences in the study of the cultural or intersubjective foundations on which the so called 'objective' physical sciences are grounded, that we can hope to make the physical sciences intelligible.

REFERENCES

1. While Kuhn, [a] Popper, [b] Polanyi, [c] Lakatos [d]
    and many other philosophers of science have argued that
    even our most basic perceptions of the facts are already
    mediated by theories, - a view that has been empirically
    demonstrated by the Gestalt psychologists and Ames and
    his colleagues, - this was already well understood by
    Heidegger [e] as the inevitable concomitant of the
    hermeneutic view of truth. Indeed it is arguable that
    even the 'early' Husserl recognised this, [f] in spite
    of his pretension that phenomenology was to be a purely
    descriptive science.

[a] Thomas Kuhn, The Structure of Scientific Revolutions,
     (1962), University of Chicago Press, Chicago, (2nd
     Edition), 1970, pp.126-7 and 132-3.

[b] Karl Popper, The Logic of Scientific Discovery, (1959),
     Hutchinson, London, (3rd Edition), 1980, pp.81, 94-5 and
     107.

[c] Michael Polanyi, Personal Kowledge, Routledge and Kegan
     Paul, London, 1958, p.167.

[d] Imre Lakatos 'The Methodology of Scientific Research
     Programmes' in Imre Lakatos and Alan Musgrave (eds.),
     Criticism and the Growth of Knowledge, Cambridge
     University Press, Cambridge, 1970, pp.98-101.

[e] Martin Heidegger, Being and Time, (1927) translated by
     J. Macquarrie and E. Robinson, Harper and Row, New York,
     1962, p.192 and 414 and 'What is a Thing' (1962)
     reprinted in part as 'Modern Science, Metaphysics and
     Mathematics' in D. Krell (ed.) and translated, Martin
     Heidegger: Basic Writings, Routledge and Kegan Paul,
     London, 1978, pp.247-8.

[f] Edmund Husserl, Logical Investigations, (1900),
     translated by J. N Findley, Routledge and Kegan Paul,
     London, 1970, p.309 and 356.

2. According to this argument advanced by, for example,
    Mary Hesse, [a] N. R. Campbell [b] and others,
    theories are no more than analogies by which we
    understand the unfamiliar by interpreting it in terms of
    analogies or metaphors drawn from our familiar
    experiences. It may be argued that gravity, for
    example, being in and of itself inexperienceable
    independently or apart from those phenomena for which it

is supposed to account, is no more nor less than a term used to describe an analogy between such phenomena as, for example, an apple falling from a tree, cups falling off tables, arrows falling to earth, meteorites falling to earth, and indeed more generally between the motions of all earthly and heavenly bodies. (This view may be maintained irrespective of recent attempts to reify this analogy by talk of 'gravitons' so called, for it is arguable that such 'particles' are in fact little more than reifications of field properties.)

[a] See for example Mary Hesse, Models and Analogies in Science, University of Notre Dame Press, Indiana, 1966, and Structures of Scientific Inference, Macmillan, London, 1974, p.222.

[b] N. R. Campbell, Physics: The Elements, Cambridge University Press, Cambridge, 1920.

3. Thus just as the interpretation of the motion of heavenly bodies in terms of an analogy (labeled gravity (see 2 above)) with the motions of earthly bodies constitutes what passes for a causal explanation of the former, so more generally the interpretation of Ohm's relation between Voltage, Ampage, and Resistance in terms of an analogy drawn from the relation between water Pressure, Flow, and Cross Sectional Constriction was also taken as an explanation, as so too was Harvey's modelling of the heart on a pump and Darwin's modelling of evolution on the struggle for survival. Therefore as Koestler, [a] Barnes, [b] and Ricoeur [c] for instance, have all argued, analogies drawn with the familiar, constitute theoretical explanation.

[a] Arthur Koestler, The Act of Creation, Hutchinson, London, 1964, see for example p.327.

[b] Barry Barnes, Scientific Knowledge and Sociological Theory, Routledge and Kegan Paul, London, 1974, p.49.

[c] Paul Ricoeur, Hermeneutics and the Human and Social Sciences, J. Thompson (ed.) and translated, Cambridge University Press, Cambridge, 1980, p.161 and Interpretation Theory: Discourse and the Surplus of Meaning, Texas Christian University, Fort Worth, 1976, p.74.

4. As Popper, [a] Kuhn, [b] and others recognise, one cannot inductively infer theories from facts, while Einstein, [c] and Hesse [d] amongst others have

argued that theories are derived by intuition. Indeed Merleau-Ponty 16 has elaborated in detail, arguing that the 'induction' of Mill and Bacon, as it is usually understood, has in fact never been practiced in science.

[a] Karl Popper, op. cit., p.31 and 458.

[b] Thomas Kuhn, 'Logic of Discovery or Psychology of Research' in Imre Lakatos and Alan Musgrave, op. cit., p.21.

[c] Albert Einstein, 'Principles of Research' in Ideas and Opinions, London, 1954, quoted by Mary Hesse in The Structures of Scientific Inference, p.254.

[d] Mary Hesse, Ibid., p.255.

[e] Maurice Merleau-Ponty, The Primary of Perception, Northwestern University Press, Evanston, Ill., 1964, pp.67-71.

5. Now as Husserl has pointed out, [a] we can have no direct experience of a (Noumenal) realm of objects existing beyond our experience, and as Heidegger [b] and the hermeneutics have shown, all facts, even the most basic, are already mediated by theoretical preconceptions (see 1 above) From this it follows as Lakatos, [c] Ricoeur, [d] Hess, [e] Quine [f] and others have argued, that theories cannot be judged by their correspondence or failure to correspond to unmediated or objective facts, but must be judged instead on the basis of their consistancy or coherence with those theories that already implicitly mediate our perceptions, and explicitly mediate our conceptions, of the world; the choice between equally intrinsically coherent yet extrinsically conflicting theories being arguably based on simplicity and/or universality.

[a] Edmund Husserl, The Idea of Phenomenology, translated by W. Alston and G. Nakhnikian, Nijhoff, the Hague, 1970, Lectures 2 and 3, and The Ideas translated by W. R. Boyce-Gibson, Collier, New York, 1962, Ch.3, Sections 30-32 and Chs. 5-6.

[b] See reference 1[e] above.

[c] Imre Lakatos, op. cit., pp.98-100 and 129-30.

[d] Paul Ricoeur, Interpretation Theory: Discourse and the Surplus of Meaning, p.79.

[e] Mary Hesse, The Structure of Scientific Inference, pp.35 ff.

[f] Willard V. O. Quine, From a Logical Point of View, Harvard University Press, Cambridge, Mass., 1953, p.16.

6. It is, I believe, precisely because scientist share with aestheticians a concern for coherence, simplicity and universality that they have the same preoccupation with aesthetic sensibilities that many scientists have. See for example:

[a] Frank Baron, Creative Person & Creative Process, Holt, Rinehart, Winston, New York, 1969, p.97.

[b] Arthur Koestler, op.cit., p.245 and 264.

[c] Henri Poincare quoted in Brewster Ghiselin (ed.) The Creative Process, Mentor, New York, 1952.

[d] H. A. Simon, Sciences of the Artificial, MIT Press, Cambridge, Mass., 1962, p.2.

7. Thomas Kuhn's Structure of Scientific Revolutions [a] stands out and has spawned a host of historical and sociological investigations, but it should be noted that the intersubjective or sociological foundation of claims to scientific objectivity, which is the main theme of this work, had already been developed in great detail many years earlier by Edmund Husserl in his book The Crisis of European Sciences and Transcendental Phenomenology.[b]

[a] Thomas Kuhn, The Structure of Scientific Revoutions, op. cit.

[b] Edmund Husserl, The Crisis of European Philosophy and Transcendental Phenomenology, (hereinafter Krisis) (1936), translated by David Carr, Northwestern University Press, Evanston, Ill., 1970. See e.g. p.32, 131 and 294-7.

8. I mean by this term the attempt to reduce human experience, action and social formations to physical and related phenomena, and as such it is to be distinguished from the 'Phenomenological Reduction, (See reference 5a) which, attempts to reduce objects and events etc. to experiential phenomena, be they physical or 'mental.'

9. Max Scheler, 'Weissensformen' in <u>Gessammelt Werke</u>, vol.8, Verlag, Bern, 1960, (2nd Edition), p.122, FN.2, as quoted by William Leiss in <u>The Domination of Nature</u>, Beacon Press, Boston, 1974, p.109.

10. Hans-Georg Gadamer, <u>Truth and Method</u>, translated by W. Glen-Doepel, Sheed and Ward, London, 1979, p.239-40.

11. See references 1 - 7 above.

12. Edmund Husserl, <u>Krisis</u>, p.216. My additon in brackets.

13. Martin Heidegger, <u>Being and Time</u>, p.72.

14. Jean-Paul Sartre, <u>Being and Nothingness</u>, translated by Hazel Barns, Philosophical Library, New York, 1956, p.440.

15. J. B. Watson in <u>Psychology Review</u>, No.20, (1913), pp.158-67, quoted by Arthur Koestler in <u>The Ghost in the Machine</u>, Pan/Picador, London 1975, pp.5-6. My addition in brackets.

16. Edmund Husserl, <u>Krisis</u>, p.223. See also p.222. My addition in brackets.

17. G. K. Chesteron, 'The Secret of Father Brown' in <u>The Father Brown Stories</u>, Cassell, London, 1974, p.465. My addition in brackets.

18. Thus Sartre tells us that, failing to recognise that in self-reflection, 'The one who is reflecting on me is...myself'[a] and that consequently 'the consciousness reflected on is not present as something outside....on which I take a point of view...'[b] in <u>impure reflection</u>, such as that practised by Descartes, [c] consciousness 'posits the consciousness reflected on as its object,'[d] as a reified ego or thing. In other words, failing to recognise that in self reflection it is itself upon which it reflects, consciousness somehow affects to stand 'outside' of itself, and consequently mistakes itself for the reflected object it precisely is not, rather than recognising itself for the reflecting subject that it has thereby become.

[a] Jean-Paul Sartre, <u>Being and Nothingness</u>, p.153.

[b] <u>Ibid</u>., p.lii.

[c] Jean-Paul Sartre, The Transcendence of the Ego,
     translated by Forrest Williams and Robert Kirkpatrick,
     Farrar, Straus and Giroux, New York, undated, pp.44-5.
[d] Jean-Paul Sartre, Being and Nothingness, p.liii.

19. Ronald D. Laing, The Divided Self, Penguin,
     Harmondsworth, 1965, p.23.

20. B. F. Skinner, Science and Human Behaviour, New York,
     1953, pp.30-31, quoted by Arthur Koestler in The Ghost
     in the Machine, p.7.

21. G. Lundberg, The Foundations of Sociology, Macmillan,
     New York, 1939, Ch.I, reprinted as 'The Postulates of
     Science and Their Implications for Sociology' in Maurice
     Natanson (ed.), Philosophy of the Social Sciences,
     Random House, New York, 1963, p.44, quoting J. H.
     Robinson in J. Jastron (ed.), The Story of Human Error,
     p.276.

22. See references 12-14 above.

23. See Edmund Husserl, Ideas, p.214 and 222-3.

24. See for example Edmund Husserl, Cartesian Meditations,
     translated by D. Cairns, Nijhoff, The Hague, 1970, p.66.

25. See Jean-Paul Sartre, Sketch for a Theory of the
     Emotions, translated by Philip Mairet, Methuen, London,
     1977.

26. If consciousness is not a Cartesian res cogitans, indeed
     is not a reified thing at all, being indistinguishable
     from those 'capacities' it is supposed to account for,
     then it has no spatial extension, and consequently no
     interiority or exteriority, in which case we cannot
     really use terms like 'introspection' in the strict
     sense. This however does not mean that we can no longer
     distinguish sensory experiences, of, for example, those
     physical objects immediately before us (which we shall
     now call third person experiences to denote the common
     view that all can experience the same physical object
     which are therefore 'public') from non-sensory
     experiences of memories, dreams, phantasies etc. (which
     we shall call first person experiences to denote that
     others cannot experience my dreams, phantasies and
     memories etc. which are therefore 'private'). Indeed it
     is to this latter group, i.e. non-sensory experiences,
     that the term 'introspection' may still be understood to
     apply, so long as we remember to ignore its original,

spatial connotations.

27. Jean-Paul Sartre, Being and Nothingness, p.476.

28. A view which interestingly enough is not shared by all phenomenologists. Merleau-Ponty for instance claims for example that '...I do not see anger or a threatening attitude as a psychic fact hidden behind the gesture, I read anger in it. The gesture does not make me think of anger, it is anger itself.'[a] This view can arguably be traced back to Max Scheler.[b] However whether it is correct or not this view is not accepted by the positivists who therefore, in their own terms, fall to our criticism.

[a] Maurice Merleau-Ponty, The Phenomenology of Perception, translated by Colin Smith, Routledge and Kegan Paul, 1962, p.186.

[b] See for instance Max Scheler, Wessen und Formen der Sympathie, p.301, as quoted by Alfred Schutz in Phenomenology of the Social World, translated by G. Walsh and F. Lehnert, Heineman, London, 1972, p.23.

29. A. Schutz, 'Common Sense and the Scientific Interpretation of Action' in Maurice Natanson (ed.), Philosophy of the Social Sciences, p.303.

30. The 'Life-world' is the world given to us in our immediate experience, a world that therefore reflects all the preconceptions and prejudices of our historico-socio-culturally relative perspective or point of view.

31. Edmund Husserl, Krisis, p.127.

32. G. Lunderg, op. cit., FN to page 34. My addition in brackets.

33. Jean-Paul Sartre, Search for a Method, Alfred Knopf/Random House/Vintage, New York, 1968, p.157.

34. Evan Waker, 'The Nature of Consciousness' in Mathematical Biosciences 7, 1970, pp.175-6 as quoted by Gary Zukav in The Dancing WuLi Masters, Fontana/Collins, London, 1982, p.88. My addition in brackets.

35. See for example Jean-Paul Sartre, Being and Nothingness, p.310.

36. David Hume, A Treatise of Human Nature, edited by L. A.

Selby-Bigge, Clarendon Press, Oxford, 1967, Book I part
III sections II-VI and XII-XVI.

37. Edmund Husserl, _Krisis_, p.218.

38. Edmund Husserl, _Logische Untersuchungen_, (revised
     edition) Halle, 1912, Vol.II, part I, p.374 quoted by H.
     Lubbe in 'Positivism and Phenomenology in Mach and
     Husserl,' in T. Luckmann (ed.) _Phenomenology and
     Sociology_, Penguin, Harmondsworth, 1978, p.103.

39. Edmund Husserl, _Krisis_, p.233.

40. _Ibid._, p.97. My addition in brackets.

41. Edmund Husserl, _Logical Investigations I_, translated by
     J. N. Findley, Routledge and Kegan Paul, London, 1970,
     p.339, as quoted by Paul Ricoeur in _Hermeneutics and the
     Human Sciences_, (ed.) J. B. Thompson, University of
     Cambridge Press, 1981. See also _Logical Investigations_,
     p.309 and 356 quoted at _Ibid._, and Edmund Husserl,
     Cartesian Mediations, p.31 and 78-80.

42. Maurice Merleau-Ponty, _The Phenomenology of Perception_
     p.36.

43. _Ibid._, p.37.

44. Thomas Kuhn, _The Structure of Scientific Revolutions_,
     pp.126-7.

45. See Michael Polanyi, _op. cit._, p.96.

46. Martin Heidegger, 'What is a Thing' reprinted in part as
     'Modern Science, Metaphysics and Mathematics' in David
     Krell, (ed.) op. cit., p.247-8.

47. See Maurice Merleau-Ponty, _The Phenomenology of
     Perception_, p.11.

48. _Ibid._, p.79.

49. Following Heideggers explication of the way in which
     circumspection (_Umsicht_) and concern (_Besorgen_)
     thematically illuminate our environment, [a] Sartre has
     developed the concepts of 'hodological space' and the
     'instrumental complex,' ways in which the world is
     revealed as reflecting rather than determining our
     choice of projects or goals, while our actions flow from
     such projects.[b]

[a] See Martin Heidegger, <u>Being and Time</u>, p.83, 96-98 and 160.

[b] See Jean-Paul Sartre, <u>Being and Nothingness</u>, pp.321-2, 437, 448-51. For a more detailed exposition see also <u>Search for a Method</u>, esp. pp.153-4.

50. And lest it be objected that the soldier's oblivion to pain is <u>merely</u> the product of physiology, let us not forget that the physiological state, for example the release of quantities of adrenalin, is, as we have already argued, a 'fight or flight' response to the perceived <u>significance</u> or <u>meaning</u> of the situation for the soldier's project of survival.

51. It is often erroneously claimed that the fact that individuals' choices of behaviour are <u>informed</u> or <u>motivated</u> by their material conditions means that they are not free, and that <u>uninformed</u> or <u>unmotivated</u>, and consequently random behaviour is a paradigm of freedom. In fact however the converse is the case, randomness being displayed, after all, by such processes as electron emission and the fall of dice, which are demonstrably unfree to choose their behaviour. Confusion arises from the spurious equation of predictability with determinism, and consequently of unpredictability with freedom. In reality however, the fact that I may be able to predict a person's behaviour if I know sufficient about them, far from demonstrating that they are unfree, merely demonstrates that if one is sufficiently familiar with another's goals and values, one may be able to predict how, in a given situation, they will exercise their freedom.

52. Jean-Paul Sartre, <u>Search for a Method</u>, p.153.

53. Jean-Paul Sartre, <u>Being and Nothingness</u>, p.448.

54. <u>Ibid.</u>, p.478.

55. <u>Ibid.</u>, p.443, 453, 480, 564.

56. See references 18 above.

57. See references 22-5 above.

58. Jean-Paul Sartre, <u>Being and Nothingness</u>, p.74.

59. <u>Ibid.</u>, p.486.

60. See references 12-14 and 22-25 above.

61. Jean-Paul Sartre, <u>Being and Northingness</u>, p.479.

62. <u>Ibid</u>., p.84

63. <u>Ibid</u>., p.28.

64. <u>Ibid</u>., p.479

65. Such a brief exposition of the major theme of Sartre's philosophy inevitably fails to do it justice and clearly raises as many questions as it answers, not least of which is how, in the absence of a 'medium' of any kind, can each consciousness unify itself and delineate itself from other consciousnesses? As these questions fall outside the immediate concerns of this paper I shall not address them here except to say that I believe that Sartre's expositions of 'transversal' intentionality[a] of the 'fundamental project,' [b] and of our perceptions of objects and events, [c] do indeed provide adequate solutions to these questions.

[a] Jean-Paul Sartre, <u>The Transcedence of the Ego</u>, pp.38-9.

[b] Jean-Paul Sartre, <u>Being and Nothingness</u>, p.443, 453, 480, 564.

[c] <u>Ibid</u>., p.liii, and <u>Transcendence of the Ego</u>, pp.38-9 and 46-51.

66. See for example Jean-Paul Sartre, <u>The Transcendence of the Ego</u>, p.46 and <u>Being and Nothingness</u>, Iiii.

67. Murry Rothbard, 'Praxeology as the Method of Economics' in Maurice Natanson (ed.) <u>Phenomenology and the Social Sciences</u>, Vol.2, Northwestern University Press, Evanston, Ill., 1973, p.317. My addition in brackets.

68. See reference 5[a]

69. Alfred Schutz, 'The Social World and the Theory of Social Action' in Alfred Schutz, <u>Collected Papers</u>, Vol.II, Nijhoff, The Hague, p.4.

70. Edmund Husserl, <u>Krisis</u>, p.319. See also pp.130-31 and p.272 for example.

71. Alfred Schutz, 'Concept and Theory Formation in the Social Sciences,' in Nathanial Lawrence and Daniel

O'Connor, Readings in Existential Phenomenology,
Prentice Hall, New Jersey, 1967, p.381. My additon in
brackets.

72. Alfred Schutz, 'The Social World and Theory of Social
Action' op. cit., p.4. My addition in brackets.

73. Edmund Husserl, Krisis, p.332.

74. See for example reference 7 above.

6 Peeping through the keyhole: Sartre and sociology*

JAMES J. VALONE

INTRODUCTION

Any effort short of heroic could not hope to adequately confront the continuing questions regarding the possibility and practice of social science. Jean Paul Sartre's philosophy of consciousness, freedom, and society is just such an heroic attempt. The following essay claims that Sartre's project to preserve the irreducibility of the subject and the irreducibility of the social offers a challenge to the social sciences, particularly sociology, to develop an approach and methodology which provide access to both subjectivity and sociality. Moreover, Sartre demands retaining respect for the phenomenon studied, a respect resulting in offering possibilities for free and critical behaviour. Whether Sartre is successful in achieving the goal of his project is important. However, success or failure aside, reflection on Sartre's philosophical enterprise has its own rewards for those interested in a dialogue between philosophy and the social sciences.

*This article was first published in International Philosophical Quarterly, vol.25, No.3, (Sept. 1985), and appears with the permission of the editor.

We begin by situating the concerns of this essay in the context of the recent development known as existential sociology. The subsequent five sections examine the implications of Sartre's challenge for the social sciences as well as specific points in his work which are relevant to sociological projects. First of all, Sartre's notion of consciousness as negativity points to the freedom and questioning which is fundamental in praxis and theory. This section of the essay also examines the concept of the self which emerges from this notion of consciousness. Consequent to these theories is Sartre's concept of freedom. In contrast to the premise that humans are the product of heredity and/or environment, Sartre posits the view that humans are radically free to make themselves who and what they are. Second, Sartre's characterisations of social relations and sociological inquiry are exposed in order to argue that social actors and the sociologists can overcome their subordination to the practico-inert.1 In so arguing, this part of the article addresses the question of the relationship between Sartre's two great works, Being and Nothingness and The Critique of Dialectical Reason. Third, the fruitfulness of the dialectical approach, the 'progressive-regressive' method, is compared with the 'analytic' method of mainstream sociologists. The fourth section includes some critical remarks on Sartre's position as well as a critique of current existential sociology. Finally, the need for a philosophical sociology is reaffirmed and the distinctive contributions of an existential orientation are articulated.

I. SOCIOLOGICAL INTEREST IN EXISTENTIAL THOUGHT

The already unorthodox flavour of Sartre's philosophy would seem to take an even stranger course by calling attention to a possible link between Sartrean thought and sociology. The emphasis on subjectivity and the apparent anti-rationalist orientation would seem to make any existentialist philosophy an unlikely source of insight for sociologists. Moreover, existentialism emerged in opposition to the very type of society, bureaucratic rationality, in which sociology was becoming an integral part. The question, then, is why does and should Sartre's work draw the attention of sociologists?

Some years ago, Peter Manning addressed the context for answering this question in his article 'Existential Sociology.'2 The article pointed to some empirical research and theoretical developments associated with the newer sociologies which he saw as critiques of 'absolutistic' types of sociology. Manning hoped at the time that a 'new creative epoch in sociology' was evolving and that existential sociology might be one of its vehicles. He wrote that existential sociology:

> characteristically is concerned with the position of man in the social world and in social theory; it considers theory and life to have an intimate and unavoidable connection; it sees the reality of human social life as situational; and it espouses a methodology that is grounded in the understandings of everyday life...3

Also among the early proponents of a rapprochment between sociology and existentialism is Edward Tiryakian. In his volume Sociologism and Existentialism 4 the author tries to link sociology and philosophy. Tiryakian claims that the co-operation between the two can lead not only to the further development of their respective studies but also to a new synthesis in our perspective on humans. He finds a mutual preoccupation of both perspectives; for sociologism, that of a crisis which threatens the existence of modern society, and, for existentialism, it is the crisis which threatens the existence of modern humans. What exactly are the grounds of rapprochment? Tiryakian sees them first of all in a convergence between Durkheim who views society as essentially an ethical-religious reality greater than the individual, and existential thinkers who stress transcendence. The respective evaluation of truth is another broad area of comparison. Durkheim, for instance, seems to gravitate toward a pragmatic conception, where what is true is what is useful. Like pragmatism, existentialism shares the same critical outlook on traditional rationalism and the notion of truth in traditional philosophy. Sociologism is further linked to existentialism through its stress on the position that the reality of the world is a process of becoming and unfolding possibilities. Professor Tiryakian, then, is primarily interested in the lines of rapprochment between existentialism and sociology as distinguished from directly working with existential notions as they might apply to empirical and theoretical considerations.

Existential sociology also has its empirically oriented adherents, including Jack Douglas, John Johnson, and Richard Brown.5 These sociologists view Existential Sociology as the study of human experience-in-the-world in all its forms. 'The goal is to construct both practical and theoretical truths about that experience, to understand how we live, how we feel, think, act.'6 This goal assumes that the usefulness of such understanding rests in its helping us arrive at realistic solutions to social problems. These proponents of existential sociology find its distinctive character in its emphasis on the freedom of the subject, the relationship between the knower and the known, and the role of feeling in human experience.

The focus on freedom counters the over-determined vision of humans which many mainstream schools of social thought promote. Existential sociology is, in part, a reaction to the predominant schools of sociology in America. Aside from Parsonian theory and structural-functionalism, it has taken part in the critique of exchange theories (Homans, Blau), ecological theories (Hawley, Duncan), experimental sociology (The Standford group), and survey research. Despite their diversity, these schools all share a number of assumptions and methodological strategies: they view the social order as non-problematic, i.e., as an enterprise of assumed rationality of shared values; they all assume a high degree of shared meanings which encompass and order transactions; and they approach the everyday world through pre-established categories, axioms and methods which overlook the reality of the life-world of everydayness.7 Existentialism, in contrast, regards social organisation as a process which involves situational destruction, reparation, or reconstruction and commits itself to exploring contradictions and conflicts within alternative systems of meaning and the conditions which give rise to, and support them.

Existentialism's outlook on the knower and their relation to the known also results in important implications. The determination that the knower is intimately and inevitably related to the known, that the subject and object are interdependent, has two consequences:

1. Traditional views about objectivity in the human sciences must be changed and abandoned.

2. Any attempt to attain the truth about the world, to be more objective, depends upon an analysis of the knower in their many aspects.

But perhaps the most distinctive, if not controversial, emphasis by the Douglas group is the attention to brute being, the dominance of feelings over the cognitive and evaluative features of social action. For these existential sociologists feelings are the foundation and goal of all thought. Yet this is not a testimony to the fundamental irrationality of human existence nor the irrationality of all action. As John Johnson argues, there is usually a fusion of thought and feeling and a fusion of both of these with action. This interfusion exhibits itself even in habitual behaviour which is too often incorrectly viewed as semi-comatose, sedimented patterns of behaviour. As one existential sociologist put it: 'Routine or custom in human life is not the result of some principle of inertia or law of least effort. Man is restless, nervous, emotional, striving primate, not an inert sloth.'8

Even more recently, and closer to the specific concerns of our essay, two book length studies on Sartre's importance for the social sciences and sociology have appeared. The first of these is Ian Craib's Existentialism and Sociology: A Study of Jean-Paul Sartre.9 Craib justifies his attention to Sartre by claiming that 'if sociology is to learn from philosophy, it must treat the philosopher seriously and make the attempt to grasp and employ his philosophy as a whole.' He argues, in fact, that when one is 'doing sociology' one is 'doing philosophy' and vice versa.

Craib sees Sartre's early work as important for the concerns of a sociology of interpersonal relations, whereas Sartre's later work takes up the issues of the type of social formations that have been the province of traditional sociology. Sartre's attempt to provide a more adequate basis for Marxism in his later work offers sociologists the opportunity to overcome their general neglect of Marx. Finally, Craib sees Sartre's attempt to understand the modern world as an effort shared by some sociology.

But perhaps most interesting is Craib's re-analysis of several empirical studies from a 'Sartrean' position in order to illuminate his originality. Among these reconstructions are an examination of Goffman's concept of the 'self' and a critique of Garfinkel's general assumptions about the nature of consciousness and the world, demonstrating how they affect his empirical studies.

Gila Hayim is the author of the second treatment of Sartre, The Existential Sociology of Jean-Paul Sartre.10 Her volume is an attempt to treat Sartre's Being and Nothingness 11 and Critique of Dialectical Reason 12 together and in relation to sociological perspectives and interest, to identify the connection between these great works, and to establish the relevance of these works for sociology and the social sciences in general, with respect to both their method and content.

Hayim finds Sartre's relevance chiefly in his combating the cultural and scientific 'spirit of seriousness' which gives priority to the world of worked matter 13 over the human world. Sartre wants to introduce a dialectic which gives primacy to the human over matter. Humans in making themselves can surpass the given. 'Sartre's Critique is a critique of the method which views and treats humanity and world as static entities (totalities) whose interconnections follow a predetermined path, in the spirit of the dogmatic version of dialectical reason.'14 Hayim focuses on Sartre's response to the malaise of modernity. The privilege of freedom can lift the weight of inauthenticity. Freedom is not an escape from matter but a praxis 15 that replaces matter with human relations. Freedom regains the world as human means instead of material destiny.

This general sketch points to some of the important influences and implications of a sociology which is sensitive to the insights and perspective of existential philosophy. Our essay, however, is neither an attempt to rehearse the way in which existential sociologists see themselves or see the general relationship between sociology and philosophy, nor is it an empirical analysis along Sartrean lines. Rather, our concerns are more philosphical and critical with particular emphasis on the integrity of the irreducible features of the human condition, subjectivity and sociality. The justification for this preoccupation rests in the fact that several important social scientific concepts, the self, freedom, social formations, theory, and methodology find their foundation in the conditions of subjectivity and sociality. It is in this light that we will examine some of the bases and tenets of Sartre's philosophy and relate them to actual and possible sociological use and relevance. Naturally, our analyses will sometimes draw from the work of the existential sociologists, particularly from Craib and Hayim.

II. THE LESSONS OF NEGATIVITY

Throughout Sartre's work there is the belief that we are responsible for and capable of self-realisation. For Sartre, this freedom springs from the distinctive processes of consciousness and our experience of the self. This relationship, among freedom, consciousness, and the self, has direct implications for sociology since Sartre's characterisation of the human as free in all situations stands in contrast to the over-socialised conception of humans and the various forms of determinism embedded in social scientific thought.

Sartre's viewpoint on freedom dictates his concern with the experiencing subject as a conscious being. He approaches freedom subjectively as opposed to regarding human action from the point of view of the Other who sees the human as but a collection of probabilities. True to his phenomenological roots, Sartre begins his exploration of the human subject with special attention to consciousness. Along with Husserl, Sartre recognises the intentional 16 character of consciousness. Yet, what Sartre makes of this is quite different from the founder of modern phenomenology. Sartre points to intentionality, which refers to consciousness as a consciousness of something, as the source of negativity; consciousness is not what it is conscious of. The locus of negativity is consciousness as intentional, for it is empty by its very character of being a 'consciousness of.' Nothing dwells at the very heart of consciousness.

In the language of Being and Nothingness, consciousness is what it is not, i.e., it is not what it is conscious of, its objects, the ego, its states and affects. On the other hand, consciousness is not what it is; consciousness is not the object of which it is conscious but neither is it a pure consciousness independent of all objects.

But what does it mean to say 'consciousness is not what it is?' Since it is according to Sartre a 'nothingness' 17 which passes over things like a 'clear wind,' consciousness adds nothing to being, only a relationship to itself. Sartre ejects all being from consciousness. Moreover, he ejects the ego from consciousness. Consciousness is not a me; it is transphenomenal, prepersonal, and prereflexive. As consciousness, I am not being, rather my consciousness separates me from what I am by nothing.

> I never am any one of my attitudes, any one of my actions. The good speaker is the one who plays at speaking, because he cannot be speaking....I cannot say either that I am here...in the sense that we say 'that box of matches is on the table'...Nor that I am standing, nor that I am seated; this would be to confuse my body with the idiosyncratic totality of which it is only one of the structures.18

What does it mean to say that 'consciousness is what it is not,' that conscious experiences are 'acts of nihilation?' For Sartre, to be conscious of something in the concrete, I must nihilate all the rest. In abstraction some property or quality is isolated from the concrete, and in perception the perceived objects emerge from and are 'detached from' their ground. Clearly, the nothingness of which he speaks is not an 'absolute nothingness' but the objective correlate of nihilating consciousness. Moreover, the experiential structure of being, the unreal, the absent, the potential, etc. which are given in and with the experience of being, has its foundation in consciousness.

A specific conception of the self unfolds from Sartre's notion of consciousness. As a consciousness, a self-reflective cogito, the self is a negativity always and continually. In Sartre's words, 'Human reality is a perpetual surpassing toward a coincidence with itself which is never given.'19 Humans are self-maintaining and a self-making in the face of the Other, the In-itself. Moreover, human action is a negativity, for it is a making of the world, which is Other than myself, something other than it is. Action is a making of what is not into what is. The self, in Sartre's philosophy, is a restlessness, a movement toward possibility.

The ontological reality of such a nihilating consciousness and self is freedom, a freedom which cements the relationship among free acts, consciousness, and the self. Freedom, says Sartre is 'the permanent possibility of dissociating oneself from the causal series which constitutes being and which can produce only being.'20 As negativity, the conscious self bears within itself the permanent possibility for freedom and disengagement. As a freedom, the human (the For-itself) surges forth from itself to the world, (the In-itself). Freedom is the very heart and soul of human reality. So much so that Sartre, in one of his many poignant phrases, claims we are 'condemned to be free.' We are born free and thereby responsible for everything except our responsibility. Referring to both the situation-bound character of freedom and our total responsibility for it, Sartre writes, 'We must regard this freedom neither as metaphysical power inherent in human nature, nor as license to do as we please, nor as some unidentified inner refuge which we would have even in bondage. We do not do as we please, yet we are responsible for what we are: that is the brute fact.'21

Sartre's powerful image of human reality seems to violate any ordinary conception of freedom, self, and consciousness found within sociological studies. Yet there is only an apparent irrelevance and impracticality for the social sciences. The Sartrean concepts of freedom, self, and consciousness are not completely unnoticed by sociologists. Ian Craib is one of the few sociologists to give serious consideration to Sartre's notions for a sociology of interpersonal relations and the issues of social formations.22

Craib re-analyses some empirical studies from a 'Sartrean'

position. In one of these re-analyses he examines Goffman's concept of the self as presented in Asylums 23 in order to provide a Sartrean corrective. Craib claims that Goffman seems to employ two conceptions of the self:

1. The self is a substantive entity or form, one can do something to the self.

2. It is possible to possess it as one possesses an item of clothing.24

Within this first conception, the self is seen as the product of others, the network of institutional relationships. Craib argues that Goffman exaggerates the radical change effected in the self upon entering total institutions. Although there are some differences between the 'inside' and the 'outside' they are not radical as Goffman portrays them. His conception of 'secondary adjustments' (these are habitual means and ends in which individuals stand apart from the self and the role taken for granted for them by the institution) overlooks the fact that these social structures are created in some ways by the persons concerned.

In light of Sartre's position, Craib counters the second concept of the self which Goffman promotes. Craib says that rather than a possession, the 'I' is a project, a pursuit of a 'self.' The human is a goal-oriented creature, a being of possibilities. There is alway a distance between the self and its projected possibilities and this distance and negativity of consciousness, are what really are at the bottom of the feeling and search for identity.

Craib presents the upshot of this re-analysis by calling for the development of a general classification of projects in terms of institutional arrangements. Although abandoning some of the individuality of meaning, the sociologist would still be working at a more specific level than someone like Goffman and would attend to and recognise the existence of even more individual 'layers' of meaning. Individual projects can then be seen as not only comprised by social structure but in terms of how these projects change the structures and the way in which these structures alienate the project. One type of example can be found in the patient who is attempting to establish an identity within the institution, and who finds that the contact with the staff necessary to express that identification and have it recognised is denied for reasons of organisational efficiency.

145

This brief glimpse at Craib's study provides some idea of the impact of Sartre's concepts for sociology. Sartre's portrayal of the self shows consciousness to be negativity, and as negativity the self can always negate the self defined by institutions and others. There is the ever present possibility of freedom and negation even in the most circumscribed conditions. Incumbent upon each human (as a For-itself) is the necessity, the obligation, to break through activity. This picture of the self stands in contrast to the image of an environmentally, socially, and genetically determined human reality. This latter conception of human reality is the predominant paradigm within social science. It is a paradigm of the human self which finds the individual at the mercy of social structures and psychological and biological laws. Where exceptions to this paradigm exist, the philosophical grounds for a conception of a free, dynamic self are lacking.

What exists at the centre of the Sartrean notion of a free, conscious self is the basis for a critical sociology. To the extent those within a society or institution mold and construct it, to that extent they are responsible for its shape and condition. The concern for the destiny of communication and freedom among people is already at work in the products, structures, and inter-relationships of subjects.

Sartre's notion that humans are shapers and reshapers of their world is co-equal with the idea that we are responsible for what we make of ourselves and our society and how we accomplish our tasks and goals. The upshot of this position is that sociology and social ethics must inform the practical activities of the common culture. Social critique translates the scientifically determined regularities into the practical context of social responsibility. The social identity rooted in past conditions is imbued with new life due to an awareness of new possibilities in light of a human future. When meanings given to social processes by scientific theories are clarified then the different theories and distinctive analyses of social reality can be ordered according to their relevance to particular kinds of problems in the practical world. This significance, however, can only be determined on the basis of and measured against a philosophical clarification of freedom, consciousness, and the self. An interpretive science and social theory which would cut itself off from the regulative idea of freedom would be nothing more than a promotion of the status quo, an abandonment to fate and inevitability. Even when it is conscious, this abandonment undercuts the very purpose which motivates it, to aid in the rational pursuit and free choice of those values best suited for human life in society.

III. THE IMPOTENCE AND IMPORTANCE OF SOCIALITY

If Sartre's notions of the self, consciousness, and freedom have direct relevance for sociological work, his treatment of sociality certainly should. Like all philosophers of his stature, Sartre gives considerable attention to sociality, thereby providing a natural convergence of philosophical and sociological interests. What would a summary of Sartre's social philosophy reveal as unique? Can we pinpoint the importance of his social philosophy for sociologists?

The following reconstruction of Sartre's social philosophy and its developments shows that what is distinctive is Sartre's continuous effort to anchor his social philosophy in individual praxis while preserving the irreducible character of sociality. Moreover, in the tradition of Hegel, Sartre examines the foundation of human alienation in his analyses of seriality and the practico-inert, and in his later work begins to discuss the possibility for authenticity. This summary of Sartre's position necessarily touches upon his account of our experience of others, the various social formations resulting from praxis, and the interpretive issues of the relationship between his early work, Being and Nothingness, and his later writing, The Critique of Dialectical Reason.

The richness of Sartre's efforts in these areas results in an equally varied set of implications for sociology. The sociological importance of his work manifests itself in three ways: first, the nature of the present sociological approach to its subject matter needs to be addressed and rethought; second, the relation of the subject matter to the sociologist should also be viewed in a new light as well as enriched and expanded; finally, the very character and organisation of the discipline must be re-examined.

Sartre is clear in his position that besides the immediate presence of the pre-reflective cogito, the conscious self, there is another equally immediately and directly experienced presence, that of the Other. I experience the Other first and foremost through shame which along with fear and pride (an attempted but impotent alternative to shame) is among the three primordial Other-revealing emotions. This immediate experience of the Other Sartre describes in his famous passage about the person peering through the keyhole.25 There is a situation, a sight to be seen behind the door because I am jealous. This is the looker's project. But as

147

looker, immersed in the subject I see through the keyhole, I fail to realise that someone is approaching. I hear a noise in the corridor behind me, and look up to find myself looked at; this affects essential modifications in my structure. I have become observed by the person behind me in the same way that the person in the room, on the other side of the keyhole, had been observed by me. I find myself before the Other through whose look I exist as a circumscribed entity, which is to say in a way that I, regarding myself as uncircumscribed potentiality, am not for-myself. The Other is revealed as a freedom (a For-itself) which is not-myself.26

> Shame - like pride -is the apprehension of myself as
> a nature although that very nature escapes me and is
> unknowable as such. Strictly speaking, it is not that
> I perceive myself losing my freedom in order to
> become a thing, but my nature is - over there,
> outside my lived freedom - as a given attribute of
> this being which I am for the Other.27

What does Sartre see as the necessary and sufficient conditions under which a theory of existence of others can be valid? First of all, the structure and existence of the Other is such that no theory or proof will or can ever be devised which will validate or invalidate its existence. Any conjecture or questioning of the Other is in fact a reflective confirmation of what I already know to be the case, Others exist.28 Second, in my own experience as a cogito, in the very depths of my being as a self, what is discovered are not merely reasons for believing the Other exists, but that the Other is not me, a being who is not me. Third, the Other is for us not as an object (as probable) but as one who 'interests' us and our being concretely and in the empirical circumstances of our facticity. Fourth, the negative relation of the Other appearing as 'not being me' is reciprocal and possesses a twofold interiority: on the one hand, the multiplicty of Others is a totality and not a collection 29 because each Other finds their being in the Other, and, on the other hand, it is a detotalised totality 30 for one's being for others is also a radical refusal of the Other.31

While in his early work he emphasised the individual, Sartre later in The Critique of Dialectical Reason, came to focus on the need to become committed and responsible within the world, not merely as an individual but as a member of a collectivity. This signals a shift in Sartre's focus, if not in his philosophical orientation, and raises the question of the relationship between his early and later work. What

exactly are the connections and discontinuities between
Being and Nothingness and The Critique?

Clearly, Sartre's fundamental emphasis on the freedom and
responsibility of the individual persists throughout all his
work. Sartre's Critique is not an attempt to integrate
Marxism into his earlier work, but to inject the notion and
reality of freedom into Marxism.

> The idea which I never ceased to develop is that in
> the end one is always responsible for what is made of
> one. Even if one can do nothing besides assume this
> responsibility. For I believe that a man can always
> make something out of what is made of him. this is
> the limit I would today accord to freedom: the small
> limit that makes of a totally conditioned social
> being someone who does not render back completely
> what his conditioning has given him...32

The continuity between Being and Nothingness and The
Critique also rests on Sartre's recognition of the existence
of the Other as an irreducible fact. The link between
freedom and sociality parallels the connection between
freedom and consciousness.

There are, nevertheless, three main differences between
Sartre's earlier and later treatises. First, Being and
Nothingness investigates the inevitable conflict of the self
and Other, while The Critique speaks of reciprocity between
oneself and the Other, and this reciprocity is recognised
only through a Third. Each of us is a third at the same time
that we are an Other and ourself. Sartre elaborates, in
The Critique, on the implications of this reciprocity.

> Reciprocity implies, first, that the Other is a means
> to the extent that I myself am a means, that is to
> say, that the Other is the means of a transcendent
> end and not my means; second, that I recognise the
> Other as praxis, that is to say, as a developing
> totalisation, at the same time as integrating him as
> an object into my totalising project; third, that I
> recognise his movement towards his own ends in the
> same movement by which I project myself towards mine;
> and fourth, that I discover myself as an object and
> instrument of his ends through the same act which
> constitutes him an objective instrument of my ends.33

Such reciprocity may be positive or negative. There is
pattern and order in human affairs, yet the contingent and
free character of human experience also ensures disorder and

149

disarray. This twofold character of human life is what makes social life and the construction of social order problematic.

A second difference between Being and Nothingness and The Critique lies in the former's affirmation of absolute freedom and the latter's talk of necessity and destiny. In The Critique the two givens of Being and Nothingness, the For-itself or human subject and its facticity are replaced by the analogue of the agent as praxis and the facticity and contingency of its field of practice, scarcity. While matter can serve to unite humans in relationships of reciprocity, it can threaten in the form of scarcity. The environment may not offer the organism what is necessary to satisfy its needs and keep it in existence. Scarcity is the contingent foundation and condition of our history, and, for Sartre, history is intelligible only as a history made in conditions of scarcity. Moreover, scarcity makes conflict intelligible since it is on the basis of interiorised scarcity that the subordination of the Other's subjectivity takes place. Humans work their environment in response to needs but the 'worked matter' has its revenge on people by producing collectives which determine them as the practico-inert. The practico-inert signals our subjection to mechanical forces which we create in the form of social instrumentalities that actually undermine genuine sociality.

The third major shift in The Critique is the possibility that the inauthenticity of role playing can become authentic. Sartre finds this possibility in internalising external action that embodies freedom. Also, the introduction of the idea of active passivity - the notion that a human being can never freely and without self-deception give themselves to anything but their freedom - is a discovery for Sartre. Sociality, like the individuality of the For-itself, can take different forms which can either stifle and cloak free activity or facilitate and promote freedom. Sartre takes the opportunity to characterise these various modes of sociality and the 'spirit of seriousness' which infects modern institutions. Captured in his notion of the 'spirit of seriousness' is the sense of granting more reality to the world than to the human, conceiving the human as a product of the world and giving values an absolute and objective reality independent of human volition. When the social group is ruled by the spirit of seriousness it abdicates its responsibility and no longer freely ascribes the values it chooses to the products of its actions.

For Sartre, the group-in-series is a primary form of inauthentic sociality. It is neither genuine praxis nor genuine effort and purposive activity toward a goal. The series is a group in which the individuals desire a common interest and the way in which they desire it is general whereby the 'members' lack individuality. Seriality is the use of simple alteriority, the physical separation of organisms, to structure one's relationships with the Other in a particular way. The series issues from the demand of the practico-inert object which is the common being. Reversing the perspective, we can view the series as the being-outside-of-itself of the practio-inert. Through the series each individual establishes their identity with the Others, as an identity of alteriority: we are each, Other than the Others. As Sartre puts it, 'Everyone is the same as the Others in so far as he is Other than himself.'34

If Sartre can be said to have a social ideal it would be the group-in-fusion. The more a society attains a character of this type, the more humane it is, but the more it approaches seriality, the more inhumane. As the paradigm form of society, the group-in-fusion provides the opportunity for the constitutive employment of human energies, allows for a great public impact of individual choice, and is more amenable to individual diversity. A group-in-fusion forms when a perceived threat from an outside party totalises the collectivity as a group, and the unity is re-interiorised by the series. Members relate to each other not as individual or Other, but as a singular incarnation of a common purpose.35 As opposed to seriality, meaningful, constructive action by the individual is at the bottom of this type of group. There can occur the development of an organisation by instituting an Oath as a means of transforming the group-in-fusion into its own permanent instrument. The Oath is both a protection against one's freedom, a freedom which threatens the group, and a means of maintaining the freedom one has gained through the group.

The previous assessment of the continuities, discontinuities, and highlights in Sartre's social philosophy ushers us into a consideration of the significance of his analyses for sociological work. At the beginning of this section we mentioned this significance manifests itself in three ways: firstly calling for a reassessment of the present approach to sociological subject matter; secondly reconsidering the relation between the sociologist and their subject matter; and thirdly re-examining the character and organisation of sociology as a discipline.

1) We have seen that the Other is 'Not-me-not-object.' The possibility of perpetual transformation, of treating the Other as subject and object, and the Other treating me as subject and object, is one of the areas of Sartre's analysis

that has immediate importance for a sociology of interaction and the relation between sociologists and their subject matter. Craib argues in his study that the sociologist is 'an ideal example of the Other as not-me-not-object, as the one who looks.'36 The sociologist is like the one who watches the person looking through the keyhole, making the sociologist part of the situation.

If we follow through on Craib's suggested comparison, Sartre's portrayal of our experience of Others places in question the typical approach in sociological studies. The typical sociological project is an attempt to possess the world through knowledge. Within this project sociologists seek to know their object as an object and treat those they study as particular types of objects which possess certain qualities and properties. Even values are normally conceived as being possessed and as having qualities. However, the more sociologists adopt the third person perspective, the less they are engaged in the field of praxis of those studied. This mode of regarding the subjectivity of the Other ruptures reciprocity and, even more, treats the ojectified subjectivity of the Other as merely a contingent factor among others in a network of group tensions and dynamics.

The Sartrean view, in contrast, regards values as created by the project, and even the sociological project is an expression of value: freedom is an expression and creation of values. Recognition of the Other is not in terms of experiencing them as 'bare existence' but in encountering the Other as an agent devising their own freedom in the world.

Craib concretises this point in a re-analysis of Alvin Gouldner's Wildcat Strike 37 and his Patterns of Industrial Democracy.38 Craib emphasises Sartre's point that while the content of human relations may be determined, the fundamental structure of the relationship is not. The basic relationship of reciprocity between myself and the Other is created through praxis and provides for the possibility of all historically present actual relationships. Rather than seeing the behaviour, roles, and conflicts of the different groups (e.g., miners, surface workers, management, owners, etc.) as the result of external forces and conditions, these behaviour patterns and conflicts are interpreted as the interiorisation of the demands of the practico-inert and the different forms of behaviour and attitudes arising from this interiorisation. For example, given the nature of the worked matter in the mine and the machines on the surface, there is a greater dominance of bureaucracy in the plant than in the mine.

A reconsideration of human action conceived as a project and related to a project can aid the sociologist in crashing through role analysis and ideal typification which tend to regard the self and consciousness as residual categories. The thrust of Sartre's concept of the situation is its recognition that the social situation is a creation by the project and the subject. Sartre's conception stands in contrast to any definition of the project imposed from the outside.

2) Any rethinking of the sociological project within the Sartrean perspective forces recognition of the possibility that those studied might 'look back' and reject the sociologist. Objectivising on the part of the sociologists, through asserting his or her freedom by the negating activity of consciousness, brings the opportunity of a reversal which transforms the sociologist into an object. Such reversals are happening, for example, in the sociology of race relations. The implications of this phenomenon include the demand for being more sensitive, realistic, and open toward those studied as well as attending to those human categories and experiences often ignored in traditional frameworks.

On this latter score, Sartre's characterisation of the relations with Others, i.e., love, indifference, sadism, masochism, hate, etc., are descriptions of the structures of interpersonal relationships that the sociologist can come across during work, providing an alternative to traditional conceptualisations of relationships as a matter of characters' 'definitions of the other,' etc. Shame, for example, is one of those experiences embedded in sociality and deserving of further attention. Shame threatens one's existential self and produces anxiety. More specifically, this feeling pervades the lives of many of the poor in America.39 Sociologically, understanding this feeling is essential to understanding the poor, dealing with them effectively, and providing them assistance.

Sociological categories, constructs, and typifications must be liberated as much as possible from stereotypes, simplicities, and strictly 'rational' determinations. If the purpose of sociological study, as we have outlined above in section one, is to increase awareness of and articulate new forms of control and choice, then it is incumbent upon sociologists to expose the full range of future possibilities and choices as well as grasp present meanings and situations.

3) Finally, Sartre's considerations of sociality and our knowledge of its formations houses implications for the very

nature of sociology as a discipline. Sartre is well aware
that the fragmentation and compartmentalisation of modern
society has its parallels in sociology. There is a notable
tendency with all branches of knowledge, including sociology,
to fragment and break down into specialised areas of concern.
The university, in fact, sanctions this development.

Within sociology this involves a knowledge of human
understanding different in nature from that sought by the
classical sociologists. What results is a partial and
inadequate type of understanding. Craib fingers the major
difference between classical and contemporary academic
sociology.

> The topics covered in most undergraduate courses as
> separate units - sociological theory, sociology of
> religion, the family, deviance, industrial sociology,
> etc. - if they are found in the work of the classic
> sociologists as identifiable topics at all are dealt
> with in a more general totalising framework. The
> last major 'totalising' theorist of academic
> sociology in the twentieth century would appear to be
> Parsons. The totalising attempt of sociology has
> declined and insofar as it remains it is directed at
> sociology itself rather than at the outside world, or
> confines itself to the elaboration of the founding
> fathers. As the attempt to grasp the world has
> become fragmented, so sociology's attempt to grasp
> itself has intensified.40

As a result of the demands of the discipline and the role,
sociologists must limit their efforts to understand
themselves or the world. These demands come in the form of
requiring the acquisition of certain 'sets' of knowledge,
choosing among pre-established topics and methods, and
producing results in an acceptable style and form of writing.

Among the general orientations or projects for the
sociologist within the context of these academic demands and
fragmentation, there is the interiorisation of the demands of
the practico-inert system as dominant. Here, the sociologist
chooses to be subordinate to the requirements of 'acceptable'
sociological practices and topics. What results is a form of
alienation where there is a projection of oneself into worked
matter in order to possess one's Being through one's being-
for-others.

Addressing this issue of sociology as a discipline Craib
points to two additional orientations which are possible
within a Sartrean perspective. The sociologist may, first of

all, choose to interiorise the demands of the practio-inert without subordinating him or her self to them in order to possess the world through understanding by using the tools given by sociology.41   In this type of project the sociologist's work is an integral feature of their relationship to the world.   There is a reciprocal reference between self-understanding and understanding of the world. A final type of orientation, says Craib, goes even a step further.   This type of project involves the interiorisation of the demands of the practico-inert in an attempt to use the tools gained as a means of furthering the understanding and praxis of some social formation.42

   What Sartre's analyses of sociality offers us are three distinct but related implications for the sociological project. The sociological task, first of all, has as its goal the explication of freedom and its possible alienation which are expressed in the actions of those studied. Secondly, this effort must be useful to those studied by providing an understanding of their activities and possible futures.   These studies must be available to those studied, especially if they question a group's serial consciousness of itself.   Third, the sociologist enagages in a process of self-discovery through his or her project.   Sociologists learn of the fruitfulness and possibilities of sociology as a discipline and learn of their real contribution as a professional.

IV THE SEARCH FOR A METHOD

Summarising up to this point, we can say that a Sartrean vision when brought to the sociological task calls for a transforming and scrutiny of the conception of the self, social relationships, the sociological project itself, and the organisation of sociology as a discipline.   But nothing as yet has been said about the cornerstone of social scientific works, methodology.

   Sartre explicitly takes up the theme of methodology in his critique of sociology.   His criticism targets on the conception of research as an activity by an 'autonomous' researcher studying the ontologically autonomous group. A good deal of sociological methodology employs a deductive model where abstractions such as 'values,' 'norms,' 'roles,' and 'social classes' are taken as real.   Theorising in this vein involves special consequences.   First, abstracting from the living reality of the life-world, 43 humans are seen as passive organisms subject to social pressures and forces and who are unaware of their social and political situations.   By minimising human agency humans are screened from alternative meaning systems and processes for change. Second, the connection between theory and practice is never adequately established thereby preventing an appropriate awareness where informed human action can help shape and construct the social world. Third, meanings are predefined and attached to events rather than disclosing the meanings constituted by individual persons. The set and complex of tacit and taken-for-granted meanings are fundamental for viewing the world and, insofar as they are basic, any sociology which neglects them distorts reality.

Research, in Sartre's view, is a living relation between people.44 Linked to his conception of a proper methodology is a reaffirmation of the phenomenological dictum: 'Back to the things themselves!' As Husserl states, 'The true method follows the nature of the things to be investigated and not our prejudices and preconceptions.'45 The difficulty of achieving this goal is complicated by the inseparability of the questioner from the questioned, the methodology from the subject matter. A methodology constructed on the basis of an accurate understanding of and respect for human experience would result in an appreciation and understanding of both the irreducibility of the human subject as a free, conscious, and total being, and the irreducible character of the social as the totality within which individuals perform and which the sociological project has as its object for totalisation.

Sartre meets this methodological demand by placing the project 46 at the centre of human reality. The project makes the future central as well as the given conditions of every event and historical period. 'Everything changes if one considers that society is presented to each man as a perspective of the future and that this future penetrates to the heart of each one as a real motivation for his behaviour.'47 The project also plunges us into immediate relations with the Other and it even issues from one's relations with others.

With the project as his focus Sartre develops the progressive-regressive method. The method is witnessed in the very nature of human conduct. Human conduct by which we strive to achieve our projects is where 'The movement of comprehension is simultaneously progressive (toward the objective result) and regressive (I go back toward the original condition).'48 In short, there is no other method than continual 'cross-reference.'49 The 'progressive-regressive' method has as its principal variables structure, person, and history. The method begins by situating an event in the social structure in which it is created. Next, biography is related to the structure. This is Sartre's existential psychology. Finally, the method seeks an integration of structure and biography into an historical movement. Sartre describes this approach:

> ...it will progressively determine a biography (for example) by examining the period, and the period by studying the biography. Far from seeking immediately to integrate one into the other, it will hold them separate until the reciprocal involvement comes to pass of itself and puts a temporary end to the research.50

The first aspect of the 'progressive-regressive' method is totalisation. Totalisation is a continual effort to relate different facets of a changing social situation into a pattern; it is making the whole social structure visible in light of its parts and its parts meaningful in light of the overall existing social network. There is 'the search for the synthetic ensemble, each fact, once established, is questioned and interpreted as part of a whole.'51 The sociological project, in attempting to possess the world through knowledge, has as its totalisation 'the world,' or 'society' or the 'social system' or some part of 'the world.' The choice of a topic is a choice from a wider set of elements and this set comprises the initial totalisation.

The impact of Sartre's position for the sociological project lies in the difference between dialectical theory and analytic theory. The former intends to totalise and the latter generalise. The process of generalisation seeks the reduction of aspects of the concrete to the lowest common denominator. Dialectical theory seeks to keep every possible and ascertainable aspect of the concrete and unite it into a whole in such a way that each particular aspect is intelligible in terms of the other. Dialectical theory regards contradictions in and between phenomena as essential to their intelligibility, whereas analytic theory aims at being logical and since it seeks what is common there must be no contradictions, unless the contradictions are common and then they become one aspect in terms of the theory.

Sociology is dialectical in structure but most likely analytic in content. But the dialectical structure can be 'filled out' by including the sociologist in the original totalisation. This means recognising one's Being-for-Others and the Others' Being-for-themselves and vice versa. The extent to which a sociologist is aware of these varies and is conditioned, in part, by the reaction of those studied. For example, certain studied populations question sociologists about their ethics and their profession, as in the area of sociology of deviance.

The second aspect of the 'progressive-regressive' method is Sartre's existential psychoanalysis. In his passion to understand humans Sartre establishes the method where his purpose seems to be primarily ethical. As opposed to those 'who wish to possess the world,' Sartre is among 'those who want to change it.'

Existential psychoanalysis is the attempt to disclose the fundamental and significant decisions, the 'projects of being,' which give unity to a particular life and enable us to understand it in the concrete. Personal life is a free project and existential psychoanalysis is the concrete science of freedom. The 'fundamental project' is a perfectly conscious, though not necessarily deliberate, choice of style of life.52 Sartre writes, 'The choice is not less conscious or less explicit than a deliberation but rather...it is the foundation of all deliberation and...as we have seen, a deliberation requires an interpretation in terms of an original choice.'53

Existential psychoanalysis can not be performed with respect to every person studied by the sociologist. Yet there are features and notions associated with this approach that can and should be carried over into the work of human scientists. Sartre believes in the positive value of biographies for discovering the principles for genuine psycho-analysis and he encourages the study of the 'successfully adjusted actions of life' as equally revealing as neurosis and psychosis. 'The goal of existential psychoanalysis is to rediscover through these empirical, concrete projects the original mode in which each man has chosen his being.'54 Also, 'existential psychoanalysis is a method destined to bring to light, in a strictly objective form, the subjective choice by which each living person makes himself a person.'55 Sartre poses this science as equal to the task of constructing an objective presentation of subjective meaning.

Sartre's position on existential psychoanalysis follows from his phenomenology of consciousness. The human person is a whole, a 'totality,' rather than a collection of drives, impulses, or forces which converge and unconsciously dictate behaviour. Sartre opposes the Freudian 'hypothesis of the unconscious' and he criticises the 'materialistic mythology of psychoanalysis.' In contrast, he offers his own basis for a psychoanalysis: 'The principle of this psychoanalysis is that man is a totality and not a collection. Consequently he expresses himself as a whole in even his most insignificant and his most superficial behaviour.'56

Existential psychoanalysis rejects the hypothesis of the unconscious but this does not mean that one knows one's fundamental project. While the subject may be conscious of the project in its concrete expression in particular acts and desires, it does not mean the same person has the necessary techniques and concepts to bring the project 'into the full light of day.' The person is not necessarily self-reflective in the full sense of the term. So Sartre is not opposed to any and all notions of the unconscious but only that notion which makes the human the mere instrument of psychophysical drives. Sartre's own notion of the prereflexive consciousness admits of psychophysical factors which are part of the facticity of a given human situation but are not the projects or choices of consciousness itself.

The method of psychoanalysis, of the existential type, is more than merely discovering the behaviour patterns, tendencies, and inclinations of the person. The method involves deciphering them and knowing how to question them. Freedom is the focus and this impacts upon existential psychoanalysis' view of hereditary dispositions, character, etc. 'Existential psychoanalysis recognises nothing before the original upsurge of human freedom; empirical psychoanalysis holds that the original affectivity of the individual is virgin wax before its history.'57 The human is a surge, a living process of history. This is why Sartre calls heredity, education, environment, and physiological constitution (which are used as explanations of human behaviour) the 'idols of our epoch.'58 In providing a psychological explanation of someone, what we are demanding is an answer to why this particular person is and acts in this way. We are demanding a veritable irreducible. 'The irreducible unification which we ought to find...this is the unification of an original project, a unification which should reveal itself to us as a non-substantial absolute.59

None of this is to say there are no serious questions regarding Sartre's position. Perhaps he goes too far in his critique of Freud, overlooking those depths of the human psyche which is the sphere of the irrational, of the repressed, hostile, and unacceptable urges, the forgotten aspects of existence. Furthermore, Sartre's exposition of the method of existential psychoanalysis is incomplete. He has performed four psychoanalyses of existential projects: Baudelaire, Anti-Semite and Jew (which is more an intersubjective and historical attitude rather than individual life-projects), Saint Genet: Actor and Martyr, and 'The Venetian Pariah.'60 These are, however, riddled with problems of interpretation and hermeneutics.

Nevertheless, the constructive aspects of Sartre's approach suggest a more integrated orientation toward structure and biography. As Jack Douglas rightly argues, one of the basic ideas of all phenomenological and existential work is 'maintaining the integrity of the phenomenon.'61 Existential sociology argues that sociology and philosophy must be moulded by the reality of one's social experience rather than forcing social reality to fit the mould of experimental methods, especially methods developed by the natural sciences used to studying a different kind of reality. What also makes the methodological work of Sartre relevant is his attempt to unify in a single theory both the approach of Methodological Individualism and Methodological Holism. There continues to be disagreement on the proper and appropriate structural approach methodologically. There is the approach concerned with micro-structures of social order as witnessed in the work of Garfinkel, Turner, and Blume, and structural analysis concerned with linking perceptual structures of the mind with the larger symbolic systems of a society, group or institution, e.g., Mauss, Hubert, and Hertz. What can be discerned from the Sartrean perspective is that the tension between society and the body is mediated by the self. This establishes the connection between the two types of structural analysis and offers an opportunity to explore complementary and innovative methodological approaches.

V CRITIQUE

In our efforts to disclose the relevant features of Sartre's work for sociology, we have naturally concentrated on the positive aspects of his work. A balanced analysis, however, calls for a critical focus on the weaknesses of this venture. A critique of existential sociology must occur on two levels. The first addresses some of the major weaknesses in the movement, weaknesses which are sighted by some of the existential sociologists in their self-critical efforts. The second level involves a correspondingly selective evaluation of Sartre's work.

There is one view fostered among some existential sociologists which distorts the value and conception of the relationship between philosophy and sociology. One of its proponents, Jack Douglas, claims that existential philosophy is the source and foundation for many of the insights and new perspectives of what has come to be existential sociology.

The philosophy, however, is not the whole cloth of existential sociology. Rather than being the impetus for observing the social world or to recognise problems in understanding the social world, existential or other types of philosophy have been used to help gain a better understanding. In contrast to this view, Craib emphasises, and rightly so, that the relevance of Sartre to sociology does not lie in choosing one or two ideas from his work and showing how they can be used by the sociologist. Rather, Sartre's significance lies in determining the fundamental importance of his method and subject matter for sociology.

We have earlier noted that perhaps the most distinctive emphasis in existential sociology is the attention to brute being, the dominance of feelings over the cognitive and evaluative features of social action. Feelings are the foundation and goal of all thought. However, the 'sociology of feelings,' which alleges this focus as the main thrust of existential sociology, finds little grounds in Sartre's philosophy for its claim. Emotions are essentially ineffective for Sartre. Although they may serve as motives for one's acts, acting on the basis of one's emotions is an abandoning of oneself to the non-rational, which of itself is not capable of effecting any change. As impotence, it cannot be a basis for rational choice, in fact, one abandons freedom in allowing oneself to be pushed and pulled by emotions. Gila Hayim also finds that Sartre's work does not justify the claim that he wanted to develop a framework for understanding the non-rational aspects of human life as opposed to goal directed rationality.62 Discerning the intelligibility of human reality is Sartre's goal.

The second level of our critique takes us directly to Sartre where our remarks are limited to those weaknesses with the greatest immediate impact for a sociology with an existential orientation. Perhaps the most severe limitation of Sartre's position emerges in the absence of a fully articulated and grounded theory of social structures. The fundamental question is whether Sartre can remain consistent with his early work and develop an ethics and a social philosophy. He cannot. Both Craib and Hayim argue cogently for the continuity in Sartre's thought. We are, as noted above, in qualified agreement. But Craib, for instance, interprets Sartre's focus on 'bad faith' and the futile character of human life in Being and Nothingness as historical and not ontological. Sartre, he claims, does not view alienation as a permanent condition, but as historically predominant. This leads Craib to bridge the apparent gap between Sartre's earlier and later work. He is much too kind to Sartre. It seems there is no other way to take Sartre's treatise, <u>Being and Nothingness</u>, other than as a philosophical statement on the human condition. Admittedly, Sartre promises an ethics and thereby implicitly calls for thinking through the possibility for authenticity and for a proper social way of living. But even where Sartre articulates his ethical posture, 63 he is ultimately driven to ground his position in freedom without providing a rational basis for authenticity. In fact, according to his view, the only freedom that is the source of my values is my freedom and therefore the only freedom that I need to choose is my own. The basic problem Sartre has in establishing the social dimension is that the freedom of others has no value for me, nor any value for that matter, unless I choose to give it some.

A related weakness is Sartre's curiously unrealistic view of freedom. As one critic puts it, for Sartre, freedom 'is not an acquisition laboriously won or intermittently exercised.64 Moreover, one's choices and freedom rise up within facticity rather than over against it as Sartre argues.

Further complicating Sartre's efforts to construct a social philosophy is his notion of consciousness. The necessary and sufficient condition for consciousness is that there be a consciousness of one's consciousness, otherwise, he argues, there would be no consciousness. This foundation is found in the pre-reflexive <u>cogito</u>. Ironically, in seeing the content of consciousness as outside itself Sartre nevertheless retains the Cartesian thesis that consciousness to be consciousness must be self-directed and self-contained.

Despite these problems, Sartre's work is a treasure-house of Western philosophy. Whether one agrees with him or not he has caught in the web of his thought the problems which continue to plague the modern sociologist and philosopher. Examination of Sartre's philosophy and the existential sociology which flows from it places us in a position to assess the need for a philosophical sociology and the distinctive contributions of an existential orientation.

CONCLUSION

If we have found the character and foundation of an existential sociology to be distinctive then we should find its contributions equally unique. We find these distinctive contributions in; firstly, its encouragement of a continued examination and understanding of the nature of the subject matter of sociological inquiry; secondly, the possibility of reconstructing and reanalysing sociological analyses by translating them into philosophy; thirdly its demand for a reflexive understanding, on the part of the sociologist, of the process and nature of sociological inquiry; and fourthly, its recognition of the need for a critical sociology, witnessed by the subject matter of investigation.

1) Sartre's descriptions and analyses are directly centered on the human reality which is the subject matter of sociological study. Sartre's work is rich in suggestions regarding the nature of the self, freedom, and the various forms of sociality. Moreover, the end of The Critique includes a number of analyses of the concrete, e.g., an analysis of mass media in terms of extero-conditioning, an analysis of imperialism as praxis-process, and an analysis of the relationship of the individual to his or her class. We find both an abundance of ideas for suggested sociological studies as well as a characterisation and analysis of the nature of the phenomena to be studied.

2) An additional thrust of turning to existentialism is that sociological analyses can be 'reconstructed' by translating them into philosophy. Such a philosophical sociology can help account for the subject of inquiry, what is to be gained and sought in such an inquiry, and provide the bases for self-reflection (including reflexive understanding by the sociologist and those studied). Even more, the type of totalising sociology called for by Sartre demands the sociologist enter into a relationship of reciprocity with the people studied. In a positive relationship sociologists must commit themselves to the ends of those studied. This is stronger than merely 'taking the point of view of those studied' since it calls for promoting the free and constructive activity of the group. In a negative relationship the sociologist must also appropriate the ends of those studied but as a moment in the struggle to overcome their alienated praxis.

3) Linked to this previous contribution is existential sociology's encouragement of reflexive understanding on the part of the sociologist. Sartre's efforts to construct a methodology and existential psychoanalysis based on free choice, though incomplete, are instructive. For example, Sartre's challenge to construct an existential psychoanalysis has been taken up by R. D. Laing and D. G. Cooper, et al, in the anti-psychiatry movement. There is no doubt that the riddles and difficulties of social scientific self-understanding persist, and it is equally without doubt that Sartre should have a voice in this process of sociological self reflection, a project clearly advanced by Craib and

Hayim.

4) Finally, Sartre reaffirms the unity of theory and practice as a goal of sociology and social philosophy. Given the historical character of human events, what the social scientist can do is determine the potentialities of current social forms and present them in such a way as to develop a critical framework by which to judge the status quo. In his analysis of the spirit of seriousness, Sartre finds the roots of critique. Reminiscent of Marx, Sartre discovers that the development of social conditions produces new needs and in the struggle to achieve these needs, ideals are forged to guide activity toward the changing of society. These ideals are outgrowths, not reflections, of material conditions of need. In turn, the struggle to achieve institutional change produces changes in those who participate in the struggle.

In summary, the thrust of existential sociology rests in the notion of reality and study as process and project. It seeks an understanding of the world as-lived-in and not just an understanding of what a theorist has had to assume in order to do his or her work. Existential sociology, in general, receives its impetus from the philosophical orientation which gives it its name, and , in particular, it does and should derive its character from Sartre's investigations. Like the person peeping through the keyhole, Sartre's investigations are not a mere looking at others and his subject matter, conferring on them the modality of object-ness. More than this, this looking takes place within a project, the purpose and meaning of which gives this looking its character and social significance. Sartre's project is an effort to establish the possibility for free, liberating praxis, and at the same time to maintain the integrity of the coequal conditions of subjectivity and sociality.

REFERENCES

1. The 'practico-inert' is Sartre's term for that which, in embodying the practices of individuals or groups in pursuit of goals, (praxis), exercises an inert force or constraint upon our spontaneous acts of freedom. Social institutions for instance would be a paradigm case of the practico-inert.

2. Peter Manning, 'Existential Sociology,' in Sociological Quarterly, vol.14, no.2, Spring, 1973, pp.200-225.

3. Ibid., p.204.

4. Edward Tiryakian, Sociologism and Existentialism: Two Perspectives on the Individual and Society, Prentice-Hall Inc., Englewood Cliffs N.J., 1962.

5. Jack D. Douglas and John M. Johnson (eds.) Existential Sociology, Cambridge University Press, 1977.

6. Ibid., p.vii.

7. Peter Manning, op. cit., pp.203-204.

8. See Jack Douglas' article, 'Existential Sociology' in Existential Sociology, p.21.

9. Ian Craib, Existentialism and Sociology: A Study of Jean-Paul Sartre, Cambridge University Press, 1976.

10. Gila Hayim, The Existential Sociology of Jean-Paul Sartre, University of Massachusetts Press, Amhurst, 1980.

11. Jean-Paul Sartre, Being and Nothingness, translated by Hazel Barnes, Washington Square Press, New York, 1966.

12. Jean-Paul Sartre The Critique of Dialectical Reason, translated by Alan Sheriden-Smith, London, 1976.

13. 'Worked matter' is the material world which, seen in practical terms as a threat to our lives, a resistance to our labour, as limiting our quest for knowledge, or as providing instruments for the satisfaction of our projects or goals for example, so far from being 'dumb matter' rather reflects or speaks to us of these projects or goals.

14. Gila Hayim, op. cit., p.82.

15. 'Praxis' is the practical activity of an individual or group in pursuit of a hitherto theoretical goal or act.

16. 'Intentionality' as used by phenomenologists refers to the fact that all consciousness is conscious of an object; that far from being isolated from the world of objects, consciousness always enjoys a cognitive relation to this world.

17. Sartre rejects the notion that consciousness is a reified entity or thing, insisting therefore that it is No-thing or nothing other than those capacities (e.g., to cognise, think, initiate action, feel, etc.) which it is hypothesised to account for.

18. Jean-Paul Sartre, 'The Paintings of Giacometti,' in Situations, translated by Benita Eisler, Fawcett Publications Inc., Greenwich, Conn., 1965, p.126.

19. Jean-Paul Sartre Being and Nothingness, p.139.

20. Ibid., p.23.

21. Quoted by Andrea Fontana and Richard van de Water. 'The Existential Thought of Jean-Paul Sartre and Maurice Merleau Ponty' in Existential Sociology, p.114.

22. See Ian Craib, op. cit., Introduction.

23. Erving Goffman, Asylums (1961), Penguin, Hamondsworth, 1968.

25. Jean-Paul Sartre, Being and Nothingness, pp.347 ff.

26. Ibid., p.350.

27. Ibid., p.352.

28. Ibid., p.337.

29. Unlike 'collections' of individuals which, related to each other in a purely external manner, are unaware of each other, and consequently depend upon an outside or independent observer for their recognition that they form a group, which is therefore nothing other than the sum of its parts, a 'totality,' by way of contrast, is present in its entirety to each of its members, and is therefore a self-constituting unity that, as such, may

consequently be regarded as more than the sum of its parts.

30. A 'detotalised totality' is a totality which, though present in its entirety as a unity to each of its members, is present as a unity which is nevertheless nothing but a multiplicty of individuals, and is consequently seen not as a self-constituting totality, but as dependent for its very existence upon its recognition by each.

31. Ibid., pp.337-339.

32. Jean-Paul Sartre, 'Itinerary of a Thought' (Interview) in New Left Review, 58, p.45.

33. Jean-Paul Sartre, Critique of Dialectical Reason, pp.112-13.

34. Ibid., p.260.

35. Ibid., pp.374 ff.

36. Ian Craib, op. cit., p.24.

37. Alvin Gouldner, Wildcat Strike, Antioch Press, Yellow Springs, Ohio, 1954.

38. Alvin Gouldner, Patterns of Industrial Democracy, Free Press, Glenco, Illinois, 1954.

39. See Jack Douglas' treatment of the experience of shame in connection with poverty in Jack Douglas, op. cit., p.45.

40. Ian Craib, op. cit., p.210.

41. Ibid., p.212.

42. Ibid., p.213.

43. The term 'life-world' implies that different individuals and groups perceive the world and their existence in it from different perspectives or 'points of view,' and consequently that the members of any group having a common historico-socio-cultural perspective may to this extent be seen as sharing a common 'life-world,' but one that is different from the one inhabited by members of another group.

44. Jean-Paul Sartre, <u>Search for a Method</u> translated by
     Hazel E. Barnes, Alfred A. Knopf, New York, 1967, p.72.

45. Edmund Husserl, <u>Phenomenology and the Crisis   of
     Philosophy</u>, translated with an introduction by Quentin
     Lauer, Harper & Row, New York, 1965, p.102.

46. For Sartre, who does not believe that the self is an
     ego, or indeed any 'thing' at all, we are ultimately no
     more nor less than bundles of capacities and activities
     which are directed towards the achievement of goals or
     projects, each hierarchy related to a 'fundamental
     project' by which each of us therefore ultimately define
     ourselves.

47. Jean-Paul Sartre, <u>Search for a Method</u>, p.96.

48. <u>Ibid</u>., p.154.

49. <u>Ibid</u>., p.135.

50. <u>Ibid</u>.

51. <u>Ibid</u>., p.26.

52. Jean-Paul Sartre, <u>Being and Nothingness</u>, p.461.

53. <u>Ibid</u>., pp.461-462.

54. <u>Ibid</u>., p.764.

55. <u>Ibid</u>., p.734.

56. <u>Ibid</u>., p.568.

57. <u>Ibid</u>., p.727.

58. <u>Ibid</u>., p.715.

59. <u>Ibid</u>., p.717.

60. Jean-Paul Sartre:- <u>Baudelaire</u>, translated by Martin
     Turnell, New Directions, Norfolk Conn., 1950; <u>Anti-
     Semite and Jews</u>, translated by George J. Becker,
     Schocken Books, New York, 1948; <u>Saint Genet: Actor and
     Martyr</u>, translated by Bernard Frechtman, New American
     Library, New York, 1963; "The Venetian Pariah"
     translated by Wade Baskin in <u>Essays in Aesthetics</u>, New
     York Philosophical Library, 1963.

61. See Jack Douglas, op. cit., p.296.

62. Gila Hayim, op. cit., p.9.

63. See Jean-Paul Sartre, Existentialism and Humanism, translated by Philip Mairet, Methnen, London, 1948.

64. Albert William Levi, 'Existentialism and the Alienation of Man' in Phenomenology and Existentialism, Edward N. Lee and Maurice Mandelbaum (eds.), The Johns Hopkins Press, Baltimore, 1967, p.257.

7 Sartre and Merleau-Ponty on phenomenological-existential psychology

ROGER McLURE

A favourite humanist argument against the use of the scientific method in psychology is that its application involves the conceptual contradiction of supposing that human reality is simply physical. To this the positivistic psychologist might reply that it is not his or her business to peer into souls but to predict behaviour by means of quantitative methods, and that this kind of inquiry may be carried out independently of considerations of the nature of the human psyche. They might even make this point while glowing with sympathy for the humanist's tender-hearted view of human being, for the more the positivist is prepared to concede, as a purely personal opinion, the 'soulful' view of human substance, the more credible will appear the contention that hard methods do not imply a hard mankind or a hard-hearted psychologist. It would, of course, be open to the humanist to allow the positivistic claim that the scientific method is ontologically uncommitted, but to argue that this is just what is wrong with applying it to the study of humanity. The humanist's complaint would now be, not that human behaviour <u>cannot</u> be interpreted by quantitative methods but that to approach it in this way is to miss out on the defining features of humanity, which, it is claimed, are not quantitative. The humanist will point out to the positivistic psychologist that it is possible to deny human specificity only at the cost of abandoning his original thesis: that the scientific method is justified by virtue of its ontological neutrality, and shifting to a very different thesis: that its application is justified because it is tailored to the study of res extensa (physical substance) from which humanity is wholly constituted.

It would be open to either party to make a conciliatory move by invoking the Identity Hypothesis. This is not, however, a move that is likely to tempt humanists since, in the first place, their faith in the irreducible character of experience is already sufficient to dispense with such gratuitous authorisation by a new theory; moreover, the humanist - and indeed the positivistic psychologist - find the idea of physical and mental talk having identical referents just as much of a puzzle as those which the Identity Hypothesis is designed to resolve.

So we may sum up as follows the humanist's case for a psychology based on self-understanding, such as phenomenological psychology. At worst - if tied to spatial reality, as Bergson claims it is - the scientific method speaks of humanity in a false language. At best - if it is ontologically neutral - it is blind to the specificity of human being. The physicists have no option but to equate explanation with prediction; they have got to tell an 'outside story' because it is not themselves that they investigate. They can only interpret nature symbolically, in terms of 'the conditions of possibility of general phenomena,'1 stated in mathematical form. But the case with human psychology is different in as much as here the nature of the subject is the same as that of the object of investigation. This 'absolute proximity'2 of the self to the self meets one necessary condition of the possibility of a psychological method based on self-understanding or Verstehen.

A further necessary condition is that the specificity of human being be in some sense rational. The method of self-understanding presupposes that experience find itself understandable. That experience does possess a concrete rationality peculiar to it is the fundamental supposition of phenomenology. This means that for an experience to be is eo ipse for it to possess a perceptible structure or meaning which defines it 'once and for all'3 as a kind of intentional 4 transaction with the world 5 and which is accessible to special types of (phenomenological) reflection. Husserl is generally taken as saying that the meaning of an experience is contained in its transcendental 6 features and that these owe nothing to existence. Sartre and Merleau-Ponty, on the other hand, refuse to separate meaning and existence. 'Essences,' they think, are modes of being-in-the-world.7 They do not, in contrast to the case with Husserl, constitute an autonomous sphere of transcendental reason. But what is common to both these orientations in phenomenology is the idea that experience yields from within itself its own meaning and that this immediate meaning, be it logically separable from existence or not, cannot be conjured away in favour of third-person or 'objectivistic' conceptual constructions. Explanation as explication of this meaning may therefore replace explanation as prediction of behaviour. It will be a matter of finding out 'what things mean,'8 a task which must precede that of finding out how language comes to mean the same as what things mean.

These transcendental meanings, which in toto make up the field of intentional consciousness, are not singular but connected in a synthetic totality. Each meaning (or essence) is a special way of signifying, and fully exemplifying, the totality of the relations of subjectivity with the world, whether 'subjectivity' be defined as an ego-bearing transcendental consciousness requiring only an intentional object (Husserl), as an ego-less transcendental consciousness requiring only some real world (Sartre), or as a body-proper anchored in this world (Merleau-Ponty). 'All of existence,' says Husserl, 'is one universal unity.'9 For an experience to have meaning is for it to signify, in the way which defines its essence, the totality of which it is a structure. Meaning is co-occurrent with self-understanding, because it is the perspectivistic embracing or comprehending of this totality by itself. 'Emotion,' says Sartre, 'signifies in its own way the whole of consciousness,or - if we place ourselves on the existential level - the whole of human-reality.'10 Indeed, an exhaustive understanding of any kind of experience (psychological essence) would issue in a perfect understanding of the totality which it signifies. Or as Sartre say: 'He who speaks of one consciousness speaks of the whole of consciousness.'11 Or again, 'To have a meaning is to point to something else, and to point to it in such a way that in developing the meaning we should discover precisely what is meant.'12 This supposition of a unitary universe of meaning is fundamental to all phenomenology, whether meaning is envisaged as logically separable from existence or not. Phenomenology therefore prescribes itself the principle that no essence has been exhaustively defined until its intrinsic signifying relations with the whole of (Husserl's) transcendental consciousness, or with the whole of (Heidegger's) human-reality have been rendered perspicuous.

Thus far I have isolated two fundamental features of the

phenomenological concept of meaning which will be espoused by any phenomenological psychology: firstly that meaning is coeval with subjectivity; secondly that this meaning is total. A third feature, namely the intentionality or world-directedness of this meaning, has already been hinted at. This, however, calls for further elucidation.

To say that phenomenological meaning is intentional is to say that it is located in the reaching out of consciousness towards a transcendent 13 world, which is the horizonally open totality of being within which all kinds of existence-positings or objects stand out. The 'home' of meaning is neither the ego nor the world as thing-in-itself, but consciousness-in-the-world. When Husserl speaks of the 'constitution' of meaning by consciousness he does not mean that the distinctions and contents of meaning that are discovered in the world are created ex nihilo by transcendental subjectivity. He means rather that constitution of meaning is indissolubly linked with the orientation of consciousness towards an irreducible transcendence, which cannot be appropriated and 'subjectivised' into a transparent system of meanings qua 'representations' having their sole source in the synthetic activity of the subject. We can put this point by saying that there would be no meaning if all we were aware of were 'mental contents.' Meaning implies the resistance of transcendence to total appropriation by consciousness. Or as Husserl says, between consciousness and reality 'there yawns an abyss of meaning.'14 Constitution is a 'creative intuition'15 inscribed in what Merleau-Ponty calls 'the paradox of immanence and transcendence.'16 Somehow consciousness is in touch with what gives itself as being beyond consciousness; somehow what is beyond consciousness is such only for consciousness. This paradox has the charm of re-discovered obviousness: nobody has the impression of perceiving 'mere appearances.' Yet nobody would claim to be able to describe genuine transcendence otherwise than from the point of view of its appearing to them. Genuine transcendence exists only for consciousness, which exists only as a meaning - realising relation to genuine transcendence. In this concept of intentionality, as implying an interdependence of meaning between the world and consciousness, the young Sartre saw a salvation from the threadbare alternatives of idealism and realism. Stressing the anti-idealist side of the interdependence in L'Imagination, Sartre writes:

> Intentionality: such is the essential structure of
> any consciousness. There naturally follows from this
> a radical distinction between consciousness and what

consciousness is of. Whatever the object of
consciousness may be, it is in principle outside of
consciousness (except in the case of reflective
consciousness): it is transcendent. This
distinction, to which Husserl reverts again and
again, is conceived with the aim of combatting a
certain immanentism which tries to constitute the
world out of the contents of consciousness (for
example, the idealism of Berkeley) .... Psychology,
basing itself on the ambiguous formula "the world is
my representation"17 causes the tree that I perceive
to evaporate into a host of sense-data, of coloured,
tactile or thermic impressions etc. With the result
that in the end the tree appears as the sum of
subjective impressions. Husserl, on the contrary,
begins by placing the tree outside of ourselves.18

Elsewhere, in an early article, it is the anti-realist
implication of intentionality that is emphasised:

But Husserl is certainly not a realist: he does not
make of this tree, which stands there in its cracked
bit of earth, an absolute which is somehow supposed
to enter into communication with us subsequently.
Consciousness and the world are given simultaneously:
in essence exterior to consciousness, the world is by
essence relative to it.19

Part of the usefulness of this principle of intentionality
to the psychologist is that it rules out in advance the kind
of accounts of experience which depend on hypostatising
either consciousness or the world. It discredits, for
example,the whole tradition of anlaysing conscious experience
in terms of 'psychic states,' 'sense-data' and other
'immanent' entities that used to furnish the 'inside' of
consciousness. For according to the principle of
intentionality, consciousness is not a container; it has no
'inside,' it is not a substance which supports
'modifications;' it exhausts itself in its transactions with
the world. The psychologist will know from the outset that
psychological experience will have to be interpreted as ways
of apprehending the world. He or she will know, for example,
that having a mental image cannot be a matter of entertaining
a copy of a past perception 'in' consciousness, and that
emotion cannot be understood as an 'inner' turmoil.
Intentionality also forewarns the psychologist against the
converse substantivist error of treating the objective
factors in psychological analysis in abstraction from their
essential relativity to the subject, an abstraction which is
presupposed by mechanistic explanation in psychology.

Once armed with the basic theory of mind provided by the principle of intentionality, the experimental psychologist will, so Sartre claims, be able to free his or her interpretation of empirical data from the deadweight of more or less unconscious metaphysical prejudices about the nature of mind which have been taken over from commonsense, language or bankrupt philosophical traditions. Concluding his study of the classical psychological theories of the image Sartre says:

> We have just seen, for example, that the classical theories of the image contain a whole implicit metaphysic and that a whole host of metaphysical prejudices, some of them going back as far as Aristotle, have been carried over into experimentation.[20]

Intentionality is both a principle and a concept: it guides research in philosophy and psychology as well as describing the essence of consciousness. We may qualify as 'ontological' those essences necessary to the existence of any consciousness. Thus, 'world,' 'situation,' time,' 'intentionality' are ontological essences in contrast to such psychological essences as 'memory,' 'imagination,' 'emotion,' 'attention' etc. (Consciousness is necessarily temporal and involved in the world from the point of view of a concrete situation, whereas it is only contingently concretised as perceiving, imagining, paying attention, etc.) Now a psychology will have a stronger claim to calling itself phenomenological if, in addition to assuming the principle of intentionality, it also operates within the framework of the ontological essences which it is the business of phenomenological philosophy to elucidate. But the psychologist will not rest content with the methods, namely the series of transcendental/eidetic reductions, through which these psychological and ontological essences are elucidated. For psychology is an empirical ('mundane') discipline concerned with 'real people in the real world,' whose behaviour presupposes the existence of the world that such reduction puts out of play.[21] On the other hand, this neutralisation of existence is a necessary preparatory strategy, since 'the essential features of consciousness revealed by the reduction do not disappear when consciousness imprisons itself in the world again.'[22] Consequently, 'the main acquisitions of phenomenology will remain valid for the psychologist, mutatis mutandis ... what is valid for the phenomenologist is also valid for the psychologist.'[23] Consider, for example, the notion 'world,' as it features in the expression 'being-in-the-world.' Whatever the world is, it is not something which the psychologist attempts to elucidate. Yet if we grant the claim of Husserl and the existentialists that to be is to be-in-the-world, and that the world is at least an ultimate horizon co-present behind every thetic positing, then understanding precisely what it is to be in the world is highly relevant to understanding the particular ways of being-in-the-world, (perceiving, imagining, etc.) with which psychology is concerned. The empirical concepts of psychology acquire their true meaning only once they are interpreted in terms of the eidetic concepts of phenomenology. Or as Sartre says:

> We still agree that psychology does not put man in question or the world between brackets.24 It takes man in the world, such as he presents himself in a host of situations: in the cafe, with his family, at war. In general, what it is concerned with is man-in-situation. As such it is, as we have seen, subordinate to phenomenology, since a really positive study of man-in-situation ought to have first elucidated the notions of man, world, being-in-the-world, situation.25

A psychological attitude is always essentially some kind of response of an individual to his or her situation in the world. Therefore, to understand these psychological attitudes fully it is necessary to understand the ontological essences 'man,' 'the world,' 'situation.' Factual information gives us no leverage on these because the essential meaning of the psychic facts we encounter is embedded in the meaning of the phenomenological essences themselves. The facts about, say, the imagination, are facts about a psychological essence which is one way of being within the world-horizon. The elucidation of the notion of world is therefore foundational in relation to psychology:

> (Psychic facts) are, in their essential structure, reactions of man in the face of the world; they therefore presuppose man and the world, and can enter into their true meaning only once those notions have been elucidated. If we want to give a foundation to psychology we should have to regress beyond the psychic, beyond the situation of man in the world, right back to the source of man , of the world and of the psychic - to the transcendental and constituting consciousness which we reach through the 'phenomenological reduction'26 or 'bracketing the world.' It is to this consciousness that we must look for answers to our questions, and what gives validity to it is precisely the fact that it is mine.27

This mention of 'the source of man, of the world and of the psychic' evokes a Husserlian doctrine which survives unscathed Sartre's critique of Husserlian subjectivity in The Transcendence of the Ego: that empirical consciousness and the world as intentional phenomenon are correlative, radically constituted products of that subjectivity. Worried by the moral more than the epistemological implications of the solipsistic tendency in Husserl's work, Sartre argues in The Transcendence of the Ego for a conception of transcendental subjectivity 'purified' of the, as he thinks, 'superfluous' and 'reifying' transcendental ego, which in Husserl supplies the unifying pole of the constituting activity of transcendental consciousness. The ego must be ousted from consciousness, but the latter must retain its transcendental dimension:

> We follow Husserl in each of his admirable descriptions where he shows transcendental consciousness constituting the world by imprisoning itself in empirical consciousness; we are, as he is, convinced that our psychic and psycho-physical me is a transcendent object which must fall within the scope of the epoche (or reduction).28

The empirical consciousness or self and the world are now to be understood as interdependent poles simultaneously constituted by a transcendental consciousness without a transcendental ego:

> The world and empirical consciousness are two objects for the impersonal, absolute (transcendental) consciousness, and it is through the latter that they come to be linked. That absolute consciousness, once it has been purified of the I, no longer has anything of a subject about it: it is simply a first condition and absolute source of existence. And the relationship of interdependence which it establishes between the Me and the World suffices ... to give a philosophical foundation to an absolutely positive morality and politics.29

Whereas

> As long as the I remains a structure of consciousness it will always be possible to oppose consciousness with its I to all other existent things. And in the end it will be Me who produces the world.30

But it is clear from Sartre's talk of 'source' and 'first condition' that the residual transcendental consciousness is no less capable of radical constitution of the world than when it enjoyed the company of a transcendental ego. What Sartre had done is to (mis)interpret Heidegger's notion of being-in-the-world in terms of a non-egological conception of radical constitution, 31 such that being-in-the-world is seen as the constituting of the world in interdependence with a co-constituted empirical subjectivity. But the point of contrast here with Merleau-Ponty is that Sartre clearly thinks that radical constitution of meaning is perfectly possible. And to believe that is to believe that the reverse process of complete reduction is at least theoretically possible; for reduction consists in progressively peeling off the layers of meaning as which the world has been constituted, with a view to showing how constituting consciousness is the ground of the world's transcendence, and so of the validity of the knowledge-claims we make about it.

Merleau-Ponty is at one with Sartre on the transcendental ego. But whereas for Sartre in his early 'psychological' period, constitution is as radical as it remains with Husserl, for Merleau-Ponty constituting consciousness operates within the horizon of a world pre-given to it. This means that the world retains a 'beyond' that cannot be appropriated as an object perfectley transparent to consciousness. The reality or transcendence of the world is therefore not a product of transcendental constitution, but simply always already made or already there, 32 'there before any analysis that I make of it.'33

But if constitution is not radical, the phenomenological reduction cannot be complete. According to Merleau-Ponty it is through trying and failing to bracket existence that we discover both that our pre-reflective faith in the world was pre-theoretical intuition of the facticity of things, and that that faith was, not justified by evidence, but the bedrock of truth back to which every appeal to evidence ultimately leads us. There is a lot more bite to this than to Dr. Johnson's stone-kicking refutation of Berkeley. For it is this logically incorrigible (not just psychologically indubitable) belief in the reality of the world that makes such intramundane judgements as 'there is a stone on the road' corrigible. Mis-perceptions and hallucinations make sense only against the background of a belief in the world that is logically secure because it founds our understanding of (at least) empirical truth. We trust the world ultimately to tell us its truth in much the same way as we trust a novelist to resolve all apparent incongruities of plot. Only, in pursuit of the world's truth we chase an ever-receding horizon beyond which it lies concealed. And our awareness of doing this is our knowledge that the world is

radically facticiel 34 and, _eo ipse_, not a fiction.
Withdrawing from the world with a view to bracketing it can
never snap the intentional threads that tie us to the world,
but only stretch them sufficiently to render the bond
visible.35 It cannot instate consciousness in a pure cogito,
in correlation with a world as pure cogitatum or essence. To
take note of this failure is, according to Merleau-Ponty, to
see that:

> far from being, as has been supposed, the formula of
> an idealist philosophy, the phenomenological
> reduction is the formula of an existential
> philosophy. The being-in-the-world (In-der-Welt-
> Sein) of Heiddeger appears only against the
> background of the phenomenological reduction.36

The visibility of our being-in-the-world afforded by the
reduction is a vision of essences, but these are to be
understood as logically a posteriori idealisations grounded
in, and allowing access to, the structure of an irreducibly
facticiel being-in-the-world. As such, they enable
provisional (pre-factual) descriptions, while not being the
'a priori forms of all possible worlds.' Merleau-Ponty's
philosophy founds the possible on the real, in that it
interprets Husserl's essences as 'bringing back the living
relationships of experience, in the way a net fetches up
quivering fish and algae from the bottom of the sea.'37

Now we can see how this difference between Sartre's and
Merleau-Ponty's reading of Husserl's reduction is going to
lead to different views of the relation, in phenomenological
psychology, between the role of phenomenological
clarification of concepts and that of empirical facts. For
considering that Merleau-Ponty's first word of clarification
of the essence 'world' is this: 'that facticity of the world
is what makes the worldliness of the world,
(Weltlichkeit der Welt) what makes the world world,'38 the
proposal to approach facts through their essential structures
ceases to be a matter of straightforward a priori explanation
(as for Sartre), and becomes the business of 'explaining'
facts through essential concepts ('man,' 'world' etc.),
which are themselves ultimately facticiel. Whether this
kind of explanation is circular or benefits from the
homogeneity it assumes between the two levels is a question
to which I shall return.

Underlying this difference, however, Sartre and Merleau-
Ponty are agreed that phenomenological psychology is an
ontological or existential psychology, in that it understands
psychological essences (whatever their relation to facts) as

ways of being-in-the-world. But how are these essences to be uncovered? Consider the essence 'perception' in relation to seeing, say, a tree. The tree I see will include many properties that are irrelevant to its status as an example of the essence 'perceived or spatio-temporal object.' Extracting the essential features of such an object requires that we vary the data imaginatively, a procedure which in recent years has attracted a great deal of controversy into which we cannot enter here. According to Husserl, however, the method of 'free imaginative variation' enables a direct intuition of the essences of experience, a 'seeing through' (Wesenschau), the contingent husk of exemplary experiences into the invariant and essential features which a concrete experience (Erlebnis) must possess in order to be the kind of experience that it is. This method has been succinctly summarised by Merleau-Ponty as follows:

> In order to grasp an essence we consider a concrete experience, and then make it change in our thought, trying to imagine it as effectively modified in all respects. That which remains invariable through these changes is the essence of the phenomenon in question.
>
> For example, if we are trying to form the idea of, or to understand the essence of, a spatial figure, such as this lamp, we must first perceive it. Then we will imagine all the aspects contained in this figure as changed. That which cannot be changed without the object itself disappearing is the essence. Suppose that we want to form the ideal of a melody. We recall a tune which we have learnt to sing, and we suppose that all the notes and all the relations between the notes are changed. That which remains invariable and without which there would no longer be a melody is the essence we are seeing.39

This differs from the inductive establishment of laws in that (a) insight into essence may, theoretically at least, be achieved on the basis of a single example; (b) eidetic insights are (for Husserl) incorrigible, whereas a valid inductive hypothesis must be falsifiable; (c) the examples on which eidetic variation operates are imaginary , save the first, which must, of course, have really occurred in order to be varied imaginatively. The cases which support inducton, on the other hand, are valued precisely for their reality.

This last distinguishing feature perhaps calls for further comment. Extracting an essence involves starting with a real or examplary experience. But according to Husserl and Sartre (though not to Merleau-Ponty), the descriptive content of the essence finally extracted must in no way affirm or presuppose that the exemplary experience actually existed. For the criterion for knowing that one is no longer thinking in terms of contingent empirical features is that the putative essence should survive even if it is imagined that supporting experience did not occur. Thus Sartre, explaining Husserl, tells us:

> It matters little whether the individual fact which serves as a basis for the essence is real or imaginary. Even if the 'exemplary' datum had been a pure fiction, the very fact that it has been able to be imagined means that it realises in itself the essence sought after, for the essence is the very condition of its possibility.40

It would be incoherent for the positivistic psychologist to claim that it is possible to get an investigation off the ground without assuming some non-empirical notion of essence: the very classifying of facts as facts about, say, emotion, presupposes a tacit and unclarified notion of the essence of emotion:

> If we did not implicitly have recourse to the essence of emotion it would be impossible to pick out from the mass of psychic facts the particular groups of facts about emotion. Therefore, since one has always had implicit recourse to the essence of emotion, phenomenology will prescribe that explicit reference be made to it and that the content of that essence be fixed once and for all in concepts.41

Thus, considering that positivistic psychologists cannot escape the hermeneutic circle, they may as well come clean and replace their habitual concepts taken over from common sense, verbal usage etc. with the eidetically clarified and correct ones made available by phenomenology. Sartre is anxious to dispel the impression that in arguing the case for an eidetic psychology he is claiming that this kind of psychology could ever be a substitute for empirical investigations. His point is rather that it is the ontologically and methodologically prior inquiry necessary to understanding and interpreting empirical data. Stating his position through his presentation of Husserl's ideas on the subject, Sartre says:

> Husserl, who has often been wrongly reproached with a hostility of principle against that discipline

(psychology), plans on the contrary, to do it a
service: he does not deny that there is a psychology
of experience;42 but he believes that in order to
meet the most urgent needs the psychologist must
above all constitute an eidetic psychology.43

This eidetic psychology would be an investigation of the
purely transcendental essences of types of psychological
experience: emotion as such, for example, as distinct from
its factually determine species - anger, jealousy, love,
hate, etc.

There will, for example, be a phenomenology of
emotion which, after having placed the world in
brackets, will study emotion as a pure transcendental
phenomenon, and this it will do not by concerning
itself with particular emotions but by trying to
reach and elucidate the transcendental essence of
emotion as an organised type of consciousness.44

This is the method which Sartre adopts in the first part of
the Psychology of Imagination where eidetic reflection is
used to isolate 'the four essential characteristics of the
image'45 while the remaining parts of the book, unlike the
first part which is titled 'The Certain,' are given over to
factual questions concerning which certainty is not possible
and which, according to Sartre, can never cause us to revise
the findings of eidetic insight presented in the first part.

Sartre concedes that the method of eidetic reflection, or
free imaginative variation, does not fully explain the
essence-species relation. Only the essence, he thinks, is
fully necessary, the species being partly determined by
factual elements not necessitated by it. He reads Husserl as
saying that the essence is a prior 'condition of possibility'
of the species, a static Kantian ground which is neither a
formal nor metaphysical necessity. This drives a wedge
between phenomenological and experimental or fact based
psychology. For if we assume that the essence is a non-
productive form or condition, then no amount of contemplating
the essence of emotion will ever tell us that emotion must
realise itself in the particular species known to us and not
in others unknown to us. The essence of emotion, as distinct
from its species, may be fully explicable as one way in which
being-in-the-world realises itself in an infinite mode, if
emotion can be shown to be an essential possibility of being-
in-the-world.   (This will seem plausible if we accept
Sartre's identification of being-in-the-world with
affectivity or the 'passion' of the for-itself to achieve
ens causa sui).   But the psychological species are not in

turn fully explicable in terms of Sartrean essences, owing to the element of facticity inherent in the species. The numerous essences or ways of being-in-the-world add nothing to being-in-the-world, which each fully exemplifies. But psychological species do add something to the essences which they in turn fully exemplify, namely the contingent features which particularise them as species. To understand these we must therefore have recourse to a fact-based psychology.

But we perceive immediately the limits of such description: the psychological theory of the emotions presupposes a prior description of affectivity, in as much as the latter constitutes the being of human reality; that is to say, in as much as it is constitutive of our human reality to be affective human reality.

In such a description, instead of departing from a study of the emotions or of the inclinations which would, both of them, point towards a not-yet-elucidated human reality as the ultimate term of all investigations - a term which, moreover, would probably remain an ideal limit for anyone who begins with the empirical - the description of affectivity would depart from human reality, as described and fixated by a priori intuition. The various disciplines of phenomenological psychology are regressive, although the limit of their regression remains for them, purely ideal; the disciplines of pure phenomenology, on the other hand, are progressive. One might wonder why, if this is so, we should continue to make simultaneous use of two disciplines. It might seem as if pure phenomenology is enough. But although pure phenomenology may be able to prove that emotion is an essential realisation of human reality, in as much as the latter is affectivity, it will be impossible for it to show that human reality must manifest itself necessarily in these-particular emotions. That there is this emotion and that emotion and only these emotions is no doubt evidence of the facticity of human existence. It is this facticity which necessitates guided recourse to the empirical; and it is this facticity which will probably prevent the psychological regression and the phenomenological progression from achieving complete convergence.46

Pure phenomenology is deductive in the sense that it moves forward from an a priori understanding, such as Sartre claims to have reached in Being and Nothingness, of the ontological essences, or 'structures' of being-in-the-world, through an understanding of psychological essences as realisations of necessary possibilities of being-in-the-world, towards the ideal limit of understanding concrete psychological reality as specifications of these essences. Phenomenological psychology is reductive, or 'regressive', in that it moves backwards from the less to the more fundamental, from the partial facticity of the species to their respective essences, and from there towards the ideal limit of explanation where essences would be grasped as essential possibilities of being-in-the-world. The two movements converge from opposite directions, but are unlikely to meet, according to Sartre, owing to the alleged inaccessibility of the ontological domain to phenomenological psychology on the one side, and to the obstacle of facticity encountered by the pure phenomenological deduction or 'progression' on the other. For that reason the two approaches cannot stand as substitutable disciplines covering exactly the same ground and confirming each other at every point. The one is needed to handle the 'blind spots' of the other.

This facticity affects the whole of the empirical world, of course, not just specific emotions. It is a necessity of the intentional essence of consciousness that there should be some contingent world. But that this particular world in which we live exists is a contingent specification of the necessity that there be some contingent world:

> After the phenomenological reduction we find ourselves face to face with transcendental consciousness, which lays itself open to our reflective descriptions. We can, in this way, fixate in concepts the results of our eidetic intuition 'consciousness.' Now the phenomenological descriptions can discover that, for example, the very structure of transcendental consciousness implies that consciousness must be constitutive of some world. But it is clear that they will not teach us that consciousness must be constitutive of this particular world; that is, precisely the one in which we live, with its animals, its men and the history of its men. We are confronted here with a primary and irreducible fact which gives itself as a contingent and irrational specification of the noematic essence 'world.'47

This stress on facticity is one respect in which Sartre departs from the Husserlian orthodoxy which he otherwise follows closely. The facticity of fact, its irreducibility to the necessity of essence, was something which Husserl consistently refused to allow, maintaining that fact is ultimately transparent, a constituted reality which it is the task of reason to lay bare. All the rationality of fact lies, ultimately in the a priori. '"Fact," with its "irrationality," is itself a structural concept within the system of the concrete a priori'.48 We shall see that this notion of a concrete a priori is close to Merleau-Ponty's conception of the relationship between fact and essence. It undermines Sartre's conception of facticity as irreducibly irrational and so opposed to the transparent realm of essence.

However, given the prestige of the scientific approach in modern psychology, it is not surprising that Sartre is much more concerned to awaken the psychologist to the importance and unavoidability of the phenomenological dimension of psychological concepts than with emphasising the limits of the phenomenological approach. To show that psychological concepts can and ought to be investigated phenomenologically - as infinite modes of being-in-the-world, 49 - is one (perhaps the more important) of Sartre's two purposes in Sketch for a Theory of the Emotions, his other major purpose being to establish that the essence of emotion is 'magical transformation of the world.' He presents his book as an experiment in method which undertakes to 'see, on the basis of a precise and concrete case - that of the emotions - whether psychology may be able to derive a method, and some lessons, from phenomenology.'50 The purpose of the experiment will be to use the emotions as a test-case for establishing the validity or otherwise of approaching psychological phenomena in general from the point of view of 'the idea of meaning.'51 In other words, the hypothesis to be tested through the study of emotions is that these phenomena - the psychic facts and purposive behaviours of people in the real world - are best understood as modes of being-in-the-world, which in Sartre's case means 'ways of relating intentionally to any real world.' If the supposition of the meaningfullness of psychological phenomena validates itself by producing a satisfactory theory, then the methods of eidetic reflection or free imaginative variation may be applied to other topics in psychology without further justificatory ado. Summarising the (positive) results of his experiment in the conclusion of Sketch for a Theory of the Emotions, Sartre says:

We have gradually ascended from the psychological considerations of James to the idea of meaning. A phenomenological psychology which would be sure of itself and which would have previously cleared the ground, would begin by straightaway fixating in an eidetic reflection the essence of the psychological reality which it is investigating. This is what we have attempted to do for the mental image, in a work which will appear shortly.52

The justifactory ado, which has restrained Sartre from straightaway establishing the essence of emotion in an eidetic reflection, has been his persuasive strategy of deriving the essence of emotion from the corpus of facts already supplied by the experimental tradition from James onwards. We can imagine the experimentalist's reaction on being presented with a theory produced by pure eidetic insight. 'Well, your purely a priori account may satisfy you but it certainly doesn't satisfy me, for you have given me no reason to suppose that your "essence" bears any relation whatsoever to the experimental data.' The only way the posivistic psychologist is likely to be converted to the benefits of eidetic reflection will be by a method which, taking account of the facts, succeeds in showing that the point of view of meaning alone enables us to articulate them into a coherent theory. The only method which will carry conviction will be one which approaches the facts in such a way as to let them speak in favour of a 'meaningful' (ontological) understanding of emotion. If such psychologists are to be converted, it will be by a method which scores on their home ground. It will be up to Sartre to show, without using eidetic reflection, that the transcendental essence of emotion may be read into the facts already supplied by the empirical tradition. The positivistic psychologists are more likely to be prevailed upon to search for essences in their transcendental consciousness, or to take them over pre-elucidated from the phenomenologist, if they can first be given a glimpse of them profiled in familiar facts. But does this attempt to convince the psychologist by taking account of facts not contradict Sartre's own thesis that facts tell us nothing about essences?

It does indeed, but let us reserve this point till later and note for the moment that reading the essence of emotion into facts requires that these be treated 'as meanings and not as pure facts.'53 Pure facts are abstractions produced by considering the structures of an experience in artificial isolation from one another. We would be producing pure facts if, for example, we were to analyse emotion into two separate orders of fact, one psychical and the other corporeal, a procedure which offends against the concrete character of lived experience. Emotion exists only as the meaning-complex as which it baptises itself in occurring, and that meaning involves the concretion of its structures: 'emotion does not exist as a corporeal phenomenon, since a body cannot be moved without conferring a meaning on its manifestations.'54 Nor, we may add, does it exist as a psychic phenomenon, because the psychic structure is lived out as, is real as, the meaning of the corporeal disturbances. It is my stomach that is afraid. We cannot legitimately abstract the psychic factor from the corporeal factor and then go on to describe each as if it still had something to do with emotion. This kind of factorial analysis does not correct or clarify our immediate understanding of psychological life. It simply obliterates the phenomenon.

To treat facts as meanings, on the other hand, will be to travel in the direction opposite to that in which abstraction moves. The noticing of facts is already and inevitably an act of abstraction, but having noticed them, our theorising about them ought to consist in reading them as perspectivistic appearances of the essence to be discovered and not as the basis of some unliveable hypothetical construction. Otherwise the facts remain dust, Humpty Dumpty will not be able to be put together again. But this method of reading essences into facts would seem to encounter a difficulty arising from the incomplete character of phenomenologcial ontology: for if the essence in which the facts have their real unity is to be understood as a way of being-in-the-world it would seem to follow that an understanding of these 'ways' presupposes a prior understanding of the ontological structures of being-in-the-world. Yet Sartre affirms that the notion of being-in-the-world is not yet clear: 'phenomenology,' he says, 'is scarcely born, and all these notions (associated with being-in-the-world) are still very far from having been definitively clarified.'55 So there would seem to be a problem about how facts can be interpreted as meaningful, given that philosphy is not yet clear about the nature of what they ultimately mean. Sartre approaches this problem by asking whether the use by psychology of a method aimed at establishing essential meaning, whether by eidetic reflection or by the reading of essences into facts, must 'wait until phenomenology has arrived at maturity.'56

He answers his question as follows:

> We do not think so. But although it (psychology) has no need to await the definitive constitution of an anthropology, it must not lose sight of the fact that such an anthropology is possible and that, should it one day be realised, all the psychological disciplines would have to draw their foundation from

it. For the present, it (psychology) must not so
much aim at gathering facts as at questioning
phenomena, that is to say, precisely psychic events,
but in so far as they are meanings and not in so far
as they are pure facts.57

The viability of treating individual facts as meaningful
(ontologically significant) in the absence of a clear
understanding of the human totality of meaning which they
signify is Sartre's major methodological premise in
Sketch for a Theory of the Emotions, his major factual
premise being that facts actually do have ontological import.
To justify his methodological premise Sartre puts up the
following argument:

If emotion can be shown to involve a total transformation
of one way of being-in-the-world into another, then despite
the obscurity attaching to this notion we shall still be able
to conclude that emotion is an event involving a sea-change
in the totality of our relations with the world. The
transformation can be grasped functionally, independently of
a complete understanding of what transforms itself.
Explaining this 'meaningful fact' method of doing psychology,
Sartre says:

(Psychology), too, will thus present itself as an
eidetic science. Only, it will not aim, through the
psychic phenomenon, at the ultimately signified as
such; that is, at the totality of man. It does not
dispose of sufficient means to attempt this study.
What will interest it, however, and this alone, is
the phenomenon in as much as it signifies (i.e. not
the phenomenon from the point of view of the ultimate
object of signification).58

The requisite for this 'meaningful' theory is duly met
when, after having reviewed 'as meanings' the facts about
emotion, Sartre arrives at the conclusion that emotion is a
magical transformation of the world.59 This enables him
proudly to announce that the study of the emotions has
validated the idea of meaning on which it was based:

We said in our introduction that the meaning of a
conscious fact ultimately comes down to this, that it
always indicates the total human reality which
makes itself moved, attentive, perceiving, willing
etc. The study of the emotions has, indeed, verified
this principle: an emotion refers to what it
signifies. And what it signifies is indeed the
totality of the relations of human-reality with the

world. The transition to emotion is a global modification of being-in-the-world, according to the very peculiar laws of magic.60

Or again:

Emotion is not an accident, it is a mode of the existence of consciousness, one of the ways it understands (in Heidegger's sense of Verstehen) its being-in-the-world.61

Because psychological attitudes are 'phenomena' of being-in-the-world, which they fully exemplify, it follows that the study of psychology can open up inroads into the study of ontology, even though the ontological domain remains an ideal limit for the viewpoint of psychology. Having established the essence of emotion:

The phenomenologist will question emotion about consciousness or about man, and he will ask it (emotion) not only what it is but also what it has to teach us about a being one of whose characteristics is, precisely, that it is capable of emotion. And conversely, he will question consciousness, human-reality, as to the nature of emotion: what must consciousness be such that emotion is possible, perhaps even necessary?62

Or again, in connection with imagination, 'what must consciousness be, such that it has the power to imagine?'63

That emotion and imagination are possible is demonstrated by their reality. But the important question is whether they are contingent or essential possibilities of consciousness: that is to say, do acts of emotion and imagination become possible only once specific empirical conditions additional to the transcendental conditions of possibility of any consciousness are given; or are the conditions of possibility of these acts the same as for any consciousness? Or to ask the question in the phenomenological idiom: could consciousness survive being imagined as not including the power to 'move itself' or make itself imagine? If the answer to this question is negative (and Sartre has given an explicit negative answer for the imagination), 64 then psychological essences are not related accidentally to being-in-the-world, and a perfect understanding of the psychological will coincide with a perfect understanding of the ontological.

One reason why Sartre's psychological study of the emotions is only a 'sketch' is that it precedes the working out of the ontological setting 65 in which a complete theory would have to be grounded:

It is not our intention to attempt a phenomenological study of emotion. Such a study, were it to be adumbrated, would have a bearing on affectivity as an existential mode of human reality.66

The positivistic psychologist might question whether introspective facts are as significant as public facts, or whether the two are complementary, or whether introspective facts ought to be got rid of all together. But that psychology should begin with facts is tacitly and universally agreed to be an inviolable principle and the basis of psychology's claim to scientific status.67 In conformity with this principle, the positivistic psychologists refuse to define human being in advance of investigation. They do not even need a working definition in order to get their investigation off the ground, for they know a human being when they see one, even though they do not know what makes him or her specifically human. The positivists' corpus of information is 'just data,' within which they have neither the desire nor the means to discriminate what is essentially human from characteristics which not all humans share or which are shared by other creatures. If pressed they will tell you that the question of human essence can be answered only at the end of the inquiry. However, as long as no distinction is made between essential and non-essential characteristics, such psychologists will never be able to know whether their final concept of humanity is too wide or too narrow.68 On this point Sartre and Merleau-Ponty agree, the latter having stated it more explicit:

One may say that 'psychology will, of course, be able to define man, but only at the end of its inquiry.' Still, this is not certain, since the investigation will be concerned with facts. Will it reveal certain characteristics that belong only to the individual that one ordinarily calls man, or will it show that these characteristics do not belong to all human individuals, or that they also belong to other individuals not usually called human. Such a factual investigation will never be able to decide whether the collection of features obtained in this way deserves to constitute a definition. Are they essential or accidental? Sooner or later the investigation of essence with which eidetic psychology is concerned should have to be

190

But the point of agreement here covers over a divergence which makes a crucial difference to our understanding of eidetic psychology. Merleau-Ponty is saying, not that essences precede facts ontologically, but only that the method of eidetic reflection must be brought to bear on factual investigations in order to sift out essential from accidental facts. But the only reason why the essence is capable of grounding this discrimination is because it holds the   essential facts together. This is the concrete a priori to which we saw Husserl allude. Sartre, on the other hand, maintains both that positivistic psychology eschews essences rendering it unable to sort out essential from accidental facts, and that all facts are accidental! So the concept of a human being that any such psychology would ultimately be able to offer would be an artificial construction out of brute bits - 'a unifying hypothesis ... a conjecture aiming at establishing connections between disparate data, and the probability of which would derive from its success (in predicting).'70

But why does Sartre think that all experiential facts are accidental to essence? And how does this, his official view, square with his talk and method of using facts as meanings (i.e. as essential)? The answer to the first question comes in the shape of a caricatural critique of the positivist rejoicing in brute facts:

> If we ask ourselves what a fact is, we shall see that it is defined by this, that it must be encountered in the course of the investigation and that it always presents itself as an unexpected enrichment and as a novelty in relation to previous facts.71

If that is what fact is, it follows that to look for them is to have eyes only for bits:

> To expect the fact is, by definition, to expect what is isolated; it is to prefer, out of sheer positivism, the accidental to the essential, the contingent to the necessary, disorder to order.72

Thus, because facts are bits, and because these are what the positivists are on the lookout for, it follows that this viewpoint precludes the possibility of human reality appearing as anything other than a collection of disparate data to be put together at the abstract level of hypothesis-formation; this point of view blinds the positivist to the possibility that experience might possess concrete rationality, a unity of being and meaning:

> We have shown that if human-reality appears to the psychologist as a collection of heteroclite data, this is because the psychologist has chosen to place himself at a point of view from which that reality must appear to him as such. This does not necessarily imply that human reality is anything other than a collection. What we have proved is that it cannot appear otherwise to the psychologist.73

It will be noted that this complaint does not depend on the assumption that human reality is a synthetic totality. Sartre's point is that '(the psychologist) must resign himself to missing human-reality, <u>if this human-reality exits</u>.'74 Whence the need for the experiment to validate the assumption.

A further prong of Sartre's critique of the experimental method impugns its poor success, even as measured against its own concept of explanation. 'Psychology, for all that it claims to be a science, is unable to supply anything more than a collection of heteroclite facts, most of which are completely unconnected.'75 This disarray is not fortuitous, but results from the artificiality of the psychologist's bits. Sartre asks somewhat facetiously what connections have been established between inferiority complexes and the stroboscopic illusion, which is a tall order to place with a young science.

A third prong of Sartre's attack points to the contradiction under which the positivistic psychologist labours in imagining that his or her factual method is capable of ultimately producing a concept of human essence:

> The psychologist does not, in fact, realise that it is just as impossible to reach the essential by amassing facts as it is to arrive at unity by indefinitely placing figures to the right of 0.99 ... This is unobjectionable if their only aim is to accumulate detailed knowledge; only, it would be hard to see the point of these collectors' items. But if they are motivated, despite their modesty, by the commendable hope of being able one day to achieve an anthropological synthesis on the basis of their monographs, then they are totally in contradiction with themselves.76

The numerical analogy is not to be taken as alluding to the idea that the positivistic psychologist will never know when they are in possession of 'all the facts.' To object to the scientific method in psychology on that score would be quite wrongheaded, since the finitude of information is a condition of all empirical inquiry and does not constitute a reason for not using the scientific method in areas where it is otherwise appropriate. We are, rather, to understand the infinite progress as showing up the psychologists' allegedly contradictory premise, namely their category mistake of supposing that the necessity of essence and significant meaning can be 'summed up' out of contingent facts. The accidental can never add up to the essential, because:

> there is incommensurability between essences and facts, and anyone who begins his investigation with the facts will never be able to recover essences. If I look for the psychic facts which are at the basis of the arithmetical attitude of the man who counts and calculates, I shall never be able to reconstruct the arithmetical essences of 'unity' of 'number' and of operations.77

This echoes Husserl's celebrated attack on psychologism in logic and the philosophy of mathematics: the necessary character of the meaning of logical and mathematical statements ceases to be intelligible if we try to account for that necessity in terms of the empirical psychological laws governing the processes of reasoning or counting. For it is not absurd to imagine that these laws could be false, whereas the laws of logic and mathematics are true by a priori necessity.

Now Sartre is simply wrong in claiming that scientific facts are 'bits,' encountered as we might find a penny on the street. The instruments of scientific investigation are admittedly selective, and to that extent designed to isolate only certain abstract or qualifying aspects of a process. But these provisionally abstract aspects are doomed to acquire reality the moment they arise, because they originate from within the corpus of knowledge which anticipated them as missing links in a chain of meaning. In arising as coherent they arise as real (what real thing is not to the left or right of something?) and in arising as coherently real they situate themselves withing the horizon of a necessarily finite corpus.

We find, in fact, two incompatible themes in Sartres' thinking on phenomenological psychology, the one implying a fundamental homogeneity between facts and essences, that legitimates his reading of the essence of the emotions into empirical data, the other asserting, with an emphasis that justifies us taking it as his 'official' position, a radical dichotomy between the two. The following pronouncement belongs to the latter, official theme:

> We must attempt to constitute an eidetic of the image, that is, to fixate and describe the essence of that psychological structure such as it appears to reflective intuition. Then, when the set of conditions which a psychological state must necessarily realise in order to be an image has been determined, then only must we pass from the certain to the probable and ask of experience what it has to teach us about such images as actually occur in a contemporary human consciousness.78

Granting that Husserl's incommensurability-thesis is true of strictly logical essences, it still remains an unargued assumption of Sartre's official position that it is true also of the sensory essences of 'lived' experience that we have of the real world. This is basically the assumption that all essences are 'exact,' and we shall see that this is not a view for which one can claim authority in Husserl. Moreover, the method employed in Sketch for a Theory of the Emotions certainly does not square with the incommensurability-thesis, as Merleau-Ponty has noted:

> As a matter of fact, Sartre does not follow the rule which he lays down here. Although he presents empirical psychology as the servant of phenomenology, he says, nonetheless, that he is embarking on the study of the emotions 'without waiting for the phenomenology of the emotions to be completed.' This means that basically experimental studies, like those of Janet, Lewin and the psychoanalysts must already reveal to us in a confused way the essence of that with which they are concerned. However it may be with his formulations, Sartre actually understands the relation of phenomenology and psychology in the way I have just now tried to explain. (i.e., as 'reciprocal envelopment').79

According to Sartre's official position essences are laid down once and for all by eidetic reflection and no amount of experimental findings can prevail against them or modify them. Empirical psychology will be concerned with relations of fact, with causal or genetic conditions, generally with everything not imaginable from the viewpoint of essence. But since none of this, according to Sartre, impinges on matters of essential meaning, it would seem that the role of inductive psychology is reduced to a filling in of detail and a mere noting of empirical curiosities. One wonders how Sartre can 'not wish to deny the essential role which experimentation and induction play in all their forms in the constitution of psychology,'80 considering in his view that these methods bear on what is precisely <u>not</u> essential. But if Merleau-Ponty is right, the species which Sartre relegates to the domain of the inessential, 'the images which are actually present in a contemporary consciousness,' are composed of factual relations that are homogeneous with essential relations. Is the angriness of anger not the concrete <u>a priori</u> of emotion itself? If it is, the fact-essence dichotomy breaks down.

Merleau-Ponty has argued that Sartre's dichotomy, and the interpretation of Husserl which seems to support it, arises from, on the one side, a 'scholastic' misunderstanding of essences unfaithful to Husserl's meaning, and, on the other side, a positivistic understanding of induction which misrepresents the way it is actually practised by all non-trivial science. Once these misunderstandings have been corrected, he claims, the two psychological strategies will be seen to be mutually complementary approaches to the same essential realities.

As regards, first, the establishing of essences, Merleau-Ponty's argument runs as follows: While it is true, on the one hand, that eidetic reflection is an 'intellectual taking over,' a process of rationalisation which ends in thought possessing and enveloping its object:

> it is also true that essential insight always understands the concrete perception of experience as something here and now which precedes and therefore envelops it. In Husserl's words, the essence presupposes 'an important part of the intuition bearing on the individual.' It presupposes that an <u>individual</u> has appeared and that one has had a view of it. It also presupposes the <u>Sichtlichkeit</u>, the visibility of this individual. Or, to put it another way, it is no insight into essence if one's reflection cannot work out a 'sense of example' to illustrate one's insight.81

Thus, although essential insight 'envelops' the concrete experience, in the sense of depicting it as only one of a number of coordinate possibilities allowed by its scope, there is also a sense in which the essence is reciprocally enveloped by the concrete experience. For 'insight into essence (involves) a recognition that it comes after something else, from which it starts (and that this

dependence) is included in its very meaning.'82 In other
words, it is part of the meaning of any essence to point back
to, and be partly obscured by, the real experience from which
it derived. Eidetic insight takes place within the
encompassing horizon of the factually real. The relation
between essence and fact is thus a structural 'double
envelopment.'83 The essence remains 'contaminated with the
facts,'84 which it envelops, for 'even when one thinks in
terms of the pure essence one still thinks in terms of the
visible, of the fact.'85

It might help at this point if we distinguish three
possible views of the essence-fact relationship. First: we
might conceive of the essence such that it prescribes
a priori the meaning-conditions of any corresponding real
psychological events. This strongly Platonic conception of
essence, which despite Merleau-Ponty's interpretation it is
hard not to attribute to at least the earlier Husserl, does
not require that an essence should have any realisations at
all. It is exemplified by Husserl's statement that:

> If we could contemplate clearly the exact laws of
> psychic processes, they would show themselves to be
> equally eternal and invariant, like the fundamental
> laws of the theoretical natural sciences. Therefore,
> they would be valid even if there were no psychic
> processes. 86

The essence here merely stipulates that if there happens to
be any realisations, then they will conform to the essential
conditions. Second, we may think of the essence as
requiring some realisation, but not the specific realisation
that it has. This we have seen, is Sartre's conception.
Thirdly, we have Merleau-Ponty's view of essence as a
concrete universal in which the species is identical with the
particular way in which the essence holds the facts together.
On this account, insight into essence is an equivalent vision
of the same factual rationality as is investigated by
inductive methods. This is a more specific existential
commitment than with Sartre: Merleau-Ponty's essences are
clouded with facticity, and his facticity is impregnated with
rationality, a view which collapses the hallowed distinctions
between the necessary and the contingent, the certain and the
probable, the possible and the real.87

Merleau-Ponty is as convinced as Sartre that experiences
are in essence particular ways of being-in-the-world.88 But
whereas for Sartre the concrete rationality of being-in-the-
world impregnates the essence but does not reach up as far as
the level of factual relations (the species), Merleau-Ponty

maintains that even this level of class-of-fact is not wholly contingent, in that it embodies a rationality that is homogeneous with that of the essence, thus ultimately with that of being-in-the-world.

This interpenetration of fact and essence supplies the ontological possibility of eidetic and experimental psychology being informative the one of the other. The two psychologies can be complementary, providing that the fundamental homogeneity of their foci is not obscured by a scholastic approach to essence and a positivistic conception of induction.

The scholasticism in question is illustrated by Sartre's a priori procedure in The Psychology of Imagination, as well as by certain formulae of Max Scheler, who says that the intuition of essences is final and indubitable for the reason that if empirical investigation should show me an image which does not conform to what I have determined to be its essence, then, of course, this is not an image. We can see from this point of view that phenomenology can be as scholastic in suppressing fact in deference to essence as linguistic philosophy was in fastening the meaningful use of language to the Procrustean bed of its ordinary use.

This scholastic corruption of phenomenology is responsible for driving a wedge between the two psychologies from the philosophical side. The same artificial dichotomy is aided and abetted on the empirical side by what, according to Merleau-Ponty, is a corrupt conception of induction. Merleau-Ponty makes an interesting connection between Husserl's critique of the empiricist (essentially Millian) conception of induction and his own attempt to show that the underlying thrust of Husserl's thinking on psychology was towards an ontological and methodological foundation of the homogeneity between eidetic and inductive psychology.[89] The actual practice of induction, he claims, does not correspond to what the positivists make of it, namely the following of the essentially eliminative methods of Mill. 'The method actually used by physicists is not the chimerical induction of Mill, which is never practised in the sciences.'[90] Contrary to what Bacon and Mill supposed, the scientist does not arrive at laws by formalising common given characteristics which recur among the otherwise heterogeneous groups of antecedents to the same phenomenon. Genuine induction is not the formalisation of the given. It is the imaginative construction of a concept suggested by the facts, the creation of what Merleau-Ponty, following Husserl, refers to as 'idealising fictions cum fundamento in re.'[91] What gives the value of probability to such fictions and shows them to be grounded in the facts is not the number of confirming instances (which presupposes the recurrence of common characteristics) but 'the intrinsic clarity which these ideas shed on the phenomena.'92 This is why, as has often been pointed out, a single experiment may suffice to establish a law.

Merleau-Ponty appeals to the example of Galileo, who did not discover the law of falling bodies by collecting arbitrary observations of real bodies, but by defining hypothetically the 'pure' concept of uniform acceleration:

Let us return to the example of Galileo and the fundamental induction which, we may say created modern physics. How does Galileo proceed? Does he consider different examples of falling bodies and then, by a method of agreement, following the theory of John Stuart Mill, abstract what is common to these examples? As a matter of fact, he proceeds in a totally different manner. The conception of the fall of bodies which guides his experiments is not found in the facts. He forms it actively; he constructs it. He freely conceives the pure case of a freely falling body, of which there is no given example in human experience. Then, having constructed this idea, he verifies it by showing how the confused empirical facts, which never represent the free fall in its pure state, can be understood through the introduction of additional conditions (friction, resistance, etc.) which explains the difference between the facts and the pure concept. On the basis of a free fall, therefore, one constructs the fall of a body on an inclined plane.93

Merleau-Ponty finds an interesting example of this creative kind of induction in his own field of psychology. The widely-used notion of behavioural 'lability' or instability refers to antithetical behaviours. An attitude is called labile both when it is too rigid and when it is not rigid enough, when it remains inflexibly the same under varying circumstances and when it is totally unpredictible. So there is no question of the notion of lability having been arrived at by abstracting a common given behavioural characteristic. We can examine the data until we are blue in the face without finding anything factual held in common. There is, of course, a common element, namely the idea of a behaviour which lacks centering; but this is an imaginative construction on the part of Goldstein, who introduced the concept, not something found among the facts. In both automatic and volatile behaviour we find different manifestations of a wholly external relation between situation and response.94

Now what Merleau-Ponty wants to conclude from his thesis that induction is the imaginative production of explanatory fictions is that, so conceived, it 'is very close to Husserl's Wesenschau,'95 the essential difference being only that the scientist's impure cases are real whereas those of the phenomenologist are imaginary.96 Where the scientist constructs an inductive fiction directly, on the basis of real cases, the phenomenologist uses the method of free imaginative variation. What is common to both these procedures is the imaginative creation of a fiction whose validity is its ability to hold the data together, be they psychic or physical.

From this Merleau-Ponty concludes that 'the Wesenschau is not the exclusive preserve of the phenomenologist,' 97 meaning that the spontaneous act of fictionalisation is central to both procedures; and we can understand Husserl to be alluding to this fact when he says, by way of trying to demystify the Wesenschau, that 'Everyone is constantly seeing ideas or essences, and everyone uses them in operations of thought, in spite of the widespread opposition put forth in the name of points of view in the theory of knowledge.'98 The empiricist theory of induction is one such point of view, according to Husserl and Merleau-Ponty.

It is, then, on the basis of the similarity of the Wesenschau and induction that Merleau-Ponty rests his methodological case for the fundamental homogeneity between the two psychologies, his ontological case being his claim that essences remain 'contaminated with the facts.' Contrary to what Sartre supposes, the pursuit of essences does not require that we 'abandon the methods of inductive introspection and external empirical observation.'99 What Merleau-Ponty claims to have shown against Sartre is that induction, far from being the slavish formalisation of 'pure facts' that Sartre implies it is, departs from 'facts as phenomena' and arrives at concepts which are complementary to the essences of phenomenology.

The difference between Sartre's and Merleau-Ponty's view of essence may be pinpointed with the help of Husserl's distinction 100 between logico-mathematical essences (the forms of inference, numbers, categories) and the generic essences (Gattungswesen) of experience, which unlike the former are dynamic forms. The crucial point here is the intuitively clear difference in type of relationship between, on the one side, the essence 'number' and its particularisation '3', or $p \supset q$ and its value 'dog $\supset$ animal', and, on the other side, the generic essence 'colour' and its species 'red', or 'emotion' and its species 'anger.' The intention or meaning of a logic-mathematical essence subsists apart from its extension, which merely 'fills out' that meaning. Now precisely the same is true of the relation Sartre postulates between the essence 'world' and this world, or between 'emotion' and its species 'anger.' He thereby betrays that he has mistaken the 'loose' relation between Husserl's logico-mathematical essences and their particularisations - a relationship which is characterised by an irrational facticity - for the very different generic relation holding between the essences of experience and their species,' different because the latter relation involves no irreducible facticity. The difference between the two kind of 'bond' may be pointed up in terms of a containment/non-containment distinction: intuitively it is evident that 'colour' lies wholly contained in 'red', or 'emotion' wholly contained in 'anger', but that there is no sense (not even part/whole sense) in which 'number' lies wholly contained in '3', or $p \supset q$ wholly contained in 'dog $\supset$ animal.' Sartre conceives of the essences of experience on the model of static logical forms (called 'Leerformen' by Husserl), whereas in fact these essences are dynamic/or generic forms that engender their extensions in differentiating themselves into concretions of facts. The essence has intention as the production of its extension, as the meaning it engenders in holding facts together to constitute species. This means that red as a 'break' from colour is just as 'essential' as red as a 'tie' to colour, whereby it becomes possible to conceive of psychological essences as the rationality of being-in-this-world, not just of being-in-some-world, as Sartre claims.

Husserl also describes generic essences as 'morphological,' to underscore the characteristic inexactness they suffer owing to their concretion with fact. It follows that there can be no 'geometry of the lived.'101 Merleau-Ponty reminds us of Husserl's warning in Ideas that the psychologist who might dream of establishing an exact eidetic of lived experience would be in a similar predicament to a geometer who might hope to give a rigorous geometrical definition of such terms as 'jagged,' 'notched like a lentil or like a sunshade.'102

It is characteristic of the notorious ability of Husserl's followers to find in his writings charters for their diametrically opposed views that Sartre should be able to quote texts from Husserl in support of a conception of essence which envisages its relation to fact on the model of the relation of geometry to physics, while Merleau-Ponty can refer to the paragraphs of Ideas where Husserl discusses the notion of inexact or morphological essences.103 Sartre quotes the following text in support of his 'official' incommensurability-thesis:

> The great epoch (of Physics) began in modern times, when suddenly and on a grand scale geometry was harnessed to physical method: a geometry which since Antiquity (and particularly in the hands of the Platonists) had been extensively elaborated as a pure eidetic. It is understood at this time that the essence of the material thing is to be res extensa and that, consequently, geometry is the ontological discipline covering an essential moment of this materiality - namely its spatial form. But it is also understood that the universal essence of the thing extends much further. This is shown by the fact that (scientific) development immediately begins to move in the direction of constituting a series of new disciplines destined to be coordinated to geometry and fulfil the same function of rationalising the empirical data.104

Then Sartre says: 'What Husserl writes about Physics may be repeated in connection with Psychology.'105 In other words, we must think of eidetic psychology as standing in the same pure a priori relation to experimental psychology as geometry does to physics. Whether or not he has Husserl's authority for extending this scheme to psychology will depend on which of Husserl's texts we choose to produce in evidence. For the disagreement between Merleau-Ponty and Sartre reflects a refinement in Husserl's own thinking on essences. In Ideas we have a Husserl who carefully distinguishes between the exact essences of logical concepts and the inexact essences of the lived world, so that whether we should demand exactness of an essence or not 'depends entirely on the particular nature of the region.'106 But we also have an earlier, 'logicist' Husserl 107 who declares that the essences of all psychic processes are as exact and ideal as the laws of the theoretical natural sciences. Merleau-Ponty takes note of Husserl's distinction between the two kinds of essences, (introduced in Ideas), whereas Sartre, quoting from the same book, mistakes the logical essence alluded to in the text above as a model for all domains, simply ignoring Husserl's later discussion of morphological essences.

As we saw, Sartre puts his official incommensurability thesis to work in The Psychology of Imagination. The results, however, are not entirely satisfactory, in that one of the major theses established by the initial eidetic investigation is controverted by questions raised in the subsequent empirical section. For example, Sartre claims that it is essential to imaging that it be a conscious excluding of perceiving, and vice versa. That this eidetically established mutual exclusion is untenable is indicated by the fact that in raising the question of illusions in the empirical section of the book 'he necessarily suggests the possibility of a situation anterior to the clear distinction between perception and imagination which was made at the start.'108 The important word here is 'possibility.' In elaborating ingenious accounts of how we come to believe, falsely, that images are sometimes mistaken for perceptions, Sartre presupposes what his eidetic descriptions deny, namely the possibility that confusion is meaningful. So asserting the contrary of his mutual exclusion-thesis is clearly not on a par with denying e.g. the phenomenologically necessary truth that all perceived objects are perspectivistically presented.

It is sometimes objected that the phenomenological method gives no guarantee against the embarrassing possibility that the supposed 'intuition of essences' is really just the unpacking of a verbal meaning and not the genuine encounter with 'what things mean' that it understands itself to be. How can I be sure that I am seeing a real essence and not a concept rooted in language, a mere Wortbegriff?. Two considerations which do not help scotch the suspicion that I might be doing the latter are that 'variation' is also a technique of linguistic analysis, and that the 'transcendental voice' which explicates the essence must be capable of translating its findings into a natural language. How do we know that the transcendental voice was from the start not just an interiorised natural voice? It would be a double irony if this philosophy of meaning, whose raison d'etre is its claim to undercut linguistic meaning and catch the meaning of 'things themselves' 109 were to turn out to be, not just a transcendental scholasticism similar to the potential scholasticism of linguistic analysis, but this very linguistic scholasticism echoing itself in a consciousness which mistakes the echo of natural language for its own transcendental soliloquy. Merleau-Ponty's solution to this problem exploits the homegeneity of essence and fact for which we have seen him argue:

The best way of arguing against this danger would be to admit that, although a knowledge of facts is never sufficient for grasping an essence and although the construction of 'idealising fictions' is always necessary, I can never be sure that my vision of an essence is anything more than a prejudice rooted in language - if it does not enable me to hold together all the facts which are known about it and which may be brought into relation with it. Failing this, it may not be an essence at all, but only a prejudice.110

Thus, the capacity of an essence to hold together the facts (and not just its own essential features) is both the guarantee of its non-verbality and the testimony of its kinship with the inductive concept. The essence is indispensible, if we are to know what inductive concepts in psychology are about, but the more it offers itself as a vision of the unity of the facts as well as of the substance of an experience, the less likely it will be that we are mistaking the conventional necessities of language for the material necessities of experience. This is as far as Merleau-Ponty can take us. To state precisely the difference and similarities between phenomenological essences and inductive concepts would require more finely-honed concepts of the imagination than are at present available, or ever will be, if the imagination continues to be a Cinderella sister of Lady Philosophy.

REFERENCES

Except where otherwise indicated, the translations from the French and German texts are Dr. McLure's

1. Jean-Paul Sartre, Esquisse d'une théorie des émotions, Hermann, Paris, 1939, p.10, (hereinafter referred to as E), translated by B. Frechtman as Outline of a Theory of the Emotions, Philosphical Library, New York, 1948, and by P. Mairet, as Sketch for a Theory of the Emotions, Methuen, London, 1962.

2. E. p.13.

3. Maurice Merleau-Ponty, La Phénomēnologie de la perception, Gallimard, Paris, 1945, p.xi, (hereinafter PP), translated by C. Smith as The Phenomenology of Perception, Routledge & Kegan Paul, London, 1962.

4. Having accepted the truism that we can have no direct experience of a world existing outside experience, Husserl recognises that we are nevertheless able to distinguish, wholly within or on the basis of experience, between the experiencing subject and the experienced object. Experiencer (subject) and experienced(object) are thus said to be 'intentionally' related in experience; the object being said to be 'intentionally' constituted in experience.

5. See PP, p.ix.

6. The term Transcendental (as distinct from transcendent) is used to refer the consciousness which constitutes meanings not given to sensory consciousness.

7. See PP, pp.viii-ix, and Jean-Paul Sartre, L'Imaginaire, Gallimard, Paris, 1940, pp.227-28, (hereinafter IRE) translated by B. Frechtmn, as The Psychology of Imagination, Rider, London, 1949.

8. PP, p.x.

9. Edmund Husserl, Parisian Lectures, translated by P. Koestenbaum, as Paris Lectures, Martinus Nijohff, The Hague, 1967, p.18.

10. E, pp.16-17.

11. Jean-Paul Sartre, La Transcendance de l'ego, (ed.)

Sylvie le Bon, Vrin, Paris, 1972, p.22, (hereinafter TE) translated by F. Williams & R.Kirkpatrick, as The Transcendence of the Ego, Noonday Press, New York, 1957.

12. E. p.16.

13. The term Transcendent (as distinct from transcendental) is used here to indicate the fact that the objects and events which we experience, while presented - as empirically speaking they of course must be - wholly in or through experience, are nevertheless experienced as distinguisable from those experiences in which they are given. It is, for example, therefore possible for me to distinguish the multiplicty of different 'appearances' of the desk in front of me, from the unity of the self-same desk that appears throughout, and this I do wholly on the basis of, or within, experience. The desk is therefore said to transcend those experiences in which it is presented to me: to be transcendent.

14. Edmund Husserl, Ideen zu einer reinen Phänomenologie und phänomenologischen Philosophie. Book I, Martinus Nijohff, The Hague, 1950, p.117 (hereinafter Ideen I), translated by W. R. Boyce-Gibson as Ideas: General Introduction to Pure Phenomenology, Collier, New York, 1962.

15. Gaston Berger, Le cogito dans la philosophie de Husserl, Aubier, Paris, 1941, p.100, translated by K. McLaughlin as The Cogito in Husserl's Philosophy, Northwestern University Press, Evanston Ill., 1972.

16. Maurice Merleau-Ponty, Le Visible et l'invisible, Gallimard, Paris, 1964, p.158, translated by A.Lingis as The Visible and the Invisible, Northwestern University Press, Evanston Ill., 1964. See also Husserl's remarks on the "mystery" of intentionality in Die Idee der Phänomenologie, W. Biemel (ed.) Martinus Nijohff, The Hague, 1958, pp.10-11, translated by W. Alston & G. Nakhnikian as The Idea of Phenomenology, Martinus Nijhoff, The Hague, 1966.

17. That is, ambiguous between the view that the object owes its being to consciousness and Sartre's view (here attributed to Husserl) that 'world' has no meaning except in so far as it is itself given to consciousness as transcending (or existing beyond) it.

18. Jean-Paul Sartre, L'Imagination, étude critique, Presses Universitaires de France, Paris, 1969, (hereinafter IM) translated by F. Williams as Imagination: A Psychological Critique, University of Michigan, Ann Arbor, 1962.

19. Jean-Paul Sartre, 'Une Idée fondamentale de la 'Phénoménologie' de Husserl, l'Intentionnalite,' in Nouvelle Revue Francaise, Paris, 1939, p.130 (hereinafter IF) translated as 'Intentionality: A Fundamental Idea of Husserl's Phenomenology,' in The Journal of the British Society for Phenomenology, vol.1, no.2, May 1970.

20. IM., p.162.

21. The reduction of the world to its essential features means that the notion of the world as somehow existing 'in itself' or without relation to our experience of it is reduced out, as being non-essential to our experience of the world and consequently to our empirical conception of it.

22. IM., p.141.

23. Ibid.

24. The putting of the world in brackets the phenomenological epoché, is a process by which we suspend all presuppositions, even or especially the 'common sense' presupposition that the world, as given to us in experience, somehow transcends (or exists beyond) such experience.

25. E., p.17.

26. The Phenomenological Reduction is the reduction of all that is given to empirical consciousness as experienceable phenomena, (e.g. objects, the world, humanity etc.)to such experienceable phenomena. It thus works hand in hand with the phenomenological epoché (See 24 above) to deliver to us the radically empirical or phenomenological world; i.e. the world as it is given to us, prior to all presuppostions, in immediate experience.

27. E., p.13.

28. TE., p.18. The description to which Sartre here refers is to be found in Ideas I.

29. <u>TE</u>., p.87.

30. <u>TE</u>., p.85.

31. In <u>On Hamanisms</u>, Heidegger protests against Sartre's interpretation of <u>Dasein</u> (or being-in-the-world) as consciousness, claiming that <u>Dasein</u> is recalcitrant to assimilation into Husserlian phenomenology.

32. <u>PP</u>., p.xii.

33. <u>PP</u>., p.iv.

34. That is, already present or pre-established fact.

35. <u>PP</u>., p.ix.

36. <u>PP</u>., p.ix.

37. <u>PP</u>., px. Many commentators have found Merleau-Ponty's reading of Husserl quite perverse. While I agree with them, it will not be necessary to pursue the matter here. The two French philosophers' conceptions of existential-phenomenological psychology may be clarified, contrasted and evaluated independently of the question which is the more faithful reading of Husserl.

38. <u>PP</u>., p.xii.

39. Maurice Merleau-Ponty, 'Phenomenology and the Sciences of Man,' in <u>The Primacy of Perception</u>, J. M. Edie (ed.), Northwestern University Press, Evanston Ill., 1964, p.70, (hereinafter <u>PSM</u>.)

40. <u>IM</u>., pp.140-141.

41. <u>E</u>., p.12.

42. Sartre's term 'expérience', means both experimentation and introspective observation of the <u>factual</u> (as opposed to essential) elements of consciousness. Introspection is focused on psychic facts, eidetic intuition on essential structures. This distinction is essential to understanding why eidetic psychology is not just another brand of introspectionism. See <u>IM</u>., p.140.

43. <u>IM</u>., pp142-43.

44. <u>E</u>., p.13.

45. <u>IRE</u>., pp.13-14.

46. <u>E</u>., p.66.

47. <u>IRE</u> p.p.227-8. Sartre understands metaphysics to be the discipline which investigates the origin of the facticities at which the explanatory power of phenomenology stops short. 'We call "metaphysics", in fact, the study of the individual processes which have given birth to <u>this</u> world, as a concrete and singular totality.' Jean-Paul Sartre, <u>L'Être et le néant</u>, Gallimard, Paris, 1943, p.713 (hereinafter <u>EN</u>) translated by H. Barnes as <u>Being and Nothingness</u>, Philosophical Library, New York, 1956.

48. Edmund Husserl, <u>Cartesianische Meditationen und Pariser Vorträge</u>, (ed.) S. Strasser, Martinus Nijhoff, The Hague, 1973, sect.64, p.181, translated by D. Cairns as <u>Cartesian Meditations</u>, Nijhoff, The Hague, 1960.

49. F. Jeanson has pointed out (with Sartre's prefaced approval) that, as I have already noted, this ontological conception of psychological essence is Sartre's attempt to reconcile Heidegger's notion of being-in-the-world with Husserl's essentialism. See F. Jeanson, <u>Le Problème Moral et la Pensée de Sartre</u>, Editions du Seuil, Paris, 1965, p.p.109-11.

50. <u>E</u>, p,17.

51. <u>E</u>., p.65. Cf. 'We are going to place ourselves on the level of meaning and study emotion as a phenomenon.'<u>E</u>., p.17. Or again, 'The theory of the emotions which we have just sketched was intended to serve as an experiment for the constitution of a phenomenological psychology. <u>E</u>., p.65.

52. The work referred to is <u>The Psychology of Imagination</u>, published one year after <u>Sketch for a Theory of the Emotions</u>.

53. <u>E</u>., p.18

54. <u>Ibid</u>.

55. <u>E</u>., p.17.

56. <u>Ibid</u>.

57. <u>E.</u>, pp.17-18

58. <u>E.</u>, p.18. My parenthesis.

59. <u>E.</u>, p.43 <u>et.seq.</u>

60. <u>E.</u>, p.66.

61. <u>E.</u>, p.62.

62. <u>E.</u>, p.15.

63. <u>IRE.</u>, p.234.

64. <u>IRE.</u>, pp.227-39.

65. Supplied by <u>Being and Nothingness</u>, which was published three years after <u>The Psychology of Imagination.</u>

66. <u>E.</u>, p.17. A further reason for the incompleteness of the theory is that the taxonomy of emotion on the purely <u>psychological</u> level is not fully mapped out in <u>Sketch for a Theory of the Emotions.</u>

67. <u>E.</u>, p.7.

68. <u>E.</u>, p.8.

69. <u>PSM.</u>, p.63.

70. <u>E.</u>, p.9.

71. <u>E.</u>, p.p.7-8 It must be acknowledged that Sartre's analysis here is uncharacteristically primitive. A brute fact is impossible. It <u>would</u> be a completely isolated thing, as Sartre says, but no such thing is 'encountered.' Such a fact would be neither perceptible nor conceiveable. Each fact is located within a methodological perspective which gives it coherence with other facts. They are not picked up randomly. As for their 'surprise-value,' all that means is that a fact is not deduced. It does not mean that it does not arise in coherence with other facts.

72. <u>E.</u>, p.9.

73. <u>E.</u>, p.19.

74. <u>E.</u>, p.16.

75. E., p.9.

76. E., p.10.

77. E., p.12.

78. IM., p.143.

79. PSM., p.74, My parenthesis.

80. IM., p.141.

81. PSM., p.68.

82. Ibid.

83. Ibid.

84. Ibid.

85. Ibid.

86. Edmund Husserl, Logische Untersuchungen I. Martinus Nijhoff, The Hague, p.199, translated in two volumes by J. N. Findley as Logical Investigations, Humanities Press, New York, 1970.

87. Merleau-Ponty owes his reputation as 'the philosopher of ambiguity' to this kind of conflation of traditionally opposed concepts.

88. 'This kind of investigation of essence is at the same time an analysis of existence, in the modern sense of the word, or at least leads towards it, since the essence of an experence is always a certain modality of our relation with the world.' PSM., p.62.

89. Merleau-Ponty admits that he is 'pushing Husserl further than he wished to go himself' and that 'he never expressly recognised the fundamental homogeneity between the two modes of knowledge, the inductive and the essential.' But Merleau-Ponty maintains that Husserl's notion of lived or inexact essence 'contains in germ the consequence I have drawn from it.'

90. PSM., p.69.

91. Ibid.

92. Ibid.

93. Ibid.

94. PSM., p.71.

95. PSM., p.72.

96. PSM., p.70.

97. PSM., p.72.

98. Husserl, quoted by Merleau-Ponty, PSM., p.72.

99. IM., p.138. See Sartre's definiton of eidetic psychology as 'empirical (in that we 'see' essences) but not inductive.' IM., p.143.

100. Ideen I., sect.13.

101. PSM., p.67-68.

102. PSM., p.67.

103. Ideen I., pp.168-70.

104. Ideen I., p.25, quoted in French translation by Jean-Paul Sartre in IM., pp.141-42.

105. IM., p.142.

106. Ideen I., p.168.

107. Husserl's Logical Investigations I, appeared in 1900, his Ideas I, in 1913.

108. PSM., p.74.

109. See Husserl's remarks on the linguistic methods which as Merleau-Ponty reiterates 'pretend to draw a real knowledge of things from the analytic judgements which we can make about the meanings of words.' PSM., p.75

110. PSM., p.75.

8 The new consciousness in the German social sciences

HELMUT LOISKANDL

INTRODUCTION

In the following pages I would like to show how general
problems of ethics in the social sciences are reflected in
some theoretical discussions in Germany today, particularly
in those discussions which integrate the transcultural
experiences of the contemporary social sciences.

It has become fashionable to reduce ethics to pragmatic
principles. The 'Revised Code of Ethics,' published by the
American Sociological Association 1 for instance shows this
quite clearly. This code of ethics is nothing but a
declaration of role expectations without even touching the
question of why exactly 'sociologists should not use their
research or consulting roles as covers for getting
intelligence for any government.' As Dahrendorf points out 2
however, the conceptual distinction between theory and praxis
does not protect theorising itself from ethical constraint.
To avoid getting intelligence for any government is not
enough. Theories can be regarded as 'off limit' as well, 3
or, to put it differently, every analysis has a critical
dimension. And, we could continue, every analysis is
characterised by a specific 'life-world.'4 Thus we could
even understand ethics as goal oriented - but what is the
goal? And how can it be justified?

The western tradition knows two answers. Ethical is, as
for instance Dupre defines it, 5 on the one hand the
acceptance of norms and rules by which a group of people
secures the conformity and the duration of the same group.
It is this conception of the social that lies at the heart of
Kant's categorical imperative; and here we find the
unquestioned functional bias of sociology. The pre-eminence
of the general over the particular is, as we know, the basis
of functional knowledge as well. Thus the 'sample of one' is
the standard joke of the social sciences. On the other hand
however, as Heintel points out, 6 such normative conformity
may offer a false security for individuality is in fact
ineliminable where ethics is concerned.7

The categorical imperative of Kant may thus be complemented
by the Shakespearian 'This above all: To thine own self be
true.' But the social and the individual may equally be in
conflict as Socrates learned to his cost! Caught in the
conflict between individual and social ethics Socrates could
see only one noble path of action: self destruction. The
inner emigration of Kierkegaard, the anarchism of Stirner and
Satori of Zen all provide ways out of the dilemma, but ways
in which society loses. Such ethical individualism, also to
be found somewhat surprisingly in many religions, goes hand
in hand with a distrust of reason, for while experience is
individual, reason is, or claims to be, universal; and this
conflict between the particular and the universal is becoming
increasingly noticeable in the contemporary social sciences
as well. Let us look at the German example, because in that
society there is a resurrection of a powerful tradition,
almost buried in the collapse of Germany in 1945.

SCHOLARS AND THE IRRATIONAL

Germany after 1945 has been characterised by re-education.
On the one hand there was the 'Anglo Saxon' tradition to be
integrated, everything from jazz to Wittgenstein; on the
other hand historical materialism became fashionable again.
Of course Marx came from Treves and Wittgenstein from Vienna,
but both became a symbol of how to cope with German idealism
and irrationalism. This idealism and irrationalism had been
diagnosed as the root of everything wrong with Germany over
the last century or so. After all didn't Hitler like
Wagner's music, and some of Nietzsche's sayings as well?

Thus not only the cultural officers of the Allied forces
but also German speaking opponents of former Nazi Germany
agreed on the importance of being positivistic, materialistic
and rationalistic. The so-called 'Positivismusstreit' in the

social sciences in the sixties pitted Sir Karl Popper against
Adorno and the Frankfurt School, but both groups agreed on
more than they disagreed on. As Habermas puts it:

> A critique of positivism leads us on the other hand
> to the insight that any theory of society has to be
> judged against the standard of research in the
> empirical sciences, and that before the bench of a
> contemporary theory of science.8

The shared enemy is thus identified as unscientific
irrationalism. The polemics of Habermas against fascism and
the New Left are based exactly on this pre-supposition as
Rohrmoser 9 has pointed out. The chance of any dialogue
free of repression rests on pervasive rationality. This is
not to say that the Frankfurt school has not long doubted the
power of such rationality as Horkheimer made abundantly
clear.10 And developments in Germany have now indeed led to
a new consciousness, a consciousness characterised by the
resurrection of the romantic tradition. Films sympathetic to
the German Red Brigades take their titles from Hoelderlin 11,
and the inspirations borrowed from German romantic painter
Caspar David Friedrich makes Strasbourg's theatre a huge
success in France 12 while much of the success of
environmentalist politics in Germany seems to rest upon
similar foundations, and books such as Hans Peter Duerr's
Der Wissenschaftler und das Irrationale 13 are receiving
increasing attention.

Now obviously, one book alone does not constitute a
conversion of the social sciences in their totality.
However, Duerr's view is that university departments in
Germany are still dominated by bland Positivists, and
Marxists concerned with nothing but their success in the
academic bureaucracy. What he attempts is to collect
together a number of opinions that express doubt in the
adequacy of previously emancipatory ideologies, opinions from
chairholders and marginal academics alike. This is the way
he sees the human sciences:

> To state that the self understanding of the human
> sciences has changed over the last dozen of years or
> so does not need excessive courage. The house of
> science, this old marvel, shows signs of getting more
> and more decrepit. And because restoration and
> rehabilitation seems too expensive to the
> inhabitants, makeshift repairs and the odd stump here
> and there help to keep the walls standing up. Ghosts
> and peculiar lights, long before declared absent, can
> be seen moving through the rooms during the night, or

heard to hammer against the cellar doors. Pests grow out of every nook and cranny and the paint is flaking from the walls. Sure, there are tenants who deny this; but even they are getting more and more into the habit of looking under their bed in the evening, and they do not dare any more to enter the cellar.14

So Duerr organises a raiding party to enter the cellar. But it turns out that a typically German battle is to be fought with the help of a foreign legion.

The first problem investigated is that faced by social scientist studying 'unscientific' topics, such as those concerned with the person and the praxis of shamans, magicians, witches, clairvoyants and the like. There is international agreement that the social sciences are faced with the problem of what 'participant observation' means under such circumstances. The observer is exposed to the inexplicable. Does his or her scholarly status allow for the admission of limits to rational explanation? The American Linton and the Englishman Boshier, the Latino Ortiz, and Oppitz who was born in Poland, give examples of these sort of experiences. Professor Hultkrantz of the University of Stockholm neatly expresses his reaction to such experiences in the title of his contributions: they are S'Things the professor does not dare to talk about!' He tells us that he has observations in his note-books which he could not possible publish without endangering his scholarly reputation.

There were things which could not be registered as facts without putting our scholarly system of values in doubt. It was a strange experience to observe the behaviour of my colleagues in such cases: while writing or lecturing about them they denied the facticity of these phenomena, reducing their reputed existence to the illusions of an aggravated mind; or to subjective religious anticipation, something not very different. In private talks, however, the same colleagues expressed their embarrassment to have observed such phenomena. And as I have to admit, my own behaviour was not much different.15

But it is not only the object of observation which is under scrutiny, it is observation itself. Murray, with a background in the sociology of knowledge, attacks the ethnological method as such.16 Not that he is the only one in this collection of essays to do so. And not that this attack is something totally new, as Murray himself cites a long list of titles and authors intrigued by the positive or negative potential of anthropological research. Obviously the times are gone when even a researcher like Margaret Mead could be assumed to have been just an objective instrument registering everything in a foreign culture with absolute reliability. Typical of the attitude now under assault was the rule that reputable anthropological work could never bring the observers and their reactions into the description. But, as Murray stresses, the problem rests with the anthropologists. What will they report? If there are a dozen phenomena just like those at home and there is just a single one different, the choice is automatic. Nor should it be overlooked that most anthropologists are marginal figures in their own culture, driven to find some better solutions, that is solutions to problems of their own existence, in some other place. But the organised scepticism of academic discussion deals with the interpretation of facts while assuming the authenticity of those facts. Rarely is there any doubt about the ability of the anthropologist to describe other cultures objectively, precisely and truthfully. And nobody would dare to imagine anthropologists who wrote down field notes listening only to their anthropological imagination.

So there are not only irrational objects of the social sciences, but the social scientists themselves are far from being perfect tools of objective rationality. Two Swiss psychologists, Zurfluh and Erdheim, work hard to elucidate this point. As Zurfluh sees it, Positivistic rationality is only able to deal with one dimension of individual experience; and simply lacks the ability to explain other equally 'real' experiences of an ecstatic nature.17 Erdheim goes a step further by undertaking an analysis of the concept 'scientific rationality' itself. He distinguishes four different tendencies in it:

1. The alienating tendency is characterised by the refusal of the 'scholar in power' to grant human status to his or her 'object of observation,' be it the mentally ill or the savage or some other class of people, which, being robbed of the basic quality of individuality and the individual consciousness, can be classified and dealt with more easily. Categories, objectivations and distancing are thus mechanisms of a basic sadism; this sort of knowledge is nothing else but rape, enabling the practitioner to indulge in a brute exercise of power. Here it is labelled irrationality not to accept this exercise of power.

2. Another paradigm of rationality has to be used if the co-operation of the 'object' or person being studied is

216

required. One could call this the instrumental tendency. The ultimate criteria of such rationality is the domination of humanity and matter. This instrumentalisation of reason in the social sciences is related to functionalism; institutions are only seen in terms of their contribution to the continuation of society. The concepts used as tools of analysis by the anthropologist are summaries of qualities common to different functional elements, and it becomes irrational to take the individual seriously.

3.   The idealising tendency, responsible for creating the 'noble savage' in anthropology, is a consequence of not perceiving the subject of study in terms of the norms of their society, but against some sort of transcendental ideal. Such a rationality is nothing but the resentiment of the looser; the negative elitism of a group of scholars not at home in their own culture any more.

4.   The Verstehen or 'understanding' tendency results from the human potential for empathy. To sympathise is to refrain from the categorisation of others in favour of applying the subjectivism of our self-experience to them. But even this understanding of rationality is not necessarily free from phantasies of power. If empathy and phantasies of power are not separated, the anthropologist again takes up a position of dominance with respect to the subject of study. The result is a form of animism in which the world becomes a screen for the projection of our inner emotive powers; the act of understanding is seen as the magic power enabling us to dominate and change the world.

The basic irrationality then is this thirst for power so typical of every mode of rationality; aggression and destructive tendencies are part of everybody's make-up; illuminating reason resides in a kingdom of darkness!18

Such discussion is typically Germanic, concerned, not as the Anglo-Saxons may be, with defining their terms and their objects of research, and with elaborations on method, but with the problem of communicative understanding. Stagl brings the discussion back to sociology and anthropology.19 He does so by using the paradigm of the stranger, something first done by Simmel in 1908.20 His central theme is the problem of categorisation, identified as of special importance in any attempt to apply power, domination or use. The stranger is seen as a typical example of a category and not as the concrete individual he or she experiences him or herself to be; more typically representative than, let's say, people in our own family or in our circle of friends. This situation shows the fundamental problem of boundaries, of the identity of social structures and of communication between these structures.

Obviously the anthropologist tries to make statements about strangers. And as Dahrendorf has pointed out so does the sociologist; the 'homo sociologicus' is a result of extreme categorisation. It is not unknown for those about whom the sociologist or anthropologist attempts to make such statements to reject the possibility of such statements. Stagl quotes an African voice:

> Obviously nobody outside a given society could decide about health or illness of this society, because he neither participates physically nor mentally in its existence.21

and from Papua, New Guinea, John Kasaipwalova, now an influential politician in the Tobriand Islands, remarks:

I have many times felt very embarrassed and awkward when I meet new people and they ask me, 'Where are you from?' and I say, 'Oh, I am from the Tobriand Islands,' and they reply excitedly, 'Ohhh, Malinowski, free love!!' What I am pointing out is that if we are going to depend on anthropological studies to define our history and our culture and our future, then we are lost.22

Indeed, the situation appears to become even more problematic if we take into consideration Malinowski's private diary from the time he was working with the Tobriand islanders. 'For me the life of the natives is without any attraction and without any importance, as far away from me as the life of a dog.'23 Could such a disinterested approach really lead to a better understanding of an object of research? Stagl thinks that the application of a sound hermeneutical approach makes understanding between cultures possible. Intersubjectivity certainly requires pedagogical mediation, but this mediation is possible on the basis of a shared humanity. Mediation though means to make an object accessible, with all the positive and negative implications, and thus it means the exercise of power.

SCHOLARS AND ETHICS

There are not many indications that scholarship creates a better human being; but scholarship certainly has created more power to change realities which are not finalised yet.

Duerr titles his contribution to this collection 'The horror of life and the desire to die,'24 thus homing in on two existential emotions beyond rational behaviour. He starts by claiming that basic life experiences are beyond rationalisation. They have to be accepted; like the Indian Sannyasin, the Zen-monk, the Shaman of the Dakota-Indians, the mentally ill open themselves up to an archaic reality. That means to 'experience death with open eyes' as Nietzsche put it, to experience the world not as the sum total of unattractive objects 'out there,' but as a mystery of thousandfold relations. Thus nature opens her eyes, as the mysticism of a Jakob Bohme predicted. If you let things be, they not only <u>are</u>, but they <u>do</u>. Thus the objects of every day life become very strange, and at the same time very close; they become more real. The <u>homo faber</u> mentality of Western tradition and especially of Marxism and Positivism is a continuous exercise of creating a world <u>a la</u> Potemkin, having our radios going full blast in order to drown out the voices talking to us. Only by listening will we hear and understand the language of things we regarded as mute before. Listening to this archaic language though will also show us the limits of language. Duerr quotes a reaction of Wittgenstein to Heidegger's statement that to be in the world is already the essence of anguish:

I think I understand what Heidegger means by Being and Anguish. Humans have a tendency to attack the limits of language. Just think of the wonder connected to the experience of existence. This wonder cannot be expressed as question, and there is no answer to it. All we can say is <u>a priori</u> strictly nonsense. But we still attack the limits of language. Kierkegaard saw that and called it, in a similar way, an attack against the paradoxon... But this tendency, this attack is significant; it signifies something ...25

To understand the normal, Duerr postulates, one has to face death and ultimate horror, the 'dark night of the soul,' the craziness of the irrational; one has to become 'mentally ill' and still remain able to return. Wisdom can only be reached through loneliness and suffering, a message that seems strange in a world which pretends to be a mechanism preventing exactly these conditions.

Thus Duerr expects the social scientist to become a shaman, a priest, a monk. The interpreter first has to learn the original, archaic language beyond words, and only then does hermeneutics make any sense. As Dostojewski puts it:

> I admit that only sick people see spirits. But the logical consequence is, that this experience is only accessible to sick people, and not that there are no spirits.26

The shaman, the prophet, the mystic, the saint and the social scientist give the world meaning, and they all understand themselves as charismatic, or members of an elite, and they all have faith.

That might be the reason why Duerr also invited the theologian and ex-priest Adolf Holl to contribute to this collection. As Holl sees it, he got caught between the institutionalisation of archaic knowledge used to legitimise societal domination, and the personal, individualised immersion in this archaic reality. As a consequence he was suspended from his priestly duties by the Catholic church:

> I have been defrocked. But I still sit in my cell like a monk and write; I experience the hidden happiness of all those clerics and nuns who return to their books after a cup of coffee in the morning. It would make no difference if I would say mass before, as previously. The privilege to hold God between two fingers has been taken from me, and I don't miss it any more. But the spiritual task of writing and scholarship remains; a sort of priestly dealing with words ... we remain ordained. Now our ecstasies happens on our writing desks, if it ever happens...27

So the social scientist has the moral obligation to take over from shaman, prophet, saint and priest, defending the archaic dimension of meaning and inner freedom. Not surprisingly Duerr presents Strasser's paper on 'Irrationalism, Meaning and Inner Freedom' as his final argument.

Strasser starts his analysis from the general agreement concerning the contemporary critique of civilisation that there is an all pervasive need for transcendental meaning in our modern society, an agreement whose only dissenters are those such as Luhmann who insist, in the face of the evidence, that there is no indication whatsoever that modern society complains about loss of meaning, alienation or similar phenomena.28 Luhmann's view is challenged by the counter-culture, whose very existence is clearly based on the need for goals, values and meaning, and a concern to live rightly or correctly.

Another aspect of this phenomenon is the increased number of people who join sectarian or fundamentalist groups in the hope of solving their life problems by sacrificing themselves totally to the service of the community. This religious perspective, though, stressing the communal nature of humanity resting on shared transcendence, is increasingly challenged by a substantial section of contemporary youth-culture, for whom the goal is not the search for values, morals or ideologies, but the inner freedom from morals and ideology and society. The goal is an individual independent from all outside influences. The free individual thinks and feels, acts or resists action as they will. This ideal is obviously a reaction to a general experience of being hemmed in or repressed by both existential and societal structures. Since Montaigne rationality and modern science have been identified as the 'scourge of mankind.' He postulates that we have to become like animals in order to gain wisdom. But can we trust nature? Since Hume our faith in a benign mother nature has been steadily eroded, with Marx and the Frankfurt School arguing that a non-repressive society or culture is our only hope. The multiplicity of roles in modern society make it almost impossible for the increasingly fragmented individual to render these partial identities cognitively and emotionally coherent. Modern society clearly shows itself deficient in enabling individual totalisation, and it seems that more and more people resent the limitations imposed on their potential for self-realisation of the sort proposed by Habermas who postulates a dialogical alienation leading to a happiness structured by dignity. Who wants to be devoured by society? The response could be an apolitical confrontation in everyday life, an anarchistic engagement, a solipsistic calculation of benefits and a total disregard for the social fabric as it exists.

Obviously this 'new' consciousness is not totally without precedent, and it may be detected in other forms elsewhere. Duerr 29 for instance points to the following:

1. The ethnomethodological dissolution of Husserl's 'life-world' into different life-worlds excluding each other.

2. The radicalisaton of life forms as developed by Peter Winch.

3. The 'dadaism' of Feyerabend as a tool to relativise the scientific method as presented by Popper and the Positivists.

4. The critique of the concept of progress in the work of Thomas Kuhn.

5. The critique of objectivistic knowledge in the hermeneutics of Gadamer.

And it is precisely in Gadamer and Heidegger where we can see how this new consciousness ties in very closely with a very potent tradition of German culture.

The antirationalism of Duerr and his concern for the individual can be traced to developments in German philosophy and literature going back hundreds of years. The domination by reason had already been criticised by August Wilhelm Schlegel, who, as Koepping points out, 30 identified the rationalistic approach of science as a barbaric exploitation of nature leading to the enslavement of people, to the expropriation of the poor and the degradation of individuals, who, like machines, are engaged in the performance of routine tasks. This concern for individual integrity led to Kierkegaard's rejection of any and all societal influence on the individual, and was heightened by the experience of industrialised Berlin and of a Hegelian adoration of The State.

It is interesting in this context to note that the modern fragmentation of the individual into a series of social roles as well as modern extreme individualism can both be traced back to the same philosophical concept, that is to philosophical talk about phenomena. Kant's insistence that we really can not approach things-in-themselves but only in their impact on us caused two strains of thought. The one, characterised by Hegel and Marx, took the position that phenomena nevertheless allow us some insight into underlying laws, be it laws based on the spirit or on matter. The other tradition stressed the point that phenomena are present to the conscious individual; hence the importance of the subject for Kierkegaard, Husserl and arguably Heidegger, as well as Schopenhauer and Nietzsche.

No wonder that overexposure to ideas stressing the eminent importance of society, be it in terms of rationalistic or materialistic functionalism, eventually created a backlash. As Duerr's book shows, the scholarly respectable search for the romantic roots in Gadamer and Heidegger, and the irrational upsurge of a counter-culture, characterised by solipsism, anarchism, the use of drugs and environmentalist concerns, share the same interest in communication freed from exploitation and domination. While such an understanding is predicated on a common existential participation in the same primordial level of lived knowledge, it also allows for the possibility of reflective meaning as well. And this dimension of meaning is definitely individualistic.

According to Heidegger you have to find your own truth:

> Hermeneutical theory, on this basis, can be no more
> than a derivative of the fundamental 'hermeneutic of
> Dasein,' in which we try to explicate and clarify an
> already existing pre-understanding that is a
> structure of our Being in the world.31

To be in the world also means however, to experience
temporality as the horizon of the understanding of Being, to
be located as an individual in the framework of past, present
and future meaning and understanding as necessary correlates
of ones perspective:

> Understanding is a fundamental existential that
> constitutes the disclosedness of being-in-the-world;
> it contains in itself the possibility of
> interpretation, i.e. the appropriation of what is
> already understood.32

The problem thus posed for the social sciences has been
anticipated by Simmel. The social sciences can be regarded
as accepting the insistence of science on the need for
general categorisation. Science by definition can not be a
'science' of the individual. And sociology has even been
interpreted as backlash against individualism:

> In widening areas of thought in the nineteenth
> century we see... individualism assailed by theories
> resting upon a reassertion of tradition, theories
> that would have been as repugnant to a Descartes or a
> Bacon as to a Locke or Rousseau. We see the historic
> premise of the innate stability of the individual
> challenged by a new social psychology that derived
> personality from the closed contexts of society and
> that made alienation the price of man's release from
> these contexts. Instead of the natural order
> cherished by the Age of Reason, it is now the
> institutional order - community, kinship, social
> class - that forms the point of departure for social
> philosophers as widely separated in their views as
> Coleridge, Marx and Tocqueville.33

But not all sociologies are like this. Simmel for
instance, still provides a basis for dealing with
individuals. The following passage ostensibly deals with two
philosophers, Schopenhauer and Nietzsche, and the problem of
comparing their thought; but implicity it poses the problem
of the social sciences in relation to the reduction of the
individual:

223

A comparison would eliminate the personal flavour, which can be discussed only in terms of the total interrelation of intertwined thoughts. This flavour is essential to the full task. Each factual statement gains its philosophical importance, its organic character only as part of a specific and structural spiritual unity, as a personal but typical aspect of the totality of life. The more 'personal' a refined individual is, the more jealously he will defend the proper meaning of every expression as but a part of the whole structure of the specific being which is himself. Certainly the essence is not automatically the sum total of all single manifestations. But to compare single manifestations always distorts, whether the result of the comparison is sameness or difference. Even comparing total personalities seems to be flawed in a similar way, thought it is more difficult to show why that is so. Personality is simply incomparable to the degree that it is personality. The problem is intrinsic to the concept and is not merely a consequence of the complications or the difficulties of the task. Every comparison has to refer to the shared denominator. Thus, a singularity which takes its measure only from its own idea of being or from norms transcending the personality is necessarily violated by comparison. But the cunning depreciation and transformation of great personalities which is accomplished by drawing parallels and correlations seems to give the epigones greater and closer access to them.34

This statement then can be applied, albeit sometimes rather loosely, to every social comparison of cultures as well as to comparisons of individuals. The hermeneutical circle is clearly evident, the part needs the whole for its interpretation, but the knowledge of the whole presupposes the knowledge of the parts.

Simmel's solution is to take personality as indicative of potential. 'Personality in the sense used here is a goal of evolution which is always imperfectly realised.'35 But what makes him so interesting for a generation bent on finding themselves in the new consciousness is his insistence that the goal of evolution is not happy community, not happy class consciousness or role identification, but total individuation. However Simmel's personal life itself argues for his point that the evolutionary time is ripe for attempting self-realisation through the playing of the institutionalised roles of a pluralistic society, while Konig, the partriarch of positivistic sociology in Germany, formulates the classical argument (including the moral exhortation) against unbridled individualism, in a way typical of Positivists and Marxists alike:

One has to admit, though, that the existence as social being, intertwined in many roles and with many groups, can not be regarded as alienating man. The individual gains his singularity as a person realising his obligations to others; cultures gain this individuality through exteriorisation in structures. Only society provides a chance to become your own real self and thus to understand yourself - and that is the only basis for freedom for any social person. The unloved fact of society does not instigate alienation; on the contrary, society shows that the only possible substantial freedom is always mediated by the same society. Here man becomes real as specific being, and what is more, here he is able to understand himself. Because man understands himself only as social being, his highest freedom is to turn his understanding to his societal existence. And the necessary consequence is to engage in normal activity controlled by society, an activity which could be labelled a social construction of the self.36

Thus the dictate of institution, class, society and societal authority stands, and Durkheim's fear of anomie is merely rephrased, as is Marx's condemnation of anarchists. But anomie, anarchism and individualism can not be declared dead by legislation. They are here to stay, and they can be expected to grow. Nor is this only a German phenomenon. But it seems rather obvious that German thought played an important role in their development. German thought in continuity with the reasoning of the early Christian tradition, to be precise.37 The essence of its break with traditional Jewish thought is the turning away from the concept of a 'chosen people,' a concept typical of all traditional religions, and the embracing of the ideal of personal freedom and responsibility, the possibilities of and individual contact with the Divine. This change also happened in other cultures (Buddha and Lao-tzu may serve as examples), but in early Christianity an additional element was added, the concept of original sin. Thus neither nature nor society are sacred entities anymore; both are awaiting change and the transformation into a new creation. The societal order of the Roman tradition was eventually able to tame these explosive tendencies, but not to eradicate them. And it was the young Luther who brought this tradition into the open again, standing up against the Pope and the Emperor (i.e. society as it was then understood). His example started a chain reaction in his own country; religious and political anarchism though eventually frightened Luther back to the fold of established society.

And in an indirect way this tradition led to Freud. As Erikson puts it:

> Luther, at the beginning of ruthless mercantilism in Church and Commerce, counterpoised praying man to the philosophy and practice of meritorious works. Subsequently, his justification by faith was absorbed into the patterns of mercantilism, and eventually turned into a justification of commercialism by faith. Freud, in the beginning of unrestricted industrialisation, offered another method of introspection, psychoanalysis. With it, he obviously warned against the mechanical socialisation of man into effective but neurotic robots. It is equally obvious that his work is to be used in furtherance of that which he warned against: the glorification of adjustment. Thus both Doctor Luther and Doctor Freud, called great by their respective ages, have been and are apt to be resisted not only by their enemies, but also by friends who subscribe to their ideas but lack what Kierkegaard called a certain strenuousness of mental and moral effort.38

So where does this leave the new consciousness in the social sciences and the ethical dimension? There is more concern now for things that were previously more or less neglected; there is a new fascination with the role of the social scientist; there is an uneasiness with the power-dimensions of mediation and of the hermeneutical endeavour. The concept of rational dialogue is under scrutiny as is the concept of rationality itself. Instrumental reason is juxtaposed to individual experience, an experience which can not be verbalised; introspection becomes equal to observation. It is probably not too far fetched to assume that Simmel did his most brilliant sociological analysis, the analysis of the stranger, by describing himself; and in a sizeable portion of the papers collected by Duerr one can observe a tendency of the contributors to see themselves in the same role. Even Duerr himself writes the introduction to the collection in Cuyamungue - 'Yo so de lejos,' as the old Indian used to say, 'Ich komme von weither.'

REFERENCES

Translation from the German text are Professor Loiskandl's

1. See Footnotes, American Sociological Association, March 1982, pp9-10.

2. Ralph Dahrendorf, Die Soziologie und der Soziologe: Zur Frage von Theorie und Praxis, Konstanz University Press, Konstanz.

3. Ibid., p.21.

4. The term 'Lebenswelt' or 'life-world' was employed by Edmund Husserl in recognition of the fact that different individuals and different groups each perceive 'the world' and their existence in it from a different historico-socio-cultural perspective or point of view, and that consequently the members of any particular such historico-socio-cultural group may be seen as sharing a common 'life-world' with other members of the same group; a 'life-world' that is different from that inhabited by members of other groups. See Edmund Husserl, The Crisis of European Sciences and Transcendental Phenomenology, translated by D. Carr, Northwestern University Press, Evanston, Ill., 1970.

4. See Edmund Husserl, The Crisis of European Sciences and Transcendental Phenomeology, translated by D. Carr, Northwestern University Press, Evanston, Ill., 1970.

5. See Wilhelm Dupre 'Kultur und Eros' in H. Ratschow, Ethik der Religionen, Kohlhammer, Stuttgart, 1980, pp79-176.

6. Erich Heintel, 'Das Einzelne, das Allgemeine und das Individuelle', in W. Ribel, Rationalitat - Phenomenalitat - Individualitat, Vienna, 1966, p.III.

7. Ibid, p.127.

8. Jürgen Habermas, Protestbewegung und Hochschulreform, Suhrkamp, Frankfurt, 1969, p.44.

9. G. Rohrmoser, Das Elend der britischen Theorie, Rombach, Freiburg, 1970, p.92.

10. Most of his statements on this matter appeared in interviews with newspapers and journals; but there are already indications of increasing doubt in the power of rationality in the statement that, 'The one hundred years since the death of Schopenhauer have clearly shown that he unveiled the hidden mystery of history.' Max Horkheimer in Max Horkheimer and Theodor Adorno, Socialogica II, Beiträge Zur Soziologie, vol.10, Frankfurt, 1962, p.126.

11. For instance a film to be titled 'Leaden Times' became 'The German Sisters.' Cf. 'German thriller hits the mark,' in the Guardian Weekly, vol.126, no.21, 1982, p.20.

12. Cf. 'Shakespeare and Von Kleist,' in the Guardian Weekly vol.126, no.21, 1982, p.13.

13. Hans Peter Duerr (ed.), Der Wissenschaftler und das Irrationale, Syndikat, Frankfurt, 1981.

14. Ibid, p.10

15. Ake Hultkrantz, 'Ritual und Geheimnis: Über die Kunst der Medizinmänner, oder: Was der Professor nicht gesagt hat' in Ibid, p.73.

16. Stephen O. Murray, 'Die ethnoromantische Versuchung' in Ibid, p.377 ff.

17. Werner Zurfluh, 'Auberkörperlich durch die Locher des Netzes fliegen' in Ibid, p.473 ff.

18. Mario Erdheim 'Die Wissenschaft, das Irrationale und die Aggression' in Ibid, p.505 ff.

19. Justin Stagl, 'Die Beschreibung des Fremden in der Wissenschaft' in Ibid, p.273 ff.

20. There have been numberous attempts to use Simmel's analysis as a new point of departure. Cf. Helmut Loiskandl, Edle Wilde, Heiden and Barbaren, St. Gabrieler Studien XXI, Modling, Vienna, 1966.

21. Justin Stagl, op. cit., p.274.

22. John Kasaipwalova, 'Modernising Melanesian Society - Why and for Whom?' in R. May, Priorities in Melanesian Development, Australian National University, Canberra 1973, p.454.

23. Joseph Agassi, 'Der flüchtige Funke in der Welt des Blabla'in Hans Duerr (ed.), op cit., p.351.

24. Hans Peter Duerr 'Die Angst vor dem Leben und die Sehnsucht nach dem Tode; in Ibid, p.621 ff.

25. Ibid., p.639.

26. Quoted by Justin Stagl, op. cit., in Ibid, p.277.

27. Adolf Holl 'Hoc est enim Corpus meum' in Ibid, p.536.

28. Quoted by Michel Oppitz 'Schamanen, Hexen, Ethnographen' in Ibid, p.49

29. Hans Peter Duerr, Ibid, Forward, p.9.

30. Klaus Peter Kopping 'Lachen und Leib, Scham und Schweigen, Sprache und Spiel: Die Ethnologie als feucht-frohliche Wissenschaft' in Ibid, p.300.

31. Josef Bleicher, Contemporary Hermeneutics, Routledge & Kegan Paul, London, 1980, p.100.

32. Ibid., p.101.

33. R. A. Nisbet, The Sociological Tradition, Basic Books, New York, 1966, p.9.

34. G. Simmel, Schopenhauer und Nietzsche, Duncker und Humblot, Leipzig, 1907, p.17.

35. Ibid.

36. Rene König in H. H. Y. Schrey (ed), Entfremdung, Wissenschaftliche Buchgesellschaft, Darmstadt, 1975, p.418.

37. Cf. H. Loiskandl, 'Japanese Ethics' in Listening, a Journal of Religion & Culture, vol.14, no.1, winter 1979, pp.73-83.

38. Erik H. Erikson, Young Man Luther, (1958) Faber, London, 1972, p.246.